THE LIFE AND LETTERS OF JAMES RENWICK

OTHER SCOTTISH TITLES FROM SGCB

In addition to *The Life and Letters of James Renwick*, Solid Ground Christian Books is delighted and honored to offer the following Scottish titles:

The Sufferings of the Church of Scotland by Robert Wodrow
The Scottish Pulpit by William Taylor
Precious Seed: Discourses of Scots Worthies
The Doctrine of Justification by James Buchanan
Paul the Preacher by John Eadie
Greek Text Commentary on Galatians by John Eadie
Greek Text Commentary on Ephesians by John Eadie
Greek Text Commentary on Philippians by John Eadie
Greek Text Commentary on Colossians by John Eadie
Greek Text Commentary on Thessalonians by John Eadie
Divine Love: A Series of Discourses by John Eadie
Lectures on the Bible for the Young by John Eadie
Opening Scripture: Hermeneutical Manual by Patrick Fairbairn
Martyrland: A Tale of Persecution by Robert Simpson
The Preacher and His Models by James Stalker
Imago Christi: The Example of Jesus Christ by James Stalker
Sabbath Scripture Readings from the OT by Thomas Chalmers
Sabbath Scripture Readings from the NT by Thomas Chalmers
Lectures on the Book of Esther by Thomas M'Crie
The Psalms in History and Biography by John Ker
A Pathway into the Psalter by William Binnie
Heroes of Israel: Abraham – Moses by William G. Blaikie
Expository Lectures on Joshua by William G. Blaikie
Expository Lectures on 1 Samuel by William G. Blaikie
Expository Lectures on 2 Samuel by William G. Blaikie
Luther's Scottish Connection by James McGoldrick

THE LIFE AND LETTERS

OF

JAMES RENWICK

The Last Scottish Martyr

BY REV. W.H. CARSLAW

From porch of the Free Church, Sanquhar.

SOLID GROUND CHRISTIAN BOOKS

BIRMINGHAM, ALABAMA USA

Solid Ground Christian Books
PO Box 660132
Vestavia Hills AL 35266
205-443-0311
sgcb@charter.net
solid-ground-books.com

The Life and Letters of James Renwick
by William Henderson Carslaw (1837 – 1926)

First Solid Ground Edition May 2009

Taken from the 1893 edition published by
Oliphant, Anderson & Ferrier, London

Cover image by Borgo Design, Tuscaloosa, AL

ISBN: 978-159925-204-9

PREFATORY NOTE.

THIS work, though a labour of love, has cost me more time and trouble than I anticipated when it was begun. Had I acted entirely on my own judgment, I would have preferred to make a selection of the letters and perhaps to enlarge the personal narrative. By others, however, it was thought desirable to reproduce these as a whole, and, so far as possible, to arrange them in order of time. This has now been done, and no pains have been spared to make this Edition a correct and reliable one.

At the close of Alexander Shields' "Life of Renwick," published at Edinburgh in 1724, four letters were given as a sample of Renwick's correspondence, the statement being also made that above sixty of these were in the publisher's hands, but that until it was known how the "Life" would be received their publication was delayed. This was at length undertaken by Mr John M'Millan of Pentland in 1764, and again by Dr Houston of Belfast in 1865. Those familiar with these editions have long felt how inaccurate and unsatisfactory they are, and, from a careful comparison of nineteen of the letters as thus published with the original autographs now in my possession, this feeling has been fully confirmed. These letters are 1, 2, 8, 10, 15, 16, 19, 23, 29, 30, 33, 35, 36, 37, 38, 39, 40, 59, 61. Letter 32 has been corrected as far as possible, but the original, which is also in my possession, is in a tattered condition and much defaced. The only other extant autographs of which I have any knowledge are two belonging to the New College, Edinburgh, one to the Free Church College, Aberdeen, and one to the Rev. Mr Thomson of Hightae. These are 7, 24, 66, 67 in this volume, and their accuracy can now be vouched for. A few obvious mistakes in some of the others have been rectified, but in the main they appear now as in previous editions.

Adapting Carlyle's words to the subject in hand, let me venture to hope that "to certain patient, earnest readers, these old dim letters of a noble Scotchman may, as they have done to myself, become dimly legible again. . . . Certainly there is historical instruction in these letters — historical and perhaps other and better. . . . Great, ever fruitful, profitable for reproof, for encouragement, for building up in manful purposes and works, are the words of those that in their day were men."

The only liberty I have taken with these letters, besides interweaving them with the thread of personal narrative, is to correct the spelling, in some cases, not in all, and occasionally to relieve the page by dividing it into paragraphs. Any words I have introduced for greater clearness, and these are very few, I have marked off by single commas, thus ' '.

To avoid the necessity of many footnotes, a short glossary of obsolete words and phrases has been placed at the end of the book, which I now send out with the hope and prayer that to many it may prove interesting and useful, and may help to stimulate them to a closer study of our Covenanting history.

W. H. CARSLAW.

HELENSBURGH,
October 20th, 1893.

CONTENTS.

Chapter VII.

Chapter VIII.

Chapter IX.

Chapter X.

GLOSSARY.

GLOSSARY.

admire	=	wonder.
airt	=	quarter.
anent	=	concerning.
angle	=	fishing tackle.
ben	=	in.
biasness	=	inclination to some side.
Carrick	=	district of Ayrshire, south of the Doon.
cess	=	tax, assessment.
construct	=	construe, interpret.
ding	=	drive.
dow	=	can, dare.
effectuated	=	effected, accomplished.
elicitly	=	publicly.
epidemical	=	prevalent, general.
evite	=	shun, escape.
fash	=	trouble.
Kyle	=	district of Ayrshire, between the Doon and the Irvine.
kyth	=	appear, shew oneself.
learn	=	teach (*lehren*, Ger.).
misconstruct	=	misconstrue, misinterpret.
organical	=	organised.
port (of the city)	=	gate.
prig	=	bargain, haggle about the price.
remnant	=	name given to the Society people.
rue	=	regret.
scrimpit	=	narrow, small.
shabble	=	short sword.
skaith	=	harm, loss.
spean	=	wean.
speer	=	enquire, seek.
stour	=	dust.
Texel	=	island off the Dutch coast.
tryst	=	agree to meet.
waiters	=	custom-house officers.

CHAPTER I.

"My boast is not that I deduce my birth
From loins enthroned and rulers of the earth ;
But higher far my proud pretensions rise,
The son of parents passed into the skies."

AMES RENWICK, the last of our martyrs, was born on February 15th, 1662, at Moniaive, in the parish of Glencairn, Dumfriesshire. His father was a weaver by trade, and an earnest Christian, while his mother was an excellent woman richly endowed both by nature and grace. She had already had several children, all of whom, however, had died in infancy, and when James was born, besides dedicating him to the Lord, she prayed fervently that he might be spared for a life of usefulness. At an early age he gave many indications of considerable precocity and of deep and tender piety.// Through the assistance of friends, he was sent to the University of Edinburgh, where he prosecuted his studies with diligence and success, maintaining a reputation also for purity and consecration to the service of Christ, though as yet he had not publicly associated himself with the Covenanters. An interesting illustration of his character and position is furnished in the fact that on 9th June 1681, while employed as tutor to a family in Lanark, he applied to be admitted as a burgess of that town. This application was generously

A

supported by Dr Mark Clifford, a Royalist, who became
security for Renwick, and succeeded, after some opposition on the part of the Magistrates and Town Council,
in getting his name added to the Burgess Roll, where it
may still be seen.   On the 27th of the following month, at
the Cross of Edinburgh, he witnessed the execution of
the Rev. Donald Cargill, and was so moved thereby that
he there and then cast in his lot with the persecuted,
and resolved to raise the standard which had that day
fallen from the brave old veteran's hands.   Six months
later, on the 12th of January 1682, he was one of about
forty armed men who rode into Lanark, and affixed to
the Cross a plain and forcible Declaration of their reasons
for renouncing allegiance to Charles II.   By this time the
more earnest and resolute among the Covenanters had
formed themselves into what were known as United
Societies, which held stated meetings in different parts
of the country, and kept up a general correspondence
for mutual protection and counsel.   It was at the first
of these meetings, held in the parish of Lesmahagow,
on the 15th December 1681, that the Lanark Declaration
was resolved upon, while at another, three months later,
it was decided to send Sir Alexander Gordon of Earlston to Holland, to represent their case to the Protestant
brethren there.   This gentleman belonged to an old and
much respected family in the South of Scotland, which,
from the days of Wickliff, had been distinguished for its
piety and patriotism.   His father was killed immediately after the battle of Bothwell Bridge in 1679 by a
party of English dragoons who were in quest of the
fugitives, while he himself was present at that battle
and narrowly escaped from falling into the enemy's
hands.   One of his own tenants, seeing him ride through
Hamilton, advised him to dismount and conceal himself,
acting on which suggestion he entered a house, arrayed

himself in female apparel, and was afterwards found rocking a cradle in which an infant lay asleep. Having by this means escaped immediate danger, he continued hiding for several years, until, in the summer of 1683, after a visit to Scotland, and on the eve of his return to Holland, he was arrested at Newcastle, and carried prisoner, first to Newgate, and then to Edinburgh. After suffering much cruelty and injustice, he was sentenced to be beheaded on the 28th of September following; but from time to time he was reprieved, although kept in close confinement, until, at the Revolution in 1688, he obtained freedom. His excellent lady, Janet Hamilton, was a daughter of Sir Thomas Hamilton of Preston, and sister of Sir Robert Hamilton, to whom the greater number of Renwick's letters are addressed. She was his constant companion in tribulation, and her meditations in the solitary dungeon of the Bass have been published under the title of "Lady Earlston's Soliloquies."

Some dissension having arisen in the Societies regarding Earlston's appointment, it was finally resolved to associate with him as Commissioner his brother-in-law, Sir Robert Hamilton, the latter being on terms of closer intimacy with some of the Dutch Ministers, and more likely to be of service to his persecuted brethren in Scotland. One of these ministers, who, for a time at least, was peculiarly friendly, was the Rev. Mr Brakell of Leewarden in Friesland, who, in a letter to "the fathers and brethren who are under the persecution in the Church of Scotland," says :—

"My heart is not a little wounded with sympathy, when I call to mind the sad things you are meeting with ; when I consider how you are deprived of all the good things and means of life, that you are put to lodge day and night in the open air, without any shelter from

the sun's heat, rain or cold (how do you live ? surely God
feeds you from heaven), when you embrace the bare rock
for a bed, having the heavens, or it may be the cold
snow for a covering ; when I consider what it is to see
the little ones (it may be) weeping for hunger and cold,
and not able to get wherewith to warm them ; when I
consider what it is to be always surrounded with deadly
foes, and to hear sometimes of the husband, sometimes
of the father or mother, wife, son, or daughter taken
to execution, and all the day as lambs allotted to the
slaughter ; what brother, what Christian, yea, what
unbiassed man can think on these things but with
excess of grief ?

"But, upon the other hand, when I consider the heavenly
abounding blessings, the great abundance of the Spirit
and spiritual joy, the deniedness to all worldly things,
the ardent love to God and your neighbour, the cheerful
martyrdom for the name of Jesus, the holiness of life,
&c., which God your Father has in a more abundant
manner bestowed on you than on any other Church in
the world in these times : when I call to mind, that God
is preserving you as a remnant of anciently a most
flourishing Church, and calling you as the first fruits,
yea, I say, the first fruits of a Church shortly to be
raised up : when I see our Lord and Master Jesus
Christ, the only head of His Church, glorified in your
miraculous preservation, and encompassing you as with
a wall of fire round about, calling you either living or
dying, and setting you forth, and preserving you to all,
either godly or ungodly, who are lurking in quiet here
and there, for to give a testimony for Himself : I say,
when I seriously ponder these things, how can I be sad ?
what shall I say, but glory to the Lord ? what shall I do,
but most willingly approve of His most holy and wise
government of His household, Who follows you with a
greater and more infinite and eternal love and good will
than I can express. Should I seem to repine by wishing
a change, and so disapproving of His dispensations ? nay,
the most holy and merciful God does all things well.

"But what shall I say unto you, my dear brethren ?   I

approve of your careful and mutual correspondence with one another, and all the Churches. I approve of your strict discipline, both as to the private life of every member, and also as to your separation from these swelling-in-pride Bishops and their adherents. And likewise I approve of your separation from those who have accepted the Indulgence from the civil magistrate, and so have acknowledged a foreign and extraneous power in the Church, and introduced it into the Church against the sole government of our only King Jesus Christ, which hath proven the destruction of the Church, and the greatest hindrance to its restoration. I approve also of your separation from the frighted and fearing though otherwise pious men, and these who are inclining to the indulged side, loving a short bodily ease, though with a check of conscience, who deprive themselves of all that open boldness they ought to have, and entrap themselves in inextricable snares, not considering how great hurt they do to the Church. O how much rather is it to be chosen to die a noble and Christ-glorifying death, and to obtain the crown of martyrdom, or to endure all sorts of injuries and oppressions in the deserts and mountains, *than to enjoy the pleasures of sin for a season.*

"Go on therefore, dear brethren, as ye have begun. Let not the devil and his instruments and followers fright you, who is come unto you full of great wrath, because he knows his time is but short, for the God of peace shall bruise him under your feet.

"Let not the cruelty nor subtilty of enemies, nor hunger, nor cold, nor the prison, nor a gallows, nor the sword, fear you. Neither let your peace entice you to comply with those, who, although they be godly men, yet they live only for themselves, and not for the good of the Church, nay rather for its hurt. O how pleasant and noble a thing is it to lay the foundation of a more pure Church, to make a way by which King Jesus shall enter to restore His Church in *Scotland.* O ! how profitable will it be to after generations to have you for a good example to follow ! and that they can say of you, so and so did our forefathers, such and such things suffered they

in such and such a case; they behaved themselves so
and so."

This interesting and sympathetic letter was followed
by one from Sir Robert Hamilton, evidently meant for
the United Societies though addressed to Mr Renwick,
who seems already to have attained a prominent and
responsible position. After referring to "worthy Mr
Brakell," and the good work he was doing in Friesland,
the writer says :—

"O let us not envy that He is enlarging His tents and
setting up in other places ; His presence is more than
able to fill heaven and earth ; there is no fear that He
wants plenishing where He comes. Let Him conquer,
let Him conquer, until He has stretched His conquest
from one end of the earth to the other, in breadth and
length, and has made a footstool of all His enemies.

"Dear and worthy Brethren, I will not further
trouble you, expecting that my brother shall write unto
you ; only this I add, that as for the number of those
that come in order to the ministry, it is condescended
upon, that four or five come at first, and they are to stay
by Mr Brakell, or else in some College here in the winter, and then receive ordination in the spring ; for once
having so many, more might be condescended upon,
as the Lord gave clearness. The Lord Himself direct
and guide you through all the parts of it, that He be
not further provoked. The Lord be with you all, and
send a joyful meeting."

We may now with advantage introduce the first three
extant letters of Renwick, which were sent from Edinburgh in July, September, and October of this year,
and which contain allusions to facts already mentioned.
They are all addressed to Sir Robert Hamilton at Leewarden, while the first refers to matters which had occasioned considerable discussion at the third general
meeting of the Societies on the 15th of the preceding
month.

Letter I.

EDIN., July 8, 1682.

Much honoured Sir, — We do not question your concernedness with us and our case at the present ; neither do we doubt of your desire to know how and what the remnant here are doing, in reference to that which God is calling them to in this day. Upon that consideration, and out of obedience to your desire, intimated to me in a letter from our friend An. Hend., I have presumed, though unacquainted, which is to my great loss, to write this line (though confused) unto you. And as to matters before your brother E.'s departure from us, whom we expect you shall see very shortly, God willing, we remit you to his information, as being more seen and perceiving than we ; and as to our procedure in matters since, I shall labour to give you a brief, yet true account. We do not question but you know already, how that, by the Lord's special providence, there is a general correspondence, which, for a while bypast, hath been kept up among the Societies of this land, who profess to own the way of God, and not to say a confederacy with this untoward generation ; for which end there have commissioners from their respective Societies met together, at least once a quarter, that they might treat and confer anent what is required in this day. As to what was done the last meeting, the first thing after prayer, which was fallen about, was this : The commissioners' names, together with the names of the shires from which they came, were written down ; and out of these, fifteen were selected, because the whole would have bred confusion, and these being thus selected went by themselves. Then it was asked at every one of them, man by man, if they knew the mind of those with whom they were embarked in Societies, and how they and their Societies carried as to the owning of our public Declarations, and if they any ways contributed brick to Babel, by actively strengthening the hands of the enemies of our Lord, and if they joined with these once ministers, who had now left their Master, and stepped aside from the way of the Lord. All professed that they and their Societies were clear for our Declarations : but there were some found, who joined with those who paid cess and locality ; which we may observe, in those who say they own our Declarations, to be a confessing God with the mouth, but denying Him in works. And though they were not guilty of those things themselves, yet being clothed with the authority of those who were guilty, they were for that time casten, and desired, if the persons in their Societies would not forbear these sinful courses, to separate from them ; and though there were none to be found in that corner where they lived, who would forbear them, by keeping at a distance from them while so, they should be received in the convention as particular persons. There were also some there, who were found to have accepted the sacrament of baptism and ordinance of marriage, administered by Mr Peden, who were for the time suspended from sitting ; but this was after a long and stiff debate. For some said, how could they upon Mr Peden's account be suspended, before trial was made, and he was found unfaithful ? Then it was replied, that he had been many times tried, and practice had proved him unfaithful in this time bypast. So the most honest thought it only best, not to trust implicitly, but after trial, to trust according as he was found to be. Then their empty places being filled with commissioners selected anew, who were not found to be guilty of these things, it was proceeded (as was ordinary) : First, to ratify and approve what had been done by the foregoing convention ; from which some receded, because it had been enacted, that your brother should go abroad, and give true information of our case, and the heads of our sufferings, to any godly Christians desirous to know, and unwilling to believe misinformation and false calumnies, which enemies of all sorts are very vigilant to cast upon us. And some (though few) who were for his going abroad at first, and would approve of his sending, were not for his continuing any longer. But as to the illegal and disorderly manner of their dissentment, having at first agreed with the thing, we remit you to our friends, your brother, or An. H. Whereupon there was great confusion, and nothing could be done, till (the dissenters drawing aside) there was a new election of those who were both for his going abroad and continuance for a while. And, the day being spent, all that was gotten done was only a ratification of what had been done by the foregoing convention, another day when to meet appointed, and some fast-days nominated.

Now, Sir, you have here a brief account of our late confusions ; but I think we ought to look upon them as the Lord breaking us by these things, aye and while we break fully off from our sinful courses, direct or indirect. But this is very observable, that those, who dissented from that duty of sending our friend your brother abroad, are the only pleaders for trusting Mr Peden before trial, and justify their joining with the abominators of the time, though they do not justify the abominations, which in them is a direct sinning, and an indirect following of their duty. But O ! Sir, wrestle much for the poor remnant, that they may be united in truth and holiness, which cannot be without separating from both the abominations and abominators of this time. For as the Lord hath said, There is no peace to the wicked, consequently there will be no peace to those who are at peace with the wicked as such. No more to trouble you at the time, but leaving you on Him who hath kept you hitherto, that He may keep you to the end, I am, Sir, your entire and obedient servant in the Lord,   JAMES RENWICK.

One cause of serious dissension among the Presbyterians is alluded to in this letter, viz., the payment of cess. This was a national assessment, imposed four years previously, for the support of a large standing army, which was raised expressly for the suppression of

Conventicles. The payment of this war-tax, or even association with those who paid it, is here described as a practical denial of God on the part of those who professed to be Covenanters, and was afterwards compared by Renwick to the supply of fuel for the furnace of persecution.

Reference is also made here to the suspicion in which the Rev. Alexander Peden, better known as Peden the Prophet, was held by some of the Societies. He was one of the most prominent among the field preachers, and greatly beloved ; but, having joined the insurgents at Lanark before the battle of Pentland, he soon left them, fearing that they were not in a condition to offer a successful resistance. This exposed him to suspicion on the part of many, who did not hesitate to accuse him of unfaithfulness. After five years' imprisonment on the Bass Rock, he was sentenced to banishment for life, but on reaching London he and his fellow-exiles were liberated, probably through the influence of Shaftesbury, whose party was then in power, and who, for reasons of his own, was seeking the support of the Presbyterians. In 1679 he returned to Scotland, where he continued to preach in the fields, and won for himself a high reputation ; but between him and the party to which Renwick belonged there remained a good deal of misunderstanding. Peden's own feelings were much embittered against Renwick, through the misrepresentations of some false brethren, though, when dying, he sent for him, and after receiving from himself an account of his conversion and call to the ministry, he said, " Sir, you have answered me to my soul's satisfaction ; I am very sorry that I should have believed any such evil reports of you, which not only quenched my love to and marred my sympathy with you, but led me to express myself so bitterly against you, for which I have sadly smarted. But, Sir, ere you go, you must pray for me, for I am old, and going to leave the world." Renwick, having prayed with more than ordinary enlargement, Peden took him by the hand, and kissed him, saying, "Sir, I find you a faithful servant to your Master; go on in a single dependence upon the Lord, and you will get honestly through and clear off the stage, when many others who hold their heads high will lie in the mire, and make foul hands and garments." ("Scots Worthies," pp. 519, 520, Carslaw's Edition).

The only other remark this letter calls for is in explanation of the initials E. and A. H. E. is Earlston, Hamilton's brother-in-law, while A. H. is Andrew Henderson, whose name is frequently mentioned with that of his brother Alexander in subsequent letters. Both brothers were imprisoned in connection with the assassination of Archbishop Sharp, and, after their escape, went to Holland, and obtained employment in Amsterdam.

LETTER II.

The "testimonies" of James Skene, referred to in the closing paragraph of this letter, are now published in the "Cloud of Witnesses" (pp. 86-98, Thomson's Edition). Though belonging to Aberdeenshire, then the stronghold of prelacy, and connected with some of the richest families of that county (his brother's estate of Skene being in the parish of that name), he was a devoted friend and follower of Richard Cameron and Donald Cargill, and suffered martyrdom at the Cross of Edinburgh on December 1st, 1680. The sermons sent were doubtless those of John Welwood, who died in 1679 at the early

age of thirty. By Mr Donald is of course meant the
Rev. Donald Cargill.

EDIN., Sept. 6, 1682.

Much honoured Sir,—The consciousness of my duty
makes me presume to write unto you ; and also your
honouring me with a particular line from your hand
(being unworthy so far as to be countenanced by you),
superadds a tie upon me thereunto. We received those
soul-refreshing letters of yours to our friends, which to
them are very encouraging, they being desirous to be
thankful to the Lord for what He hath done, and to cry
that He would carry on what He hath so nobly begun,
and to be co-wrestlers with all that wrestle for Zion,
upon the account of her desolation.   And according to
your desire, all friends, having occasion to come to this
place, see what you wrote ; and I also take some copies
thereof, and send them to several corners of the country.
But indeed I cannot express how all that hear thereof are
refreshed and overjoyed. But, O ! Sir, pray that we may
not be abusers of mercies, and that we may get the Lord
put and kept in His room, and because of these things
that our hearts may only rejoice in the Lord. I cannot indeed admire * enough how some behaved toward you while here ; but we may have peace, because
it was upon the account of duty.   But this I think is
observable in such cases, that the Lord then lets out Himself to refresh the souls of His people ; and it is ordinary
with Him when there is least outward encouragement
to give most inward encouragement from Himself. He
stays His rough wind in the day of His east wind. O !
does not this magnify His wisdom and graciousness,
who killeth, and yet maketh alive ? and does it not tell
us that He is unwilling to afflict ? and should it not
teach us only to look to Himself for encouragement,
with whom there is no shadow of change ? And as to your
call abroad, and especially your staying where you are
surely the Lord's hand hath been only in it, which His
dispensations since have confirmed. But, O ! labour to

* Wonder.

be thankful to the Lord, who hath made you any ways useful where He casts your lot. And (if my heart deceives me not) my soul shall be thankful to Him upon your account; and whatever He does, or whoever He makes use of to do any thing for Him, let us only attribute the praise thereof to His free grace and mercy that honours any so far.

When these refreshing news came to our hands, my spirit was overjoyed with the hearing of them, but immediately this thought struck into my mind, that what if the Lord be now going to leave Scotland, seeing He is making His candle shine so clear in another place! But this got no abode, for it was greatly resented in the time; and the thought of the many noble testimonies that He honoured a remnant here to give for Him, and the precious blood that He had taken in fields and on scaffolds, to seal His cause and quarrel,—I say, the cries of those, I thought (though there were no more) would not let Him give up altogether with this land, especially seeing it was married to Him, and His keeping a remnant in it even to this very day speaketh good unto us. Then, again, I was made to think that this rather might be the thing which the Lord would do because we have been generally so treacherous a people, that He might not possibly honour any of us to have any hand in the delivery; yet He would deliver, and could command deliverance from afar. However I desire to believe, that He who hitherto hath preserved a remnant here to contend for Him will do so still. But Oh! He is a sovereign God. Well would it become us to put a blank in His hand, and to leave the filling up thereof to Himself, and not to limit the Holy One of Israel, but rather believe in His word, who hath condescended so far as to tell us, that all shall work together for good to those that love and fear Him. He is wise and mighty. His end (which is His own glory, and the good of His people) cannot be frustrated, and He can and will make means work together for that end, when the contrary is intended by them. And what you wrote,

Sir, amongst many things, I think, to me it speaks this,—
the making out of His word, that He shall see of the
travail of His soul ; and that He is able (if it were) out
of the stones to raise up children to Abraham ; and that
He will not want a testimony ; yea, that if these were
silent the stones would cry out. So this should learn *
us to credit Him with the cause, who is the main-
tainer thereof, and will show Himself to be the avenger
thereof also.

Be pleased to show Mr Brakell that some friends
here, and I, have our services presented to him ; and
that, when friends meet, I think they will write to him
in particular, from them in general, and show him that
the last day of the last month was nominated by some
friends, having met in this place, a day of thanksgiving,
for the noble testimony the Lord had helped him to give,
and for His enabling him so signally to stand out, and
not to quit any of his Master's rights. The relation of
the whole business (which you wrote) being in the entry
of the day read in their hearing, that it might prove a
mean to frame them for that duty, and show that they
are not omitters of what he desires of them (they
seeing it greatly their duty), and rejoice in the Lord
upon his account. And that you, and friends with you,
and friends here, may be one in the Lord, and one in all
our duties, I thought it fit to intimate here, that (as
we reckon)† the last Thursday of this instant, and the
second Thursday of October, are denominated days of
public fasting by the remnant here, and that the next
general meeting of our friends is to be on the second day
of November. And as to what was done the last meeting, we refer you to the confused account thereof in your
brother's letter.

You shall receive from the bearer all our martyrs'

---

* Teach.

† There is an allusion here to the different methods of reckoning
time, the old style and the new. An illustration of both is furnished
in Letter XIX., and, by keeping in mind that a different practice
prevailed in different countries, we shall often be able to reconcile
apparently inconsistent dates.

testimonies that are unprinted ; but there are written in with the rest two particular testimonies, or rather letters, of James Skene, which he never intended to publish as testimonies. So, if you think it fit (it being congruous with reason) they need not be printed, or at least, not as such ; the one whereof is directed to all professors in the shire of Aberdeen ; the other, to all and sundry professors in the South. Receive also some sermons of Mr Welwood's in a little book ; but let the sermons, and also the testimonies, be well noticed, for, not having correct copies, though I wrote them I cannot answer for the correctness of them.—We have sent you also a letter with a paper written by Mr Donald's own hand in answer thereunto : but it is unperfected, he being taken away before he got time to finish it. But as for that book which is in Glasgow, it is not as yet come to our hands, but when corrected it is promised, and when gotten it shall be sent, with all the (so called) Acts of parliament. So, leaving you and all His people upon the Lord for counsel and direction, I am, Sir, yours, to my full power to serve you in the Lord,

JAMES RENWICK.

' *P.S.*'—Receive moreover, according to your desire, Manning upon the Romans.

LETTER III.

Mr Brakell's letter has already been mentioned. He was an earnest minister of Leewarden in Holland, and an intimate friend of Sir Robert Hamilton. Renwick's humility is seen in his surprise at so early a date being suggested for ordination. Others, however, took a different view, at least of his qualifications for the ministry, as he was ordained early next year after a few months' study at Groningen.

EDIN., October 3, 1682.

Much honoured Sir,—We received yours, which was
very refreshful unto us, and also very seasonable, because of the many wholesome advices therein given unto
us, whereof we greatly stand in need, especially in this
juncture of time. But O that we could get the Lord
acknowledged in all our ways! then He would direct
our paths; for they are only well led and guided whom
the Lord leads and guides. O noble guide! O sufficient
guide! O true guide! and O constant guide! He is
nearer than a brother; though father and mother should
both forsake, yet He will not; He will not leave us, nor
forsake us. Though oftentimes we be so unperceiving
that we know not that it is the Lord who upholdeth, yet
afterwards we will be made to say, that when our feet
were slipping, God's mercy held us up (Psal. xciv. 17,
18); and when we were as beasts and fools in many respects, God held us by the hand (Psal. lxxiii. 22, 23).
O is not such a Guide well worth the following with all
joy and alacrity? Is not such a Master well worth the
serving, with all the soul, heart, mind, and strength?
He is not like other masters; for there is an infinite
disproportion betwixt His work and His reward; and
He gives no work, but He gives also a heart for the
same, and all furniture suitable and requisite for the
doing thereof, which is the thing that other masters
cannot do. And the more He gives, the more we may
expect; for, the more He gives, there is not the less behind; because that which is infinite cannot be exhausted,
yea, not diminished. O this is not after the manner of
man! that the more He gives, the more we may expect.
And doth He not many times lay abundantly whatever
we need unto our hand, when we dare not say, that
either we were right in seeking thereof, or in exercising
faith and dependence upon Him for the same? O! does
not this hold forth the freedom of His free, free grace?
Should not this stop our mouths, and cause us be silent
before Him? Should not this shame us out of our mis-
belief, and cause us to credit Him fully and freely with

all His matters, and our matters? His foundation standeth sure; He knows who are His; and whom He loves, He loves unto the end. There is no shadow of change with Him. O let us follow Him! O let us serve Him! O noble Master! O noble service! In serving of Him, therein we shall get all our ambition satisfied. O let us follow Him, and serve Him in His own way. He cannot be found out of His own way. In His light we shall see light; in the light of His paths, and there only, we shall see the comfortable light of His countenance. O light! O comfortable light! There be many that say, who will shew us any good? but let us say, "Lord, lift thou up the light of thy countenance upon us." He can, yea, doth gladden our hearts more than the enemies' hearts in the time when their corn and wine are increased. O let us leave the world and follow Him. Is he not saying, "Come with me from Lebanon, my spouse, with me from Lebanon!" O if His company will not allure us, surely nothing will; and both to ravish us therewith, and make us sure thereof, He says, "With me from Lebanon, with me from Lebanon."—O worthy Sir, the Lord hath been kind unto you, and made you an instrument of much good. O you are the more obliged to His free grace! Therefore, be humble, and be thankful, and my soul shall desire to be thankful to Him on your account. The more He does for you, and by you, be you the more engaged to Him, and for Him only.

We have no news to write unto you: but this is very observable now, and clearly to be seen, that the fear and terror of the Lord is legibly written upon the consciences of malignants and backslidden professors. There is not so much heart and hand to be seen amongst any, as amongst the poor remnant. How can it be otherwise with these backslidden and backsliding professors? for they are suffering and sinning, sinning and suffering; and in their suffering they want the world's peace; and by their sinning, they want the sweet, sweet enjoyment of a peaceable conscience, and this breaks and mars all their peace with God. They are really deadened; their hearts are stricken with fainting, and their knees with feebleness; and any life or heart, that is to be seen, is among the poor remnant, whom the Lord helps, in any measure, to make Moses' and Joshua's choice. O! what means all this terror? Is it not the forerunner of sudden and sore judgments? He is on His way, He is on His way. Blessed are they, who, when He comes, shall be found in His way, and prepared to meet Him. Worthy Mr Brakell's letter was very refreshful to all who have heard it, and there are copies thereof Englished and sent to several corners of the country. He may expect a line from the remnant when they meet, which, God willing, will be on the eleventh of this instant, it being called sooner than expectation, for choosing out of these young men. But, go who will, the work they are to go for is most weighty, and their going in such a manner is also most weighty: but there is all furniture with Him who is the life and the light of men. O that none may go but those whom the Lord sends and goes along with, and whom He helps and will help to look to Himself, and to Himself only, for all frame and furniture suitable. But we marvel greatly what you mean in your letters, by speaking of ordination against the Spring; for your worthy brother knows assuredly, that we have none of whom that, or anything like unto it, can be expected.

The Acts of the pretended parliament (according to your desire), and the book that you wrote for, shall come by the next occasion, God willing. Let us know if you received those papers, and that book which we sent with your cousins. We know it is the desire of the people, and we expect it will be done at the meeting, that you should be conjoined with your brother in his commission. We hope we need not desire you, and friends with you, to mind us. So leaving you on Him who is wise, mighty, and gracious, with my endeared love to yourself, and worthy Mr Brakell, and all our godly and concerned friends in our Lord Jesus, I am, much honoured Sir, yours, to my full power, to serve you in the Lord, JAMES RENWICK.

CHAPTER II.

ON THE WING.

HOLLAND, which at an earlier period had secured its liberty at a great price, was now a harbour of refuge for the persecuted. In most of its cities many of our country-men had found a settled abode, and Scotch churches were already established in Rotterdam, Campvere, Leyden, Amsterdam, Delft, Dordrecht, the Hague, and Middleburg. There was also full ministerial Communion between the Reformed Church of Holland and that of Scotland. Scotch probationers were readily received by the Dutch Synods, and the local "Classis" or Presby-tery conferred ordination or induction when required on the ministers elected by the Scotch congregations within their bounds. We need not therefore be surprised at the action of the Societies in sending Commissioners to Holland, or at the steps subsequently taken by some of the Dutch ministers in ordaining Renwick to the ministry.

The first suggestion which ultimately led to this result was made by Sir Robert Hamilton in the letter already quoted in the previous chapter. Two months later, at a general meeting of the Societies in Edinburgh, the work of selecting suitable men to go abroad to study with a view to the ministry was proceeded with, when, after solemn prayer,

"The young men who were present, and to be put in the list, were desired to speak their minds, which they did satisfyingly, first of the work they were to go about, next of the going in such a manner, which was not ordinary. There were six put in the list (all of a blameless life, and not only of one judgment with themselves, but forward and zealous then, in adhering to, and promoting the Testimony), of whom four were present, viz., James Renwick, John Smith, John Flint, and William Hardy : and two absent, viz., William Boyd and John Nisbet. Then there were six pieces of paper taken, all of one magnitude and form ; and upon four of them were four figures, each of them having a figure a-piece, and two wanted, in order to the electing of four out of the six, which was the number judged fit to be sent abroad at that time. Whereupon the four young men were called in (being before desired to remove) and gave an account of their ages to the meeting. Then after praying again that the Lord would determine as He saw fit, these young men, presenting themselves, drew the pieces of paper out of a bonnet, the oldest being still preferred to draw first. As for those who were absent, two drew for them. Those who got the papers wanting the figures were to stay at home, which fell to be John Smith and William Hardy ; and of those who got the papers with the figures and who were to go abroad, two were present, viz., James Renwick and John Flint, and two were absent, viz., William Boyd and John Nisbet. Then praying that the Lord would bless those on whom the lots had fallen, this work was closed. Thereafter it was concluded, that 100 Pounds Scots, should be allowed to the four young men called to go abroad (to each 25 Pounds Scots) in order to defray their expenses in their voyage, and that what was needful to provide them in clothes and other necessaries was, over and above, to be taken off for them at Edinburgh. The collection for this effect was to be sent with those who were to come from the societies to the next General Meeting, and the young men were desired to be ready for their voyage betwixt and the second week of November. This conclusion was cheerfully consented unto, and as willingly and readily put in practice ; for immediately thereafter, not only the money was given to the young men which was allowed them, but also what was needful was provided for them at Edinburgh. Two of them, William Boyd and John Flint, in November thereafter took ship, and went to the Netherlands, to the University of Groningen, but Mr James Renwick was not ready to go until December."

In the meantime this important change in his prospects did not prevent Renwick from keeping a vigilant eye on all that was transpiring around, and particularly on anything that might injuriously or otherwise affect the cause he had so much at heart. Of this an illustration is furnished in the following letter addressed to Mr Henry Jenkinson and other friends at Newcastle.

Letter IV.

EDIN., October 3, 1682.

Endeared Friends,—We wrote to you, and gave you notice of our appointed public fast days, but we never heard if our letter came to your hands, and our still waiting to hear from you in answer to ours was the cause of our so long delay now. But, however, at this time, our concernedness with you, and the great love we have unto you in the Lord, puts us to it, that we can no longer forbear ; and that because we have heard, that one Mr John Hepburn, a preacher, was amongst you, and we see it assuredly to be our duty to desire you to beware of him. For he is one of those who handle the word of God deceitfully : and though he is not altogether so guilty of the public defection, and of compliance, as some, yet he condemns the laudable

practices of the godly party, who were helped to give
testimony for truth, and against the enemies thereof:
and he is incorporated with the rest in calumniating,
reproaching and condemning those, who, in any
measure, were kept faithful to their Lord and Master
Jesus Christ; and his incorporation with them therein
is enough to us, though there be other variances
amongst themselves. *Let us not own the way of God by
halves, but wholly, fully, and in all things.* And
particularly, he is against our noble and faithful
Declaration published at Sanquhar, whereby that
wretched tyrant, Charles Stuart, and all his accomplices were cast off by us, as we ought; which, alas!
was too long a-doing: and by this he buries the blood,
and condemns the faithful testimonies of so many
worthies who have died upon that head, and therein
have been eminently owned and assisted of the Lord.
Indeed, herein he will run this subterfuge, and say, he
acknowledges he ought to be rejected and deposed;
yea, he may possibly grant, that he deserveth death,
both by the laws of God, and the just laws of man; yet
he cannot see how that can be done without another
magistrate or magistrates. But we would answer,—if
he sees no other ways than those, he is but blind, and
that is deceitful and double dealing. For magistrates
have no power but what is derivative from the people,
and magistrates have nothing actually, but what the
people have virtually; yea, and more than virtually,
for they may actually confer it upon whom they think
most fit,—for the power of government is natural and
radical to them, being unitedly in the whole, and
singularly in every one. So whatever magistrates may
do the people may do the same, either when they want
magistrates, or when the magistrates fail or refuse to
do their duty.

We need insist no further upon the lawfulness of the
thing; for is not this most consonant to the law of
God, and the law of nature? It is also sufficiently
cleared by all our most sound divines, particularly

worthy Mr Knox, who herein had the approbation of Calvin, and other learned divines of his time, under their hand-writing : and it is likewise clear enough by the laudable practice of resolute and worthy reformers. But as to the necessity of the thing, to wit, of the rejecting Charles Stuart, as he is installed this day ; hath he any power to govern, but what is established upon the ruins of the land's engagements ? and hath not the exercise thereof been still according thereunto ? What then can we own in him, if neither the establishment nor the exercise of his authority ? And does he not act in all things by virtue of his own blasphemous supremacy ? The owning of him, in less or in more, is the owning thereof, because the supremacy is made the essential of the crown ; and it is but one supremacy that he arrogantly hath both in matters civil and ecclesiastical, which is clear from the Explanatory Act of the Supremacy : so that it is essential to the crown, is the same with the crown, and that which is one cannot be divided.

Now, dear friends, what you have done in this, to wit, in your joining with Mr Hepburn, we do not impute it to your wilful stepping aside, but to the insinuation, or unreasonable recommendation of Mr Young, who was hugely overseen therein,—which is both a grief and an offence to the remnant. But, O ! stand still, go not you to them, but let them come to you. *Join with none out of the way of God, but labour to bring all into it that ye can, yet go not out of it yourselves to fetch them thither, and give not ear to the instruction that causeth to err.*

We hope we need not bid you beware of Mr James Welch, for he will soon kyth* in his own colours. Labour to walk according to that paper sent by you unto us, and walk with none but those who will walk according thereunto. We are sure if you would pose Mr Hepburn upon these things in your paper, you

---

* Appear (Psalm xviii. 26, metrical version).

should not find him to satisfy you. And if you will defend, or continue in your joining with him, or any other who stands where he is, or where he was while he was here, we must deny correspondence with you. But hoping for better things of you, and desiring an answer hereof, we leave you on the Lord for light and life. I am, your friend and servant in the Lord,

JAMES RENWICK.

In this letter three men are mentioned about whom little is known, namely,—John Hepburn, Andrew Young, and James Welch. The first was a minister who claimed connection with the Societies, but does not seem to have been pronounced enough in his opposition to the king. The second was one of the objectors to Earlston's appointment as Commissioner, partly on the ground of expense. As for Welch, he was evidently, in Renwick's opinion, not to be trusted.

That there were persons in Newcastle, who were familiar with the Sanquhar Declaration and approved of the principles therein, is obvious both from this letter and from a sermon which Renwick subsequently preached in that neighbourhood, and which appears among his published writings. The sermon was founded on Hosea viii. 11, and contains the following sentences:—"The Lord hath no more to do with the wicked powers in these covenanted lands than to make them monuments of His displeasure and objects of His justice, and that He may shew forth His wonders and power in breaking of their power which they, Pharaoh-like, exercise against Him. In plain terms, they are much worse than Pharaoh was, for we read of Pharaoh's oppressing the Israelites in their persons and estates, though not in their consciences, and he took not their lives; but the present wicked powers cannot be satisfied

except they get estates, lives, consciences and all."
Those who could listen with approval to such words
had evidently not been much influenced by John
Hepburn and his friends. The Sanquhar Declaration
is frequently referred to in the history of the Cove-
nanters. It was nailed to the Cross of Sanquhar by
Richard Cameron and other brave men on the 22nd of
June 1680, the first anniversary of the battle of
Bothwell Bridge, and was meant as a public protest
against the continuance of the Stuart dynasty.

About the same time, Renwick sent the following
letter to the Rev. Mr Brakell of Leewarden.

LETTER V.

EDIN., October 5, 1682.

Most Rev. Sir,—Our friends when met are intended
with one consent to write unto you, in token of
thankfulness unto the Lord for what He hath helped
and honoured you to do for Himself; and in token of
their soul concernedness with, and real affection for, all
those whom the Lord helps and honours to follow in
His own way, in owning of, adhering to, and contending for the faith once delivered to the saints. Especially,
they purpose to write in token of their soul concernedness with you, whom the Lord hath so signally helped
to advance in His own way and contend for all His
rights and privileges, being carried above the fear of
frail mortal man whose breath is in his nostrils, and
only fearing Him who is "Lord of lords, and King of
kings," the terrible Majesty of heaven and earth, "the
high and lofty One who inhabiteth eternity." Yet my
soul is so united unto you upon that account, and
because of your real concernedness and soul sympathy
with all of us in Scotland, who desire to be helped of
the Lord, to espouse His quarrel to be only ours, and

His concernments to be only ours; I say, so united (though little or nothing I can say as I ought) that I cannot keep silent.

But, O! what shall I say? Is not the Lord God of hosts worthy and only worthy of all service, if we could serve Him? May not that infinite and transcendant love (in the profound depth of the admiration whereof angels are drowned) which He bore unto man before the foundations of the world were laid so ravish and fill our souls, as that we might say, Him only will we serve Who loved us, nothing present or to come shall be able to separate us from the love of God that is in Christ Jesus? O! is not "His yoke easy, and His burden light?" His cross is no cross, for He bears it Himself, and also those who take it up. His will is holy, just, good, and spiritual in all that He does. O! what is more desirable than to live and die with Him and for Him?—"For our light affliction which is but for a moment, worketh for us a far more exceeding and eternal weight of glory; while we look not at the things which are seen, but at the things which are not seen." "Let us not be weary in well doing, for in due season we shall reap if we faint not." "It is a faithful saying, if we be dead with Him, we shall also live with Him; if we suffer, we shall also reign with Him; if we deny Him, He will also deny us." O! is not Moses' choice very desirable? Are not "all His ways pleasantness, and His paths peace?" Where is peace to be found? is it not in His way? and when He gives peace, who can create trouble? He gives, and can give joy which no man can take from us. Now,

Most Reverend Sir, my soul desires, while I live, to praise the Lord for what great things He hath helped you to do, in so nobly, faithfully, and freely witnessing for His noble cause, and sweet Scotland's cause. My soul desires to honour you, because He hath so honoured you; and to love you, because He loves you, and hath caused you to love and own His cause and receive His truths in love, and also to be afflicted in all the afflictions of His people, and to be such a sympathiser, and a burden-bearer with His poor remnant in this land, as that we may say of you, as Paul of the Hebrews,— "Ye have had compassion on us in our bonds." O Sir, go on in His way, and advance valiantly; be zealous for Him and He shall animate you. "Cast not away your confidence, which hath great recompence of reward; for ye have need of patience, that after ye have done the will of God, ye might receive the promise. For yet a little while, and He that shall come will come, and will not tarry. Now the just shall live by faith; but if any man draw back, my soul shall have no pleasure in him," saith the Lord. O! who is he that will harm you if ye be followers of that which is good? Therefore, "cease from man, whose breath in his nostrils, for wherein is he to be accounted of?" Now, the Lord let you feed upon His all-sufficiency, and give all suitable frame and furniture unto you for His work in your hands; and give you His Spirit, whereby you may go on in His way, with all magnanimity, Christian boldness, and free speaking for Him unto the sons of men!

O Sir! do not impute any thing said to you in this short and confused line to arrogance in me; for what may, if mistaken, give occasion thereof flows only from my concernedness and soul-unison with you. So, at the time, I shall trouble you no farther. But this I must tell you, and I think it is to be remarked, and may be clearly seen all this time, that the terror of the Lord is greatly engraven and legibly written upon the consciences of the compliers with the horrid abominations of this land. They are really deadened, and it is no wonder, for they have forsaken the Lord, and He hath forsaken them. He cannot be found out of His own way. *A guilty conscience is bad company*, and what means all this terror of sudden and sore judgments from the Lord? There is not so much spirit, courage, and voidness of slavish fear among any, whether avowed malignants or compliers with them, as amongst the poor remnant, who are desiring to be helped of the Lord, in

all things to make a right choice.   O! pray for the
Lord's return to poor Scotland, and for His appearance
unto the rejoicing of His people, and confusion of His
adversaries.   And pray for him, who is, most Reverend
Sir, yours, to his full power to serve you in the Lord,

JAMES RENWICK.

We have now reached a transition period in Renwick's
life, when he is about to leave his native land for a
season, that he may prosecute his studies, and be
prepared for a still more active and prominent part in
the Lord's work in Scotland.   According to a statement
already made, he was not ready to go to the University
of Groningen until December, while his companions
succeeded in getting away during the previous month.
But from the letter which we now insert, if we can
depend, as we believe we can, on the accuracy of the date
and place of writing, it would seem that he had either
accompanied them to Holland, and then returned for a
few weeks to Scotland, or that he had found it necessary
in connection with other important matters to make
this voyage.   The letter is addressed to "the honourable,
the Laird of Earlston at Leewarden," and appears to
have been written at Rotterdam, in November 1682.
It also refers to an unexpected delay in that city, and
to the necessity of a letter being written which he is to
bring with him on his return to Holland, presumably a
letter of recommendation to the ministers and professors
of Groningen.

LETTER VI.

ROTTERDAM, Nov. 20, 1682.

Much honoured Sir,—It is not a little troublesome
to me that I should be in this place so long, but I
have occasion to go away whenever the wind offers :

and I hope your Honour will be careful to get conveyed
unto Scotland, with all expedition, an account of what
you think fit to be contained in that letter which is to
be written, for out of Scotland I cannot come, if once
it pleases the Lord that I were there, until that I get
that letter with me.   It will be also very necessary
that some should be pitched upon for catechising, and
this must be recommended to the carefulness of some
who will see it done at the General Meeting.   And if J.
V. be gotten reclaimed—for your Honour knows that he
walked contrary to his own duty, and our appointments,
in joining with Mr Hepburn while he was out of the
way of God ;—I say, if he be gotten reclaimed, amongst
others he may be one, as I think.   It is reported in the
Scottish news, that the actually Indulged (so called)
ministers are required, either immediately to take their
test, otherwise to lay down their charges at the feet of
those men of whom they took them up : and if it be so,
let the world think what they will, I dare not be sorry
thereat, but on¦ the contrary rejoice, because that Indulgence hath been, and is yet a stumbling-block unto the
people of God.   Is not the removing of stumbling-blocks
a token of sudden good to His people, how low soever
they be brought?   It is also reported, that Charles
Stuart hath ordained his Council in Scotland to proceed
against Haltoun, in making him accountable for the
mint.   Haman's rejoicing is short.

O Sir, I cannot get the thoughts of the weighty
case I left you in, when we parted, out of my mind.
But this I think, the Lord is taking several ways with
your Honour, in discommending all other things unto
you, that so He may commend Himself unto your soul,
and that you may be kept from rejoicing in anything but
Himself alone.   When He is the matter of our joy,
that is the joy that no man can take from us.   O ! 'tis
Himself that is the portion of His people, and the world
cannot deprive them thereof, and this is our comfort.

Remember me to your worthy brother, your lady,
and her sister : and as I have been partly an eye but

more an ear witness unto some of the troubles you have
been put to upon our blessed Lord's account, so I hope
also to be a witness of the everlasting inconceivable joy
you shall be filled with, when those who overcome shall be
sitting in white robes upon thrones with crowns upon
their heads, judging the world. O are you not high up
now ? are you not far ben in the King's palace, when you
are sitting upon thrones, giving your "amen" to the
sentence, which He will pass upon the world ? Walk
worthy of the name by which you are called. So leaving you on Him who is the Rock of Ages, Whose work
is perfect, for perfecting what concerns you, I am,
your Honour's servant in all Christian duty,

JAMES RENWICK.

Who J. V. was we cannot tell : only it is evident he
was a friend of Mr Hepburn already mentioned in
Letter IV. The Indulgence here referred to was one of
three Acts of Charles's Government, which were osten-
sibly meant to grant a larger measure of liberty to the
outed ministers, but whose chief result, if not design,
was either to favour the Papists or to produce dissension
among the Presbyterians. These Acts were passed in
1669, 1672, and 1679. Probably it is the last of the three
which is referred to in this letter. The Test was the
oath enjoined by Parliament in 1681 to be taken by all
persons in public trust, and which among other things
declared it to be "unlawful for subjects, upon pretence
of reformation or any pretence whatsoever, to enter into
covenants or leagues, or to convocate, convene, or
assemble in any councils, conventions, or assemblies, to
treat, consult, or determine, in any matter of state, civil
or ecclesiastic, without his majesty's special command,
or express license had thereunto." The reference to
Haltoun or the Earl of Lauderdale in this letter is
interesting, and tends to confirm the accuracy of the

date about which at first we were somewhat doubtful.
From the minutes of Privy Council we learn that, on
August 31st, orders were given to prosecute the Lord
Haltoun and others for some serious offence ; and that,
on November 7th, a letter came from the king himself
commanding them "to execute these orders, and to
pursue the Lord Haltoun, *now* Earl of Lauderdale, and
other officers of the mint." Renwick's feelings on receipt
of this report are clearly enough expressed in the terse
saying, "Haman's rejoicing is short."

We now insert a hitherto unpublished letter, for
which we are indebted to the Rev. John H. Thomson of
Hightae, and which helps to explain Renwick's move-
ments about this time. This autograph letter was
found by Mr Thomson at Waterside, in the loft of
Robert Calderwood's house, in a trunk with a number
of other documents. It was exhibited by him at the
Inverness Assembly in 1888. Like so many others, it
is addressed to Sir Robert Hamilton at Leewarden.

LETTER VII.

EDIN., Dec. 6, 1682.

Much honoured Sir,—It was the fourth of this instant
before I arrived at this place, being ten days upon the
sea, and that will cause my return to be the longer
procrastinated. But I shall not take ease so long as I
am here, and Mr J. F. being ready it was thought fit that
he should not wait any further.

Our case this day is more trying than ever heretofore,
but I think that is that the Lord make His strength to
be the more seen. But of all things this is the most
weighty to think upon, the vigilance and diligence of
some in persecuting as much one way as the enemy doth
another. For Mr Young upon the one hand deals as we

were set off at the right hand, and J. Russel as we were gone off at the left. But may not this give occasion to know that we are (in some measure) helped to stand in the middle way ? But now James is beginning to modify his former sayings anent these customs, not affirming any conclusion thereanent (as heretofore he did say), but that they were made an interrogation : but unto this I reply no other thing than what I have already. And (mainly by And. Y. his instigation) that Society at Newcastle are at the time lost. But being presently going away to the West, I cannot get (as I would) my mind of things told : neither can I get it told what strange providences the Lord hath (and that of late) trysted me with. O I shall be inexcusable if I shall not make money of such pennyworths ! But I remit you to the information of the bearer of what I cannot get written. So leaving you on the Lord with my love to your worthy brother and all his family, I am, Sir, yours at command in the Lord,   JAMES RENWICK.

The persecution of enemies was bad enough, but the strife and suspicion of friends were still worse, and these Renwick is now suffering from. Of Andrew Young mention has already been made. He seems to have represented the Society of Teviotdale, and is said to have been "a man of no despicable parts." James Russel is described by the same writer as "a man of a hot and fiery spirit." Besides maintaining the unlawfulness of "the Cess," he denounced the payment of dues at "ports and bridges," and separated from the Societies on this ground. We now begin to understand how difficult it was for Renwick to get away from Scotland ; but we shall soon see him making up for the delay by increased diligence, and even outstripping those who preceded him at Groningen, one of whom was John Flint, the J. F. mentioned in this letter.

CHAPTER III.

GRONINGEN.

RONINGEN is a large and strongly fortified town in the north-east of Holland, and is the capital of the province of the same name. Situated at the junction of two rivers, the Hunse and the Aa, it is, like other Dutch towns, traversed by numerous canals, which are crossed by eighteen bridges. Its market-place, which is said to be the largest in Holland, contains the beautiful Gothic church of St Martin's, with a noble tower three hundred and forty-three feet high, the highest in Holland. It has also a University which, at the time of which we write, was comparatively new, having been founded in 1614, but had already succeeded in attracting to its chairs some of the most distinguished theological professors in Europe.

Here in the early months of 1683, Renwick is busily occupied with his theological studies, which, however interesting, cannot prevent him from thinking much and often about the Lord's cause in Scotland, as the following letters to his friends in the neighbouring province of Friesland amply testify. Four of these, viz., 8, 10, 11, 13, are addressed to Sir Robert Hamilton, while the others, viz., 9, 12, 14, 15 are addressed to Sir Robert's two sisters who resided also at Leewarden.

C

LETTER VIII.

GRONINGEN, February 6, 1683.

Much honoured Sir,—O that now when I write to
you there were, for every drop of ink that falls from my
pen, a tear falling from my eyes! There is more than
cause enough for it, yea, and I cannot say but I am made
to see the same; for (in some measure) I see and know
the poor afflicted, tossing, and wandering remnant, in
such a case as the waters have flowed over their heads,
the Lord having covered Himself with a cloud. But for
all this (woe is me) my eye doth not rightly and
thoroughly affect my heart. O! if we would consider,
that the Lord doth not willingly afflict, nor grieve the
children of men, and then reflect upon our griefs and
afflictions in this day, we would be put, with amazement,
to wonder at the greatness of our sins. And instead of
coming to the Lord with this in our mouths and in our
hearts, That which we see not, teach thou us : Wherein
we have offended, we will offend no more, we are still
adding sin to sin, which are both the tokens and the
causes of the Lord's displeasure. O! there is nothing
(I think) that is so sad as the spiritual judgments of the
Lord, and nothing betokens so much of his displeasure.
O Sir! cry and wrestle and desire all that love Zion to
cry and wrestle with the Lord that He would preserve
a remnant from being swallowed up by this weighty
cloud of wrath hanging over our heads, ready to break
forth now when we are so ripening for the same.

I shall let you know my mind in all our particulars,
but (as yet) I can say nothing. But as for my own present case, you may know that from what I have said; for
those things that ought, and that I see, do not rightly
affect my heart. And by my seeing this also, I am at
present in a confused, anxious, and disconsolate condition; yet I dare not say but the Lord is kind, though I
be froward : and (I think) that which my soul would take
as the greatest proof of His kindness, would be a melting frame of spirit from Himself. But O! in all cases,

let us have our recourse to that Rock that is higher than we, where we shall find comfort for our perplexed hearts ; and let us lay our all under the feet of all men, but quit a hoof of God's matters to no man. LET US BE LIONS IN GOD'S CAUSE, AND LAMBS IN OUR OWN. Remember me to your brother and sisters. I hope (God willing) to write to him shortly. Remember 'me' to worthy Mr Brakell. I am, much honoured Sir, your soul's sympathiser, JAMES RENWICK.

'*P.S.*'—Mr Flint assures me that Mr Brakell's letter came by post. O ! Sir, let me have your counsel, and you may direct your letter for me to be found in the Volterlinge Straet, in the montremaoker's huys.

One would like to know about this montremaoker or watchmaker, to whose house in the straet or street bearing this peculiar name Renwick's letters were to be directed. Was it here he lodged during his stay in Groningen, or was this only a house of call ? Watchmakers, like printers, were then generally favourable to the cause of liberty, and were frequently remarkable for their intelligence and learning. It would be interesting were it possible to get a glimpse into this Dutch household, and to ascertain the exact relation between its members and this young Scotch student.

The next letter is addressed to Mrs Jean Hamilton, who resided with her brother at Leewarden, and to whom a few months later her sister, Lady Earlston, was obliged to entrust the care of her young family.

LETTER IX.

GRONINGEN, Feb. 13, 1683.

Worthy Madam,—The sense of my duty will not let me omit writing unto you ; although, if it would please the Lord, I would desire a clearer sight of some things than I have at present, that so I might be admitted to

tell you my thoughts more distinctly : but His way with
me is in the depths. I cannot tell what method He
would have me to take in some things ; for I find my
ordinary studies, that are more directly for exercitation
than for edification, put me out of a concerned frame
with the afflictions of Joseph. And then seeing this,
when I set upon other things, my thoughts begin to
slight these ordinary means. What the Lord would have
me to do therein, as yet I wot not. O that He that
hitherto hath condescended would condescend to let me
know what course He would have me to take, and make
me willing to follow the same. O it is hard to carry
within measure, and to give every thing its own place.
O let us earnestly labour to get a sympathising frame of
spirit kept up, with that poor, afflicted, scattered, and
broken remnant in Scotland ; for I observe this palpably,
that I am never in any sort of a good frame, but when
they are lying near my heart, and when their afflictions
are touching me. There are many things that are very
discouraging like ; but there is comfort, Jesus Christ
is a King, and seeing He is a King, He will have
subjects ; yea, He will reign till He put all His enemies
under His feet. Shall not the pleasure of the Lord
prosper in His hand ? "He will see of the travail of his
soul, and be satisfied." And may not our souls feed
upon the ravishing thoughts of the pureness of that
church which He will have in Scotland ? What shall
be the end of all these things ? shall they not all tend to
the purging of Jacob from his sin ?

O Madam, live near the Lord, and labour to get Him
present with you. His presence will make all trials
sweet. Who would not come with Him from Amana,
I say with Him from Amana ? He is the chief among
ten thousand ; His countenance is comely as Lebanon,
excellent as the cedars ; yea, He is altogether lovely. A
sight of the preciousness that is in Him will cause
us to go through fire and water with Him and for Him.
Will not the consolations of His Spirit bear up the soul
in all its difficulties ? especially when it is aye made

to see in the end, that it could not want one dram
weight of its cup? And O the great need that there is
of the consolations of His Spirit in this day! For I have
these thoughts this long time, that many would be
trysted with such dispensations, as would not so much
call for light to lead them, as for heart comforting grace
to bear up their spirits in them. I think some of our
dispensations will be to some more discouraging than
darkening. O mind sweet Scotland, and him who is
your Ladyship's servant in all Christian duty,

JAMES RENWICK.

LETTER X.

GRONINGEN, Feb. 22, 1683.

Much honoured Sir,—I cannot express my obligations
to you for writing to me, a poor empty nothing; and
considering my present case, your letter was very
seasonable; for my great exercise is, and was, how to
know the motions of the Lord's Spirit, and what He
would have me do in the circumstances wherein I stand:
and you have given some marks thereof, which I think
indeed are very holding. But in this I must reverence
a higher hand than yours. I have (since I saw you last)
had as sad conflicts, yea more sad than ever I had heretofore. But O that I could bless and praise the name
of the only holy and wise God, there is not one dram in
the mixture of my cup that I can want, yea, I see a
necessity for all that I meet with. And though I have
had very sad conflicts, the Lord (O infinite condescend
ence!) hath made me to possess sweet hours both in the
night and day. And as to my own case, I may say,
"The Lord stays his rough wind in the day of his east
wind;" for notwithstanding that "deep calleth unto
deep," yet the Lord keeps my spirit, in some measure,
stayed and stablished as to that. But when I ponder
other circumstances, I am put to many strange
thoughts; yet the Lord makes me even feed many times
upon this, and that even with great joy, that as He is

dealing with His church this day, so is He dealing with
me ; yea, I see not one circumstance in the one, but I
also see it in the other : yea, and is not this great
matter of joy ?   The Lord forbid that I should desire to
be otherways dealt with than His church is.   O how
unnatural-like and unchild-like would that desire be.
When His way is in the deeps with His church why
should it not be so with us ?   But, O Sir, I see a cloud
of wrath ready to fall out ; and I fear, I fear that we will
not be found free of it.   O may not anything be easily
borne ? but how can this be borne ?   O for grace to turn
speedily and repent, may be the Lord would repent him
of the evil.   There is mourning and humiliation that
the Lord is calling for ; and the Lord will aye (I think)
give us stroke upon stroke, and blow upon blow, until
He get that effectuated.   If my heart deceive me not, I
could submit (at least desire to submit) to any thing in
time ; but to this, to wit, to have a deep hand in drawing
more wrath forth, I cannot submit, and I ought not to
submit.   O that the Lord would rather take me away in
the midst of my days !   But I ought not to misbelieve ;
He can keep my feet from falling, He can perfect
strength in my weakness.   But this is the way that the
Lord would have me to take ; yea I think assuredly, this
is the course He would have me to fall upon, to seek all
that I need from Himself by prayer.   For to the praise of
His free grace I must speak it, when He helps me either
to pray or meditate, He is not wanting ; but in other
things I do not find Him.   However, I think, this may
be the cause of it.   I cannot win to use them and keep
them in their own places.   But there are some things
good in themselves, and good when made right use of ;
but to me they are as Saul's armour to David.   I can put
them on, but I cannot walk with them : and I cannot
say, but I could put them on, unless I should lie of the
Lord, who (blessed be His name) hath given me, in some
measure, a disposition.

O Sir, as your letter was very refreshful, on the one
hand, so, upon the other, it was very weighting unto me ;
because you say the trouble you told me of is not yet

away. But O I fear there may be much of a tentation in it, for I cannot see cause for trouble upon that account. But my hearing that you are troubled is no surprisal to me ; for you were often brought before me since I parted from you, and you were aye represented as one overwhelmed and weighted, and this was sometimes troublesome to me. But when I thought upon the case of the Lord's Church, I was then made to think, why should I wish it to be otherwise with you, than it is with your mother? But is not the Lord taking all ways with us, to spean* us from all things ; yea, even to make us denied to one another? He will have us to take Himself for all our contentment and satisfaction. O noble contentment! O sweet satisfaction! Other airts may fail us, and will fail, but the Lord will never fail any that put their trust in Him : and whatever the Lord hath to do with you in any place, as He calls you forth, so He will also, in His own blessed time, lead you whither you should go. Heb. xi. 8, "By faith Abraham, when he was called to go out unto a place which he should after receive for an inheritance, obeyed ; and he went out, not knowing whither he went." O Sir, pray for sweet Scotland ; pray that zeal and tenderness may be kept there : and pray for him who is,

Much honoured Sir,

your soul's sympathizer,

and servant in the Lord,

JAMES RENWICK.

'*P.S.*'—I cannot understand what you mean by the enclosed that you speak of, which was refreshing to you, and which you desire to be sent back again, for I received nothing enclosed but a line to Mr William.

Master Flint and Mr Boyd remember you. Your brother will tell you how it is with us. Also I had written more largely ; however we expect to see you here shortly for there is much work ado here.

My love and service to your sisters, the Lady and Mistress Jean.

* Wean.

In this letter reference is made to "sad conflicts," evidently of a spiritual nature, through which he had recently passed. His studies probably had become engrossing and distracting, and were occasionally felt by him to be a hindrance rather than a help to his spiritual life. That he did not neglect them is certified by Mr Brakell, the minister of Leewarden, who, in a letter to the United Societies, remarks, "the three students chosen by you to the pastoral office are busy at their studies." But from a remark which one of these companions made to Sir Robert Hamilton regarding him, we are permitted to infer that he spent much time in prayer and other spiritual exercises. Of this his own letters leave us in no doubt whatever.

Letter XI.

GRONINGEN, March 6, 1683.

Much honoured Sir,—I received your letter with worthy Mr Brakell's, which were very surprising to me, in respect of the circumstances of the times. The sense of the work, together with my own unfitness, came so upon my spirit, that I began to give place to this resolution, that I would desire some more time ; but therein I could find no peace, the mind being tortured and racked. Upon the other hand, when I considered the afflicted and affecting case of the remnant, both in respect of open adversaries, and of treacherous sitters at ease, who stand in the cross way ; I say, when I considered how the glorious truths of God were wronged, by cruelty against them, on the one hand, and perfidious treachery and double-dealing on the other, I thought it would be an honourable thing,— the Lord calling me thereto, and fitting me therefor,— if it were but to give one public testimony against the same. Yet many objections arose in the heart, flowing

all from the sense of my unfitness; but the Lord (O
praise be to His holy name!) answered them all with
your letters, and with that word, Ps. lxxxix. 19.
"I have laid help upon one that is mighty." Also I
thought, that it was so like the way of His dealing with
His church, and I saw so much of glorious wisdom
and infinite love toward me in it (for if I had anything
in me, I would be ready to forget Him, and not to
resort to that inexhaustible and precious treasure,
but now I was put to run to Himself, having no other
airt to betake me to), that I could find no place for my
objections more. But oh! a weighty work indeed; I
see that we can never run to Him to get the weight of
anything taken off our spirits and laid on Himself, till
He let us once find somewhat of the weightiness thereof,
and get it, as it were, laid heavy upon us. O! I say,
a weighty work indeed! Who is fit for opening up the
mysteries of salvation? Who is fit for declaring our
sweet Lord Jesus Christ, prophet, priest, and king in
Zion, without any competitor, and for opening up the
same? Who is fit for dispensing those glorious benefits of the covenant of redemption? O! who is sufficient for these things? And why is He calling poor
unworthy nothing me out to such a great and glorious
work? I think that He is saying, that the excellency of the power may be of Himself, and not of me.
So, having the mouth of all objections stopped, I offer
myself in all trembling, fear, and humility; yet having
great reason to believe in Him for all things, though I
be altogether unfit. O dear Sir, wrestle, wrestle, and
desire all true lovers of Zion to wrestle with the Lord,
that you and we may be directed in this great affair.
O set time apart, and seek the mind of the Lord
therein. You will meet with difficulties in it; but I
hope the Lord will have a care of His own work, and
direct you wisely. For my own part, I desire nothing
but what may be for the advantage of the cause; but
I hope the Lord hath so framed my affections, that whatever is seen not to be advantageous, I shall not desire.

We desire humbly to thank you for your books. The Lord will repay you : and as for your letter from Scotland, which you sent to me, it was very refreshful. I am sure the Lord moved you to send it ; for I was made therein to see a great proof of the Lord's condescendency to poor me. That which it contains of Andrew Young was the thing which I was expecting, for he was still brought before me, and represented as a man full of bitter passion ; yea, he was so brought still in my way, that the day, or two days before I received the letter, I said several times to my neighbours, that I was sure I would hear something of him. O ! that I had the tongue of the learned, to set forth the praise of that so glorious and excellent, yet so condescending God. O ! there is none that know Him but they will love Him. The many proofs of His kindness and condescendency, make me many times to cry out, "What is man that He is mindful of him, or the son of man that He should visit him ?" But He loves, because He loves ; and there can be no other reason given for it. I shall trouble you no further at the time, but present my love and service to your worthy brother. I hope he is not unconcerned at this time. As for his going to Scotland, the Lord will direct him what to do : and I shall labour, through the Lord's strength, to obey your answer hereof. O Sir ! wrestle, wrestle, and desire all to wrestle with the Lord, that He would carry on His own work, and get glory to Himself in fitting instruments, and in making His people a zealous people, a holy people, a self-denied people. I am, much honoured Sir, your sympathising friend, and servant in the Lord, JAMES RENWICK.

The next is pre-eminently a letter of consolation, and is addressed to Mrs Jean Hamilton. It contains some quaint expressions, and reveals an intimate acquaintance with the life of faith.

Letter XII.

Groningen, March 31, 1683.

Worthy Madam,—I have no time to write any thing to you, but I hope you will not think me so far out of my duty as to be unmindful of your case ; for I am very sensible of the circumstances wherein you stand. However, though your trials be many, and your fears not few, yet I think not your case strange—the like hath happened to the Lord's people. O take all well out of the Lord's hand. Look to His purposes in His dispensations, and then you will be made to read love to you in the saddest of them. Away with scrimpit sense, which constructs * aye God's heart to be as His face is. Faith is a noble thing, it soars high, and can read love in God's heart when His face frowns. Have you not reason to construct well of Him? Bode † good upon His hand. Your evening of sorrow shall be turned into an everlasting morning of joy. Let the faith of this sweeten your present case unto you. The Lord be with you all. Mind him who is, worthy Madam, your friend and servant in the Lord, and a sympathiser with you in your trials,   James Renwick.

From a letter which Sir Robert Hamilton afterwards wrote to some friends in Scotland, we learn that it was about this time, and as the result of the previous correspondence on his own mind, that he began to exert himself to procure ordination for Mr Renwick. He went first to his friend Mr Brakell, and laid the whole case before him, "who no sooner heard of it, but was as one out of himself with the great satisfaction and joy he had in it, which" (says Sir Robert) "helped to my strengthening. Whereupon we resolved to write presently to Mr Renwick." It is doubtless to this communication that the following letter refers.

* Judges.   † Expect.

LETTER XIII.

GRONINGEN, April 23, 1683.

Much honoured Sir,—I received the enclosed yesterday, but I have no time to write any thing, for the occasion is now going. Only I have written this day to Mr Brakell at L., and by the Lord's gracious free condescension, I was put and kept in a good frame all the while. O! that I could praise Him for His free, free love! He lets me see much sin, and yet lets me see also, that He does not contend for the same, which cannot but be great matter of wonder. No sight, I think, is so sweet as that sight, for it is backed with admiration of His free love, and also with self-loathing. Hoping that you will be mindful of poor unworthy me, as with my whole heart I desire to be of you, I am, much honoured Sir, yours at command, to serve you in the Lord,

JAMES RENWICK.

After various difficulties had been overcome, which are minutely described by Sir Robert Hamilton in the letter already referred to, Mr Renwick's ordination was fixed for the 10th of May. On that day, after an examination by the "Classis" or Presbytery, which lasted for four hours, he was ordained by the laying on of hands, the only Scotchmen present being Sir Robert Hamilton, Sir Alexander Gordon, and another friend frequently mentioned in these letters, George Hill. It was while these preliminary negotiations were proceeding, and in view of the solemn act of ordination which had been promised, that the next two letters were penned, the first to Mrs Jean Hamilton and the other to her sister, Lady Earlston.

Letter XIV.

GRONINGEN, April 25, 1683.

Worthy Madam,—I thought it my duty to acquaint you with what great things the Lord hath done in this place, for His own noble cause, and for us poor, weak, empty nothings. For when upon Thursday last, being the 19th of this instant, Mr John Flint and I went in before the Synod, which was then sitting, and sought ordination from them ; they, for the most part, not knowing us, after we had removed for a little space, began to ask among themselves what we were seeking, having heard something thereof from ourselves. Whereupon, first, Dominus Philingius, then Dominus Albringha rose up and declared unto them somewhat of the case of our church : at which, some of them fell out into tears, and said,—Though the kings of the earth should be against them, they would go on in our affairs. Whereupon we were called in again unto them, and three men were appointed for our trials ; and the tenth of the next month, for the day 'of ordination' ; the ministers of this town having undertaken the expense which we ought to have been at. So having many things to do, I shall detain your Ladyship no farther. But O ! is not this great matter of praise, that the Lord should let His own hand be so much seen in procuring such testimonies to His noble cause. Yea, before He want a testimony, the very stones shall be made to cry out. Therefore, come and let us worship Him, come and let us exalt His name together. He reigns, and therefore let His followers be glad.

Recommending you to His fatherly care, hoping that you will not be unmindful of poor unworthy me, upon whom the Lord hath laid so many obligations to be for Him, and whom He is now calling forth to His vineyard in such a weak condition (but my sufficiency is of Him, and to be found faithful is all my desire). 'I send' my love and service to your worthy sister, the

Lady, and her children. Worthy Madam, yours to my
full power to serve you in the Lord,

JAMES RENWICK.

LETTER XV.

GRONINGEN, May 5, 1683.

Worthy Madam,—I received your Ladyship's letter ;
but I am sorry that I had not the time to write sooner
back to you. However, I hope you will excuse me, considering the circumstances I stand in at this time. Your
letter represents unto me a troubled case, but (I think)
not a bad case, because you have the lively sense of it
on your spirit. You say, a hiding God, who can bear it ?
O that I could see those pleasant days, to hear many
crying that cry ; to hear many signifying their desire after
Himself, by crying out, that they could not want Him,
that they could not be content without Him : yea, and
that they would not be content with anything else, being
wilful in the matter ! It is true, indeed, they who know
what His sensible presence is, they will not get borne
up in His conceived absence, and, if I could, I would
desire to mourn over their unperceiving temper, who
can equally bear up in both. But when the soul, not
being filled with sense, pants after Him as the hart
after the brooks of water, and, getting up, and running
through the whole fields, cries out, "Saw ye Him
whom my soul loveth," I cannot but think, that the
Lord is eminently present with that soul, though not
to its own apprehension. Yea, and though there be no
changes in the Lord, nor in His love, yet of all times
(as to the outletting thereof) He is at such a time most
fasht to keep it in, and who knows not that love, the
more it is covered, the more it burns, as fire, the more
it be covered, the more it smokes, unless it be extin-
guished ? But here is our comfort, He cannot change
His love, nothing can extinguish it : for whom He
loves He loves unto the end. O let us not miscon-

struct * Him, for He dow † not abide it ! And, for mine own part, I am made many times to go and bless His holy name, because of His withdrawing, for I see much more of His love manifested therein, than if He were sensibly present; because then I am made to see many things in myself which I saw not before. For it is most difficult to carry aright upon the mount. Do we not find this, in such cases, that we forget ourselves many times?—as Peter, when he was with our Lord on the mount and saw His glory, said, It is good for us to be here, let us make three tabernacles, one for Thee, one for Moses, and one for Elias; which Luke notes with that, that he knew not what he said. O! let us study that noble life of faith, which the Lord is at so great pains to teach us; for it is faith followed with holiness that all the promises are made unto, not one unto sense.

Your Ladyship writes, that since you came to this land, the Lord's way hath not been ordinary with you, and I think, it looks the liker His way that it is so. And though (possibly) at the time you cannot see what is the language thereof, yet I am sure that afterwards He will let you see it. We have the swellings of Jordan to pass through yet, and the Lord seems to be training you up for what may be before your hand, and learning you only to live the life of faith. O let us wait on Him, for we many times lose our alms ‡ because we want patience to wait on but a little. Let us lie near Himself, that we may not be surprised or confused in a day of fiery trial, not knowing whither to run. And as for that trouble which ariseth from the finding of friends like to take offence at your not going to the kirk, I confess, in its own place, it is some matter of concernment. But we have One who is higher, whom we must look unto that we offend not; and to seek their countenance such a way, I dare not, nor will not counsel you to it. Labour to follow the Lord's leading of you,

* Misjudge.   † Can.
‡ *i.e.*, the favours we might have got from His hand.

for I think your case in that particular must be of Himself, although that ye are not humbled with your Sabbath days being your worst days, for the Lord herein seems only to be trying you. And if Satan get in his foot, and make you to question duty for your want of sense, he will get his end mightily gained. O what is the matter though all the world should forsake, though all men should forsake, though all men should turn against us,—if He be for us, what need we care? O sweet word, Though father and mother should forsake, yet He will not; and though our flesh and heart fainteth and faileth, yet He never faileth us. O Madam! I have no time to say what I would, but shall omit the rest until meeting, which (if the Lord will) shall be shortly. Our ordination is going on; but, for ought I think, Mr John Flint will not go through. O! pray, pray that the Lord may let His hand be seen with poor, weak, unworthy me: without Him I can do nothing. O what excessive madness will it be to go on without Himself! If He go not with me, I pray that He may not carry me up. My love and service to your worthy sister and all your family. I am, your Ladyship's servant to serve you in all things in the Lord, JAMES RENWICK.

'*P.S.*'—I have written a short line to your worthy husband, but I durst not be very particular with him, lest he should be troubled: but if the Lord so order it I shall be free at meeting. I have left it without a direction, because I know not how to direct it. Your Ladyship may do it, but if you fear that it will be miscarried, I entreat not to send it lest it do harm.

CHAPTER IV.

AFTER ORDINATION.

SOON after his ordination, Renwick proceeded to make arrangements for returning to Scotland and entering upon his public ministry. At the close of the month we find him at Amsterdam, after a visit to his friends at Leewarden. The letter which immediately follows refers to sundry commissions which he had undertaken for Sir Robert Hamilton, and shows how intimate their friendship had become and how thankful Renwick was for any opportunity of serving his friend and benefactor.

LETTER XVI.

AMSTERDAM, May 30, 1683.

Much honoured Sir,—I am sorry that those things could not be sooner had to have been sent unto you. However, I used all diligence for that effect, but could not accomplish my desire : for it was five hours of Tuesday morning when we came to Amsterdam, and having taken up our lodgings in a Dutch house and made ready to go forth, I went seeking Alexander and Andrew Henderson, but could get nothing done by them until afternoon. But there was much of the Lord's providence to be seen in everything ; for when I spoke anent the changing of some money into gold, they (thinking it was for ourselves in our passage) said

D

they thought it was a very good motion because it would be both easy to carry and to hide, signifying that they themselves had done the like. I am sorry that you should have so little, but I thought that from your tender sympathising affection towards your brethren, you would not be content if more had been sent. However, I was exceedingly troubled after I parted with you that I should have left you so as I did, but I hope you will have me excused, my mind being much taken up with the leaving you. Moreover, you shall receive three Dutch and English Grammars : but I know not what sort you were desirous to have, and therefore I am afraid that two of them be not so full as they should be, I not having the third to compare with them when they were bought, and they who sold them said they were as good and as full as any. However, if they be not good enough, or if you desire more, I think you may employ therein Alexr. or Andrew Henderson. Receive also these heads that the worthy Ladies Van Heermaen desired me to write, but you may look them through yourself before that you deliver them. And as for your French mael* it was very ill to be had and stands 9 gild. 4 st., for I could get none that was so good any cheaper. I might have had one less, but I thought you would need it this great. But if it be not according to your mind, you must not be offended at me, for I did everything therein for the best. Also I used all diligence in seeking unto you an English Wollebius but could not get it : but if it be to yourself, I think it would be no loss to read it in Latin, and one of these you can have in any place. Now, much honoured Sir, if there be anything that you desired me to do, which I have omitted, you must excuse me therein, for I can remember no more, my thoughts being taken up with many things.

After I met with Andrew Henderson I asked him

---

* A valise or trunk, costing nine guilders four stivers, or fifteen shillings and fourpence. The word was also spelt *male*, and is probably a corruption of the French *malle*.

anent his service, and told him my mind freely of it
and what I saw therein : whereunto he assented, saying
if he had seen ill in it or yet have thought that it
should have offended any, he had not gone to it : albeit
his liberty in the Sabbath day was the thing which
overcame him. However, he says now that he resolves
not to stay with it ; but oh it is a difficulty to know
how to carry toward people.

George Hill went away this morning unto Utrecht,
but I hope he will be watchful. Yet I know not
whether Mr Cameron cometh to speak with me or not,
for I could not have freedom to desire anything therein
to be done, but according to your letter and as George
shall find him in converse. And I determine (if the
Lord will) to stay in this place until Friday at twelve
of the clock, to see whether or not he comes, and
then to take the mercat Scout to Rotterdam, where
I can be about six of the clock on Saturday morning,
George being gone thither before and resolved to wait
upon the Scout, that I may know what he hath done
and where he hath taken up his quarters ; and then
to accept the first occasion that offers.

O, much honoured Sir, you know what a great work
the Lord hath laid upon me, and how He hath laid so
many obligations upon me to be for Him and Him
only. I hope that you will be mindful thereof,
praying that he would endue me with zeal, courage,
resoluteness, constancy, wisdom, tenderness, and
humility, and give a door of utterance that with all
boldness I may speak all His words, and that He may
follow the same with His rich blessing. I do not
think but difficulties and trials are abiding me, but
if He be with me I shall not care. We must not this
day seek to ourselves great things, when the Lord is
bringing evil upon all flesh, and is breaking down
that He may plant. O I must say this indeed to the
praise of His free grace, that He is continuing and
increasing His kindly dealing with my soul. O that I
could praise Him and commend Him to all flesh !

Remember me to all our friends in the Lord, particularly worthy Mr Brakell, if you have occasion, your worthy sister and the worthy ladies Van Heermaen whom I am singularly obliged to be mindful of, and not only I but the Church of God. The Lord's blessing be with you and the earnest good wishes of him who is, much honoured Sir, yours to serve in the Lord while I have a being in time,   JAMES RENWICK.

The two ladies Van Heermaen are frequently mentioned by Renwick in his correspondence, and two of his letters are addressed to them. They showed great kindness to the refugees from Scotland, and at a later date they were specially thanked by the Societies for their attention to Sir Robert Hamilton and his sisters. The Mr Cameron, about whose coming he is uncertain, was Andrew Cameron, a brother of the famous Richard Cameron. After studying in Holland for the ministry, he seems to have returned to Scotland in 1685, and to have been very eager in trying to induce the Societies to join the ill-fated expedition of Argyle. Ultimately he threw in his lot with the indulged ministers. By "Wollebius" we are to understand one of the works of a famous Swiss professor, Jean Wolleb, who was born at Basle in 1536, and held the chair of New Testament Exegesis in that city.

The next letter is a shorter one, and both in MacMillan's and Houston's Edition of these letters is dated March 30th. There can be no doubt that this is a misprint for May 30th. Similar mistakes occur in the case of other two letters which were written from Rotterdam, and in those editions have been referred to the month of January instead of June.

Letter XVII.

Much honoured Sir,—After I had sent away your French mael,* and a letter with it, I received yours, but the post being just now going away, I have no time to write. But what would I, or could I say, but only desire to be submissive to the Lord's will, who hath made a necessary separation betwixt us, that I cannot have the comfort and advantage of your company. But, though you be absent from me as to bodily presence, you are not long out of my mind. I wish I may get you kept in your own place, and kept from murmuring and discontent at my want. I resolve to pass for a while under the name of James Bruce. I have no time now to write to these worthy ladies; but before I go to Scotland I shall see to get it done, yet if once I were there, I think, I would know better how to write of matters. The Lord Himself be with you. I am, much honoured Sir, yours to serve you in the Lord, while I have a being in time,   JAMES RENWICK.

Several days before the next letter was written, Earlston had already been arrested at Newcastle, though the fact had not yet become known in Holland. By E. A. is meant Edward Aitken, his servant, who was with him at the time, and was also apprehended. Earlston's non-appearance at Leewarden was evidently creating anxiety among his friends. By J. N. we are probably to understand John Nisbet, one of the young men selected to go to Groningen. He had before this been appointed by the Societies to accompany Earlston as their Commissioner, but had remained in London while the latter went to Holland.

John Gibb and his companions were commonly known as the "sweet singers." He was the leader of a

* Referred to on page 50.

small sect of crack-brained enthusiasts, who, in some respects, resembled the Anabaptists of Luther's time, and like them, by their blasphemous speech and conduct, brought discredit on the cause of religion. Cargill sought in vain to reclaim them from their sinful extravagances, and his letter addressed to them while in the Canongate prison may be read in the "Cloud of Witnesses," pp. 20-26. (Thomson's Ed.)

LETTER XVIII.

AMSTERDAM, May 31, 1683.

Much honoured Sir,—Having met with E. D. who is coming to be your sister's servant, I thought it my duty to acquaint you, that your worthy brother, Earlston, is a long while ago come from Scotland, having met with friends there. And, as I hear, there are three papers drawn up; one including some reasons why we have rejected the tyrant; another, some reasons of our separating from those (so-called) ministers; and the third, she says, is a call to, and a protestation against them. I wish it may be a bringing us out of the mire (and not a casting us into it over again) as I hope it will be. But the reason of your brother's not coming hither ere this time, is his coming by London. I hope he knows his errand and call thereunto, though I cannot see it. E. A. is also coming alongst with him; but I hope you will not meddle with J. N. The Lord counsel him and lead him, for that land is a valley of snares, especially at this time. Of the seven who were apprehended, four have taken the Test; whereof one is Alexander Millar, a young man. O! all flesh is grass; for I thought once, if there was a zealous man in Scotland, he was one. Yet the Lord hath not left us so; for He hath accepted a bloody sacrifice of our hands, two men being executed, viz.: John Wilson in Lanark, a young gentleman, and David M'Millan in Galloway, of whom I hear nothing but what is matter of praise, and cause of encouragement. O! let us go on and run our race rejoicing, and with patience. The cup of the Amorites is fast filling, and their day is near at hand, when they shall get their own blood to drink, for they are worthy. Robert Lawson is saying he will not die at this time, but I like not such prophecies as our case stands. John Gibb and his companions are freed both from death and banishment, and have their liberty to go through all the prison, and large expense allowed daily unto them, by him whom they call the Chancellor. If the enemies had done otherwise, they would not act like themselves. Courage, dear Sir, they will drop ripe very suddenly.

I have sent you, with the said E. D., the exposition of the text which you desired, and shall take care to get a true copy of your letter secured unto you. I shall add no further at the time, but pray that the Lord may be unto you a present help in all times of need; for I think difficulties and discouragements are many, but you know where your strength lies, and what must comfort you. O! hitherto He hath not been wanting, neither will He be wanting, for He is a faithful God, who keepeth covenant; and He knows this, that if He had not now put other work in mine hand, and were He not calling me to another place, it would be my heart's desire to serve you (as, indeed, is my duty many ways) and to take part with you in all your troubles. But what I cannot do by bodily presence, I hope the Lord will help me to do it by heart sympathy and willingness. Leaving you on your Master's hand, I am, much honoured Sir, yours to serve you in the Lord, while I have a being in time, JAMES RENWICK.

During this time of waiting and anxiety Renwick seems to have removed to Rotterdam, from which the next four letters in our collection are written. They are all addressed to his friend, Sir Robert Hamilton, and testify strongly to his distress at the sad tidings which were then reaching him from Scotland, as also to his earnest longing to be with his suffering and oppressed brethren. The first is dated according to both the old and new styles, between which there was a difference of ten days. Renwick was familiar with both, as the new style was adopted in Scotland in 1600, though not in England till 1752.

Letter XIX.

Rotterdam, June $\frac{16}{26}$, 1683.

Much honoured Sir,—I received your letter, but the intervening of some dispensations put me so that I was not in case for answering it; and our friend George* having written unto you, therefore I shall not now speak neither of our own progress, nor of what sad news otherways we have heard. The Lord help us to patience, for we have need of it, and make us submissive to His will who can do nothing but good! O they are happy who are well away, and they are happy who will be carried through, for there are sad days coming, and these lands shall not escape. I cannot express the weighty impression I have of it especially since the last fast day that they had in this province, in the morning whereof I fell in a dream, and thought that I was preaching upon these words, Zech. vii. 5. at the end of the verse, "Did ye at all fast unto me, even unto me?" (spoken by the Lord) and thought that I brought in this from it, that they who were but hypocritical, formal and outward, or outside folk only in their fastings, did not fast unto the Lord. And 2dly, 'I brought in this that' They who fasted, and yet retained sin, and refused to let it go 'did not fast unto the Lord': and then made application to many particular sins in these lands. I think little of this as a dream, however it hath some impression upon me. O to be helped to obey our Lord's command, and to exhort others there-

* George Hill, who was present at his ordination.

unto, Luke xxi. 36. Watch ye therefore, &c. O dear Sir! I cannot express the case I am in, partly with our dear friends falling into the hands of our Lord's enemies, and partly with my being so long detained from my brethren. I cannot tell what may be before my hand, but my longings to be in Scotland I cannot express. I would spare no pains or travel, and fear no hazard; only, I do not think it duty to go on deliberately in a seen hazard, where there is no probability of safety. O! (I say) that the Lord would be pleased to provide some occasion which might be my duty to embrace; and that He would order all things aright for the enlargement of His kingdom. O precious kingdom! and O noble way that He is taking this day to enlarge it, by stretching out the borders thereof with blood! His house is a costly house, and it is well worth costly cementing. I hope I need not bid you labour to submit cheerfully to the holy and wise will of the Lord, and be strengthening unto those with you. The Lord strengthen, the Lord comfort and give Himself instead of all things to them and to you, is, and shall be the earnest prayer of him who is, much honoured Sir, yours, to serve you in the Lord, while he hath a being in time.

JAMES RENWICK.

'P.S.' Remember me to all our dear friends, particularly to those worthy ladies Van Heermaen. I am resolved (if the Lord will) to write to them the beginning of the next week, and to our friend Mr Muntandam.* I would desire to signify my sympathy by writing a line to your worthy sister, but I hope to see her shortly.

LETTER XX.

ROTTERDAM, June 18, 1683.

Honourable Sir,—I have received both your former and later letters. But you may see an emblem of the case I was in when I last wrote unto you, by my not

* This gentleman had the oversight of our students in Groningen.

answering some particulars in your former letter, which I ought to have done. However, I have heard that our friend G. has written to you, wherein, I hope, he has given you a full account of his passage at Utrecht ; and also of some strange disappointments that have happened unto us since, which made me often remember a word of yours to myself, that you thought I should meet with some strange things in my going home. I have met with some strange things, indeed, and have nothing to boast of, but only of the Lord, who is to be admired in all His doings ; for they are works of wonder. And O that He would help me to submit to His holy and wise will, in keeping me so long here ; yet I think the work is the liker His work that there are so many difficulties in the way of it. But as for Mr A. Cameron, I did not see him, but I hear that he is come unto you. The Lord, I hope, will let you know your duty, and will clear that best unto you, by conversing with himself. O ! add not drunkenness to thirst ; but if the Lord call, see that you bestir yourself in it all that you can. He that hath had his hand singularly with you in many pieces of great service, will not leave you in this. And as for A. H., and A. H., they know, indeed, of my ordination ; and the way they came to know it was, by their peremptory questions, to which I could not negatively answer ; and then, finding them gather the affirmative, I told them it was so, and enjoined silence upon them. But as for other particulars of our affairs, they know none by me, save that James Russel and we, when we met, could not agree.

You wrote anent Mr Flint and Mr Boyd, their bestowing three hours each day upon James Russel and his comrade, in teaching of them ; but as matters stand, I cannot approve of it, upon many considerations. For it is both encouraging and hardening to them. I say, encouraging to them to hold on their courses, for I see very little hope of what they pretend unto. I fear that there is rather in it a faction, seeking to make a party. And as for Mr Binning's being employed to teach our expectants, the Lord, I hope, will give me to know my duty in it, abstracting from all persons whatsoever.

As for what you wrote of fairs and markets on saints' days, I agree heartily with it; it was my own thought before, but confusedly. However, I desire to bless the Lord, who hath made you a mean in that (as in some other things) to make me more distinct therein. O! I cannot express what I owe unto you, — I say, I cannot express what I owe the Lord, whom I desire to bless while I live, that ever I saw your face. The Lord hath also made you to back what I was resolved on before, by your wholesome advice, in counselling me to take up an inventory of the Lord's way of dealing with friends and enemies in their persons and families, particularly and generally. And be assured, much honoured and dear Sir, that I shall, as I ought, keep nothing back from you. For, under the Lord Himself, I have none that I can expect such counsel from as from you, therefore, you must still be giving me your advice, and lay it out before the Lord ere you give it to me; for, indeed, I will lay much weight upon it : however, I desire to weigh it in the balance of the sanctuary. As for your going further away, I desire, indeed, to believe, that the Lord hath some work to do further abroad ; but I think the change of dispensations calls you to stay still a while with our friends that are with you ; for assuredly they will be much affected with the news of our dear friend Earlston, your dear brother, being taken. And also, I think, you cannot move until you hear what comes of him, (the Lord, I think, hath a great kindness for him, and will honour him), and till you receive letters from Scotland, both to yourself, to the presbytery of Groningen, and other friends.

I am not a little sorrowful at the very heart, that I am not in Scotland to obey all your commands anent your dear brother. The Lord Himself knows, that

nothing that ever I was trusted with was such an
exercise to me, as my being detained now out of it is.
My longings and earnest desires to be in that land, and
with that pleasant remnant, are very great. I cannot
tell what may be in it, but I hope the Lord hath either
some work to work, or else is minded presently to call
for a testimony at my hand ; and if He give frame and
furniture, I desire to welcome either of them. O ! dear
Sir, mind me, become of me what will. I have much
ado, many obligations lying upon me ; and the Lord
hath laid on not a few of them by your hands, and
therefore you are the more engaged to be mindful of
me. And, I may say it, your God lets me not be unmindful of you ; and I am of the mind, that sometimes He is
very kind unto you, putting mixtures of joy and
rejoicing in Himself, into your cup of sorrow.

When I am writing this line, I received from Scotland
a packet of letters, directed for your sister, the Lady
Earlston. But, expecting that there were letters for
myself therein, I presumed to break up the packet,
but did not read her letter. I found three for myself,
but none from one that I most expected a line from,
viz , M. B., neither hear I any word of news, for they
are not dated, but I think it is long since they were
written. However, I hear that all the forces of Scotland, the rendezvous of hell, are afoot, because there is
one Alexander Smith, a member of one of our Societies,
and a godly youth, who was apprehended, but rescued
from the enemy, who were taking him from Edinburgh
to Glasgow to be executed, and one of their guard
being slain. The Lord be thanked, that He is stirring
up any to vex the Midianites, and to account their
brother's case to be their own. I must also tell you this,
that I hear in one of my letters, that the Lord is making
the increase of the persecution a mean to blow up the
zeal of some to a greater height. O good news ! dear
Sir, it minds me of Paul's words, Phil. i. 28. "And in
nothing terrified by your adversaries," &c. It is not
long till the cup of the Amorite and Edomite shall be

brimful. *Courage yet, for all that is come and gone ; the loss of men is not the loss of the cause. What is the matter though we should all fall ? I assure all men that the cause shall not fall.*

I thought fit also to send you the Martyrs' Testimonies (not having gotten one of them read). Although my letters speak nothing of them, yet I know none else that they are ordained for, or that should have them, but you. As for the taking away of that every way abused oath, if it be not already taken away, through the Lord's strength, I shall see unto it. But do not think, much honoured and dear Sir, that Mr Boyd will get any thing done, as he vents himself ; for no presbytery will ordain him, unless he be called by the remnant of the Church of Scotland. And if they shall now write to the contrary, he will have no ground to plead upon from their sending of him hither, and giving him a commission. I shall say no more, but my love and service to Mr Brakell, and the ladies V. H. whom, I hope, the Lord will help to sympathise with you in your present condition. The blessing of the God of Jacob be with you, and the earnest good wishes of him who is, honoured and dear Sir, yours to serve you in the Lord, while he hath a being in time.

JAMES RENWICK.

LETTER XXI.

ROTTERDAM, June 22, 1683.

Right hon. and dear Sir,—This afternoon I received two letters from you, wherein you call me unto you, by the desire of that worthy lady and her family. I am very sorry I cannot get you so soon answered as I would desire : for this day or to-morrow I cannot come, being detained here by a certain dispensation fallen out, of which I cannot now write. But when met (if the Lord will) I shall give you an account of the matter and manner of it. However, upon Monday I resolve to come away, and shall stay so long as I may and can be serviceable to any there. But Oh! that I could commend the Lord and His noble way to the world. I must say this to His praise, that He is daily giving me confirmations of His way, and engaging me thereunto, and folding me in all circumstances with His own concernments. Being in haste, I shall say no more. Recommending you and that worthy family to the Lord, for all you stand in need of, I am, yours to serve you in the Lord, JAMES RENWICK.

LETTER XXII.

ROTTERDAM, June 23, 1683.

Honoured and dear sir,—I thought it fit (supposing that possibly you may not see it nor hear of it) to write to you, that I have seen in the English Newspapers, that there was a company of grenadiers appointed to meet Meldrum's troop, that they might receive from them our worthy friend Earlston, in order to the bringing of him to Edinburgh; but it is also inserted, that some say he is escaped. Oh! if it hath pleased the Lord so to order it, both his taking and his escape may have many languages unto us. But what I think I see is in the one, and will be in the other (if it be true, as I would gladly hope it will, because they never use to insert such things but when they are true) I forbear to mention until meeting, which, if the Lord will shall be on Monday night or Tuesday morning. O dear and honourable Sir, we have many enemies. Let us lie near our strength. Wicked men and back-sliders will do more and more wickedly. I shall say no more, having many things to tell you when we meet; but we think it fit that notice hereof be sent to your worthy sister Mrs Jean, if so be that you think she will not otherwise hear. Leaving you on our Master, I am, honourable and dear Sir, yours to serve you in the Lord, while I am,

JAMES RENWICK.

CHAPTER V.

HIS RETURN TO SCOTLAND.

EAVING Holland in the summer of 1683, Renwick had many dangers to encounter before he reached his native shores. First, while waiting for a favourable wind, he was so annoyed by some of his fellow-passengers, who urged him to drink the king's health, and threatened to denounce him when he refused to do so, that he was at length forced to leave the ship in which he had embarked and take another bound for Ireland. Having got out safely to sea, a violent storm compelled them to seek refuge in Rye harbour, in the south of England, where fresh dangers awaited him. It was a time of public suspicion and alarm, Lord Russell and many other noble patriots having recently been apprehended for conspiracy against the King. Russell was brought to trial on July 13, and on July 21, was executed. He was a man greatly beloved, and the narrative of his last hours by Bishop Burnet, his intimate friend and companion, is justly considered one of the most pathetic passages in English history. Algernon Sydney, another of the conspirators, was also executed a few months later, while Monmouth, whom the King loved passionately, was pardoned, and Hampden was fined. Others who were implicated in the "Rye House Plot," as this conspiracy was called,

fell one by one into the hands of the Government
and suffered on the scaffold. As some of these were
seized abroad and brought to England for trial and
conviction, we can well believe that Renwick was in
no small danger of apprehension during his enforced
stay at Rye, and that his relief was great when the
state of the weather allowed him to proceed on his
voyage. Holland was at this time a general harbour
for refugees from England as well as Scotland, and
every Dutch ship became very naturally an object of
suspicion to the Government. Continuing his voyage,
he reached Dublin in safety, where he found many
good friends, as appears from a letter subsequently
sent to them from a General Meeting of the Societies,
of date October 3, 1683. At the close of this letter the
following sentences occur :—" We shall trouble you no
further at this time but heartily and fully approve of
the carriage of your hearty friend and well-wisher in
the Lord, Mr James Renwick, among you, who is for
us a faithful minister of Jesus Christ . . . We hold
ourselves obliged in duty to satisfy you who have been
his hearers, therefore we have sent unto you a true
transcript of the certificate of his ordination in Latin,
and the English version thereof, with some other
papers for your clearing and information in the Lord's
cause, thanking you heartily for the great kindness he
reports that ye showed unto him, taking it as if it had
been done to all of us."

LETTER XXIII.

DUBLIN, Aug. 24, 1683.

Right Honourable Sir,—I am assured that you will
think it strange that ere this time I should not have
written unto you. But many hindrances have been

cast in my way, by reason of the difficulties and dangers of this time, all these lands being (in a manner) in an uproar by reason of challenging and suspecting all persons, and the transmitting of any letters. However, I can no longer forbear to write, though it should never come to your hand, having many things to say to the commendation of the Lord's wisdom and power in outwitting and restraining men. For after being several days tossed at sea and in great hazard by reason of the insufficiency of the vessel, we were forced to go in to Rye in England, where we were much noticed by the wicked in that place, who (I fear), had our skipper's concurrence in laying snares for us. But blessed be the holy Lord who brought the counsel of the heathen to none effect. For upon the Saturday the men who are called waiters * in that place came aboard, asking the skipper for us, if that we were ashore or not, and if he did know us; who replied that we were aboard (we being in the cabin over-hearing their discourse), and that he did not know what we were, which was the only way to make them take notice of us; and when even they came to us they by the holy wise Lord were so restrained that they were suffered to say nothing but ask how we did. Then on the Sabbath day the skipper used all means to get us ashore, pretending an invitation to a dinner, wherein we refused him. But after that time of day was passed, he being detained by an excessive rain, he told us that it was to the Church he was desiring us. But what shall I say of the Lord's wise providence, who immediately struck him so with sickness that he was not able to go and tell that we would not come? But O I think, the Lord hath had a special hand in my coming to this place, for He hath not suffered me to be idle; and, blessed be His name, He hath kindled a fire, which, I hope, Satan shall not quench. For all the people of this place were following men who did not follow the Lord, and thought they were right

* *i.e.*, custom-house officers.

enough. Yet now, some of them are saying, we have been misled; we never knew before this, that we were standing betwixt the Lord's camp and His adversary's. O! what shall I say? blessed be the name of the Lord, who lets me see that He will see of the travail of His soul and be satisfied, and gives me many confirmations of His calling me to this work, wherein my desire is only to be faithful. O I rejoice in Him who hath called me forth to fight against those who oppose themselves, notwithstanding of all their malice at me, and pretended friends there meeting to consult upon my apprehending. I shall say no more. He hath found some who have engaged to do for me, in taking me home to Scotland. But I have the more patience here, because of the Lord's doing great things. The Lord be with you, and with all His Israel. I am, Right Honourable Sir, yours, to serve you in the Lord, while I am,

JAMES BRUCE.

'*P.S.*'—My neighbour George is gone home, having got an occasion of some who would not at all take me. My love to all my dear friends. 'Pray for me,' and be mindful of Zion, and 'I shall not be' unmindful of you.

Leaving Dublin in a ship bound for the Clyde, he succeeded only with great difficulty in reaching Scotland, as all the harbours were then strictly watched, and the captain at first refused to land him except at a regular port. However, in answer to his earnest solicitations, he at length succeeded in overcoming the captain's scruples, and was put ashore, tradition says, somewhere below Gourock. From this point he seems to have made his way as speedily as possible to Edinburgh, where on September 26, 1683, we find him writing to the following effect :—

LETTER XXIV.

EDIN., Sept. 26, 1683.

Right Honourable and dear Sir,—I have been thinking much long for an opportunity of writing unto you, but I hope your goodness will not draw any wrong constructions from my necessitated delay. For (blest be the only holy and wise Lord) I am made to rejoice in Him thereanent, and have been kept (by His grace) from murmuring and quarrelling against Him, because I saw so much of Himself, and of His holy and wise purposes, yea, even toward me, in the circumstances I stand in, in every step, since my departure from your Honour. For, being kept some days at the Texel, where I was (in some measure) exercised to know what might be the language thereof, which I could not know till afterwards, we launched forth into the sea, where we were tossed for some days with a violent contrary wind, and driven within uptaking of the coast of France, before that we could get the English coast taken up. And all with very great hazard, for the vessel was but little, and not at all firm, which occasioned our setting into a harbour in England called Rye, where we went ashore and were much noticed by the tyrant's waiters, it being upon the back of the discovery of their plot. Yet the Lord so restrained them that we were not challenged. However, we thought it not fit (fearing snares) to stay ashore, and therefore went aboard again. But, after some days, the said waiters in their passing by came aboard of us, and asked very rudely of the skipper, where we were, who replied, that we were aboard; and then, asking what men we were, were answered by the skipper, that he knew not; which I, overhearing, thought that his answer would make the said waiters more inquisitive. However the Lord so restrained them, that when they came unto us, they had no power to challenge us. Now all this time, we still concluded that we were already apprehended, seeing no probability of shun-

ning it. But, blest be the Lord, it was no way terrifying
unto me ; for, notwithstanding of His other special assistance, I saw so much of His hand in it, (we being driven
seven leagues back unto that place) that I could not
quarrel, but was much refreshed with that word—
It is the Lord, let Him do what seemeth Him good.
Then, after this, the skipper did what he could to en-
snare us on the Sabbath-day, but the Lord so struck
him with His own hand, that he was not able to go forth
to give any information of us. And on the Monday
morning the Lord sent a fair wind, which was embraced,
and so brought us safe away, far beyond our expectation. O ! all this should learn us to credit Him with
His own cause, and with our case, and may let us see
that enemies, further than is permitted, shall not prevail.   Then after this winning forward unto Dublin,
from whence there was no way of departing without a
pass, but desiring to wait the Lord's time, and to
commit our case unto Him, He wonderfully provided an
occasion for our friend George. But in no ways they
would condescend to take me with them, which was a
piece of exercise unto me to know what might be the
language of it ; yet at the time, I could not see it fully,
but afterwards was made to see, that the Lord had
some piece of work to do there.   O ! blest be His
name, for He set some upon a search of their ways,
and to know that they had not been right ; who were
so affected with my departure from them, (when the
Lord had wonderfully provided an occasion, whereby I
was cast out in the night-time at a hillside, some few
miles below Greenock), that they entreating me with
tears to stay, saying, that their necessity was greater
than Scotland's necessity, would not part with me,
until that upon some suppositions I promised to return
again. But, as the Lord stirred up some people to all
this, their (so called) ministers increased their malice,
especially one Mr Jack, the ring-leader of the rest,
who sought to speak with me ; which I would not, nor
could not, without stumbling of the people, refuse ; who,

when met, we reasoned upon several heads, particularly this, Whether or not a person attacked for duty
might choose a punishment? whereof I held the nega-
tive. But, in a second conference, he (having some of
his companions trysted with him) fell to more briskly,
and asked, How came I to draw away his congregation and to preach to them without his call, and satisfying him anent mine ordination? To which I replied,
that I denied him to have a congregation, and did only
labour and desire to draw the people from sin unto
their duty; and for accepting his call to preach, that
I ought not, nor would not, because I could not own
him as a faithful minister of Jesus Christ, for he
had betrayed the cause of the Lord. And, for satisfying him anent my ordination, I told, when I met
with faithful ministers of Christ, I should subject
myself to them, but him I declined as competent to
require that of me; and also, that I behoved first to
be satisfied anent his entry to that congregation, the
exercise of his ministry during his continuance therein,
and now his yielding it up at the enemy's command—all
which had to be reconciled with the work of God, our
engagements, and the duty of a minister. Which when
he heard, he grew mightily passionate, falling out in
bitter reflections; and I, perceiving the dishonour done
to God thereby, told him that I would speak no more
to such men in such a frame, and so departed. I had
also some battles upon your account, but the Lord
assisted in that, as in all other things; for I saw it
was not you, but the cause and party which they reviled. O! honourable and dear Sir, what shall I say
to all these things? It is good keeping the Lord's
way, for He will not leave nor forsake.

Now, since I came to mine own land and people, I
have seen several things which are encouraging and
promising, as the Lord's helping some, of whom little
was expected, to show both zeal and stedfastness
in His cause, and other things which speak out
wrath to be at the doors, as the neutrality and luke-

warmness, yea declining of many, who have been helped
to be hitherto valiant. O! blessed be the Lord, who
will not give His glory to another, and blasts every
thing that our eyes are upon.

As for news, the Lord is wonderfully to be seen in
every thing, and assists in what He calls unto. For, in
coming through the country, we had two field-meetings,
which made me to think, that, if the Lord could be tied
to any place, it is to the mosses and muirs of Scotland.
O! He will have a day of His power to be seen in this
land. I say, He is to be seen in hiding, preserving and
providing for His people in such a day of the enemy's
cruelty, and He seems to have some strange thing upon
the wheels, especially in your honoured dear brother's
case, which we desire to wait upon and behold. For
his enemies' cruelty and threatenings against him are
great, and their snares and subtilities no less; however,
they are wonderfully restrained, and he strangely reproached, but very causelessly. And as for Robert
Lawson (so sad and sweet in several respects), he is
suffered to cast all his former doings, to the hardening
of backsliders and the grieving of the godly. But
Edward Aitken he is escaped, and intends to come to
you and follow his books : but his carriage in the public
matters hath been very hurtful to the cause, and in
private very unchristian, opening mouths to reproach
and blaspheme ; therefore, I hope you will not move
in it, without the Church of Scotland's advice. Also, I
expect that Thomas Linning will be sent unto you, and
I hope you will be satisfied with him, for he hath been
very satisfying, refreshing and encouraging to me since
I came home.

Likewise (according to your direction) I challenged
Mrs Binning upon her intimacy with your sister; but
she says there is no ground for it, and I think not such
as your Honour apprehends. As also I challenged her
upon the commendation she gave John Wilson in her
letter unto you ; but she says that, when she saw it, it
was so contrary both to her thoughts and commendation
of him.

We are in some confusion now through the want of time, and upon other accounts. However, as occasion offers, I will labour to get full information of every thing sent unto you ; for I am sensible of the advantage that it will be unto the Lord's cause.

Now, the Lord be with your Honour, making you a brazen wall and an iron pillar against all enemies and forsakers of His truth, as hitherto (by His grace) He hath done, and point out unto you your duty in every case, helping you to follow it. Write to friends, for your letter was very refreshing, rejoicing, and strengthening unto them, and to him who looks upon you as his master, his father, and brother, and remains your Honour's assured friend, sympathizer, and servant in the Lord, JAMES RENWICK.

Edward Aitken we already know. He was arrested with Earlston at Newcastle, but seems now to have made his escape. Thomas Linning's name occurs frequently in subsequent letters. Renwick was strongly attached to him, and succeeded at length in getting him sent to Holland for study. This seems a suitable place for introducing another letter which was written, probably about this time, although the exact date is unknown. It is addressed to "the Ladies Van Heermaen at Leewarden in Friesland" (1683), and bears testimony to their warm sympathy with our persecuted brethren.

LETTER XXV.

Worthy Ladies, beloved in the Lord,—Though it hath pleased the holy God, in His wise providence, to carve out my lot unto me, since my departure from you, that I had no time and occasion of writing, yet the Searcher of hearts knows (as I hope your goodness will construct it) that I have not been forgetful of you, nor of your heart-concernedness with Zion's case, and sympathy with her afflicted children, particularly as in Scotland ; whereof I have seen great tokens and evidences. O go on in holy tenderness : go on in zeal, for therein lies your peace, as to duty. Follow the Captain of Salvation fully, for He makes all His followers to enjoy the prize. His soldiers He makes overcomers, and His servants kings, to reign with him for evermore, in His inheritance, whereunto He, their elder Brother, hath entered to take possession in their names. What shall we say of these unspeakable privileges of His people ? Shall we not stand still, struck with wonder and admiration, having our mouths filled with the praise of Him, who left the glory of heaven, and the bosom of the Father, to come down, and to take upon Him our nature, that therein He might interpose Himself betwixt the Father's wrath and us, both by His suffering, and fulfilling of the law for us ; that we might not only be freed from sin and the consequents thereof, but be made partakers of inconceivable privileges, and be restored to a more happy and sure estate than what we fell from ? It is angels' work to desire to look into this, and it will be our work throughout all eternity. Should we not study to be more in it now, viz., in praising of Him for His covenant of free grace, and "for His works of wonder done unto the sons of men," who delighteth to manifest His mercy, His power, and His holy wisdom, and to let poor things find something of Himself in all His attributes, in their own experience, so that they are made to say, He is good, and does good ? For mine own part, I may say, that though, when I had the occasion to see your Ladyships, He had done great things for poor unworthy me, so that I had great reason to set forth His praise, if I could have done it, yet now He hath done much more, which may furnish new matter of praise : for, since my departure from you, the Lord has been pleased to tryst me with several difficulties, that He might have occasion of manifesting Himself, in bringing

me through the same. In fire or water I dare not say
He hath left or forsaken me; and though perils by sea,
and perils by land, and the snares of enemies to the
cause and cross of Christ, have been many, yet He hath
wonderfully brought me hitherto through the same, and
frustrated the expectations of the wicked; and not only
hath been at great cost and pains to lay obligations
on me to be for Him, but also hath taken many ways
to train me up for the work that He has laid upon me,
in the circumstances of the times wherein my lot is fallen. But the greatest of all, I think, is the many confirmations He hath given me of His own cause, and
also of His call to such a weighty business, and His
letting me see what hath been a great part of His end
in detaining me so long from my own land and people;
which was, to cast me and keep me a little space in
Ireland, where He hath kindled a fire, which, I hope,
He will not suffer to die out; and hath put some people
upon a searching of their ways, wherein they had
turned from Him. O! blessed be His name, who will
see of the travail of His soul, and be satisfied, and
who is that good Shepherd, out of whose hand none
shall pluck the sheep; for the gates of hell shall not
prevail against His church, and no wonder, for it is
a rock, and built upon a rock. O! come, let us enlist
ourselves under His banner, and take His part against
a lukewarm generation, and resolve upon trials; for, I
think, He loves none whom He lets want them. But
consider for whom it is. It is for His name's sake, who
is "the chief among ten thousand," and is "altogether
lovely."

Now, the Lord, who is not unrighteous to forget your
labour of love, be all things unto you, and reward you
for your sympathy and concernedness with the Lord's
people in this land, who are very sensible of your becoming companions with them in their tribulations, and
that you have had compassion upon them in their bonds.
We desire still the help of your prayers for the desolations
of the Lord's holy mountain. So, no more at the time,

being assured of your concernedness with our much honoured friend, Robert Hamilton, of whose courage, constancy, and zeal for the Lord's cause you have proof; for, what is done to him is, as it were, done to us all. Mind poor me, and the great work the Lord hath laid upon me. The Lord be with you, Madams, your Ladyships' affectionate servant, and sympathiser in the Lord, JAMES RENWICK.

CHAPTER VI.

THE FIRST YEAR OF HIS MINISTRY.

THOUGH ordained on May 10th 1683, Renwick had not as yet received a formal call to the work of the ministry in Scotland. This however was given and accepted on Oct. 3rd at Darmead in the parish of Cambusnethan, on which day a general meeting of the United Societies was held according to appointment. Having first given an account of his ordination, and having also presented a certificate thereof, a formal call to act as their minister was then received and accepted by him, after which what is generally known as his "Testimony" was read to the meeting, although on various grounds some who were present strongly objected to it. This had been previously written and subscribed by him at Groningen, and a copy left for safe keeping in the hands of Sir Robert Hamilton. In it a very free and full expression had been given of his views regarding the controversies of that day, and, though in substance he adhered to it till the very close of his life, he seems on maturer consideration to have regretted the manner of it, and especially the unnecessary introduction of certain names. To this there is an affecting reference in a letter to his friend Sir Robert Hamilton written on the very day of his death. "Now as to my Testimony" (he says) "which I left in your hands, when

I entered into the work of the ministry, I do still
adhere unto the *matter* of it, but I think the *manner of
expression* is in some things too tart, and it containeth
sundry men's names, some whereof are now in eternity.
It is not so pertinent to our present affairs, for the
state of our controversies is altered. Therefore I judge
it may be destroyed, for I have testimony sufficient
left behind me in my written sermons and in my letters.
But if this trouble you, and if you desire to keep it for
yourself and your own use, you should keep this letter
with it and not publish it further abroad. Yet you
may make use of any part of the matter of it that may
conduce to the clearing of any controversy. As for the
direction of it unto you, if I had lived and been qualified
for writing a book, and if it had been dedicated to any
man, you would have been the man. For I have loved
you and I have peace before God in that, and I bless
His name that I have been acquainted with you."

The following two letters belong to this period, and
breathe a spirit of deep devotion and unreserved
consecration to his Master's service. The first is
addressed to "The honourable society of strangers at
Leewarden, in Friesland," and the second to Sir
Robert Hamilton.

LETTER XXVI.

Nov. 13, 1683.

Honourable and dear Friends in our Lord,—I have
not only heard, but also, in the little space I was
amongst you, I saw many tokens and evidences of your
love to our lovely Lord, and tender sympathy with His
afflicted sufferers; which was no small refreshing and
encouragement to me, also a great engaging and endearing of my heart unto you; so that I know not

how to unfold my thoughts, and unbosom my ardent
affections. But as my heart is much with you, so, I
may say, you are frequently with me, and that in the
times which you most require, when I desire to pros-
trate myself at the footstool of the throne of grace.
However, I could not forbear, neither thought I it my
duty to omit writing unto you. But, what shall I say,
but that which you yourselves know ? The Lord, being
the only object whereupon all our desires can satisfyingly terminate, is worthy of all honour, fear, love,
and service ; yea, and at the mention of this, we may
stand astonished, and wonder, that He in Himself,
supertranscendently and infinitely glorious, incapable
of receiving any additional glory from His creatures,
should call such unworthy worms, and self-destroyed
creatures, to serve Him ; which, though He had not
freely and graciously promised any reward after time,
would be a reward of itself. But, O ! what can be His
end in calling and drawing out such self-destroyed and
unworthy creatures, as any of the lost posterity of
Adam, to love and serve Him ? It is not that He may
get good (of which He is incapable) but that He may
give good. O ! praised be His free grace, He hath
provided and laid open a way whereby we may have
both access and right unto Him, by the mediation of
His Son, our Lord Jesus Christ. Therefore, let us
answer His call, and come unto Him, where all our
happiness lies, with hearts so enlarged, and conceptions
so framed and shapen out, as that nothing less than
Himself may satisfy ; for more cannot be desired.
Let us come unto Him, follow Him fully, take up
His cross and our engagements against the world,
the devil, and the flesh ; for He is a noble and glorious
Captain whose banner we have to fight under, who
not only bears His soldiers' charges sufficiently here,
all their stock being only in His own hand, but also
makes them sure of the victory, and of the kingdom
and crown in the end of the battle, they being to
walk with Him in glorious white robes, throughout

all eternity. Let us espouse His quarrel for our own, and not be discouraged for what opposites can do; for, in all their intended actings against Him, they are but pulling down themselves, and setting up His kingdom. Neither let us be annoyed with the difficulties in time, but look above and beyond these unto the rich recompense of reward. For the day is near at hand, when these tabernacles of clay shall fall down about our ears, and we shall be set at liberty, made incapable of grieving His ˙Spirit, or sorrowing any more, and fitted for the blessed, full and eternal enjoyment of Father, Son, and Holy Ghost. O what a day will that be, when the saints shall get their fill of Him, encircling Him with both their arms, or rather, being encircled by Him! Let us wait and look out for it, longing for the day when that shall be heard in heaven—O how sweetly will it be sung!— "Arise, arise, arise, my love, my dove, my fair one, and come away; for behold your winter is past, and your everlasting summer is come." O let the thoughts of that summer, and tasting of the first fruits thereof, sweeten this our winter unto us, making us cheerfully to travel through the same, with songs of our Beloved in our mouths, and patiently to endure what travail or tribulations, either for our chastisement or instruction, He who doeth all things well may be pleased to let out upon us. And as you have been helped through grace to become companions with us in our tribulation, so I would have you look out for the same upon yourselves; for the Lord will come and shake terribly the earth, and punish the inhabitants thereof for their iniquity, lay waste cities, and desolate lands; for all nations are overspread with a supine and loathsome formality, yea, avowed profanity, and dreadful blasphemy against the heavens. I say not this, my honourable and dear friends, to discourage you, but rather for the continuance and increase of your holy zeal, which you manifest towards the Lord's cause and interest. Oh! go on in it, for therein shall be your peace as to duty, and He Himself is your exceeding rich reward.

Now, for your great kindness, love unto, and sympathy with our bleeding and wounded mother-church, which I saw amongst you; and particularly for your heart love and tender respect towards myself, though altogether undeserved, I cannot express how I am engaged to the Lord, and obliged unto you; yea, it passeth my apprehension. But I am singularly obliged indeed; so I must beg further matter (though already enough be had) by the continuance of your mindfulness of our distressed and wounded church, and of that exceeding great and weighty work, which you know the Lord hath laid upon me. But why should I fear? The work is His own; and He sends none a warfare on their own charges: and, ever blessed be His holy name, I may say this from sweet experience; for I have found Him a present help in all my necessities, and many ways beyond my expectation, confirming my call, and countenancing His work both at home, and elsewhere, where He was pleased to cast and detain me. Now, the Lord be with you. Again, mind me, as I desire to do you. Remaining, honourable and dear friends, your hearty wellwisher, assured and obliged friend and servant, to my full power in the Lord,

JAMES RENWICK.

LETTER XXVII.

EDIN., Nov. 14, 1683.

Honourable and dear Sir,—Though I have many things that I would and could say, yet I am so busied, which I think you may know, that I cannot be so large in writing to you as I would. However, I see many encouragements and discouragements; encouragements from the Lord's omnipotency, condescendency, and faithfulness, yea, the glory that is to be seen in His noble way of managing His own cause; and discouragements from several airts which I expected not. For since I came home, I have found some, of whom I expected better things, cleaving to crooked and perverse ways; yea, and they are turned very imbittered against us. At the present (oh sad! but too true) we are pestered with a company of prejudiced evil persons, who join hand and issue with backsliders, and make known every thing unto them; wherein I only desire and labour, that the particular persons may be found out, so that we may proceed against them according to the word of God, and our duty.

My coming home hath had such effects as I expected indeed, for enemies are more cruel and eager in persecution than ever, and backsliders more embittered with malice than heretofore. But some whom I expected to be cordial with, I have not found them so; neither should I in the ways that they are upon. And this hath been chiefly occasioned by my Testimony; which as it hath, by the Lord's goodness, been refreshing, encouraging, and strengthening to some, so it hath made others vent more what they were. And herein I rejoice, yea, and will rejoice (there being not an article in it, but what I am more and more confirmed of) because it hath a tendency to the siding of us either for or against the Lord. But among all friends none is so helpful and strengthening unto me, as our friend George Hill. However, I must say, that I find the Lord countenancing and blessing His work, yea, and giving testimonies for His cause. O! ever blessed be His holy name therefore!

As for information in other things, there is little to give your Honour. Only at our last meeting, all that we did was the reading of the Testimony, some papers for coming to you, and subscribing them, laying aside the abused oath of secrecy, and ordaining John Binning to teach our scholars. At the meeting presently ensuing, I know of nothing to be done, but some other papers to be subscribed; our scholars, some of whom we were jealous of, examined; and some sought out to be sent unto your Honour, with our letters and papers; and (that which will be our continual work) a way thought upon for the finding out of those whose tongues and hands are so against the Lord. As for myself, in other things, since I came home, I have been more pained and indisposed of body, than for several years before. However, it was made sweet unto me, for I saw two things in it. First, when before I was casting up, and counting all pieces of cost, I thought I saw my all in the Lord's hand, but only bodily strength, thinking that there was enough of that in mine own; and He takes that way with me, which, O! is glorious, that I may have strength as well as other furniture from His hand, in more than an ordinary manner, that so His name may get the more praise therefore. Secondly, I saw this in it, that though I have been in some places of the country, yet I have but won through little of it; and, where I have not been, I fear more an anxiety after the ordinances, than a thirsting after the Lord, so that, I think, the Lord is seeking to get His people both to prize, and yet to be denied, to the means.

O! dear Sir, the thought of our long absence is frequently troublesome unto me; but shall we not have a joyful meeting in heaven? and who knows but we may meet in time? In the mean time, only be mindful of me, and the work which you know the Lord hath laid upon me, as I am and desire to be of you, both in public and private. The Lord be with you. I am, your Honour's hearty wellwisher, real sympathizer, greatly endeared friend, and most obliged servant in the Lord, JAMES RENWICK.

Nine days after this letter was written, on Nov. 23, 1683, there was a great gathering of people at Darmead to hear their young minister deliver his first public discourse in the fields. After a short preface he

lectured on Isaiah xl. 1-8 and preached from Isaiah xxvi.
20. Those who have been led to think of him chiefly
as a controversialist will be surprised to meet with
such tender and pathetic appeals as are found in the
following passage from his sermon. He is pressing
home the doctrine that "there is both ability and
willingness in the Lord to give you whatsoever your
necessity requires," and he says, "*There is ability.* What
would you have? Salvation and deliverance? then He
is able to save to the uttermost all that come unto Him.
Lift up your eyes and behold a wonder which you
cannot know and put forth this question, 'Who is this
that cometh from Edom, with dyed garments from
Bozrah? this that is glorious in His apparel, travelling
in the greatness of His strength?' And His answer will
be, 'It is I that speak in righteousness, mighty to save!'
Gainsay it who will, the pleasure of the Lord shall
prosper in His hand. He shall see of the travail of
His soul and be satisfied. And now methinks I hear
some of you saying, 'All this is true; we can set our
seals to it; but is He willing? This is our question.'
Willing He is indeed. He is not more able than He is
willing. What are all His promises but declarations of
His willingness? What are all His sweet invitations but
to tell you that you are welcome? Let him that is
athirst come, and whosoever will let him take of the
water of life freely. Ah! what say you to it? Give
us your seal to His willingness also. Go, say you, why
not? you have it. Then Come away, there is no more
wanting save Come; we know He is willing and we set
to our seal to His willingness. But is He willing to
receive me? Satisfy me in this, and then I will be right.
Ah, cheat! you are taking your word back again now,
and lifting off your seals. If you except not yourself

He will not except you. His invitation is unto all:
'Every one, Come; he that thirsteth, Come; he that
hath no money, Come.' . . . We must preach this word
'Come' to you so long as you are here, until you be
transplanted out of this spiritual warfare into celestial
triumph. Oh! Sirs, Come, Come; ask what you will
and He shall give it. Oh! Come, Come!"

Need we wonder that Renwick at once became a
favourite preacher among the persecuted Covenanters,
and that in a few months in the first year of his
ministry he is said to have baptised more than six
hundred children.

James Nisbet, son of Nisbet of Hardhill, gives the
following account of his style of preaching :—"After this
I went sixteen miles to hear a sermon preached by the
great Mr James Renwick, a faithful servant of Christ
Jesus, who was a young man, endued with great piety,
prudence, and moderation. The meeting was held in a
very large, desolate muir. The minister appeared to be
accompanied with much of his Master's presence. He
prefaced on the 7th Psalm, and lectured on 2nd Chron.
chap. 19th, from which he uttered a sad applicatory
regret that the rulers of our day were as great enemies
to religion as those of that day were friends to it. He
preached from Mark xii. 34 in the forenoon. After
explaining the words, he gave thirteen marks of a
hypocrite, backed with pertinent and suitable applica-
tions. In the afternoon he gave the marks of a sound
believer, backed with a large, full, and free offer of Christ
to all sorts of perishing sinners that would come and
accept of Him for their Lord and Saviour, and for the
Lord and Lawgiver. His method was both plain and
well digested, suiting the substance and simplicity of the
Gospel. This was a great day of the Son of Man to

many serious souls, who got a Pisgah view of the Prince of Life, and of that pleasant land that lies beyond the banks of death."

Busy as he was in seeking to answer the many calls now addressed to him to preach in different parts of the land, he still found time to write to his friends at Lee-warden, who, notwithstanding Earlston's imprisonment, remained as devoted as ever to the cause of the sufferers.

The two following letters are addressed to Sir Robert Hamilton, the first being probably written from Edin-burgh, where Lady Earlston was sharing her husband's imprisonment.

LETTER XXVIII.

Jan., 1684.

Right Honourable and dear Sir,—Being by the Lord's providence with the Lady Earlston, when sending away her letters, I behoved to salute you with this line, show-ing you that (blessed be the Lord) I am well every way, though my case is singular, and my trials no less such. Yet I may turn my complaints into triumphant songs, for I have seen the Lord's wonders in the land of the living, and He is still increasing the number of His fol-lowers : for, though I should go over and over again to any countryside, at every time there come others aye out who did not come out before. But enemies are in-tending sad things against us, for they are now lead-ing out their forces to the West, threatening to lay it desolate, saying, That we will never be curbed till they make that country a hunting-field. But, let them prate, a higher hand rules all ; and I am persuaded, that we shall thereby be more affrighted than scathed, though our fears be not great, whatever be the fears of the apostate party. Know also, that Mr Shields is brought to Scotland. I know that he and Mr Andrew Cameron and Mr Flint were joined together in seeking after ordination, that they might come home to Scotland. But when I heard it, I was not satisfied that you were not owned in it. However, this hath a strange language. The Lord hath crushed it; for their papers anent the same, and many books, were cast away at sea. O! the majesty of your God and my God, that shines in His management of affairs. Let you and me stand still and admire this. So, leaving you to His all-sufficiency, with my love to all my friends with you, I am, as formerly,   JAMES RENWICK.

LETTER XXIX.

March 29, 1684.

Right honourable and dear Sir,—I have much to say, but have no time to express myself. However, though I had ten thousand times ten thousand years, yea, the faculty of angels, I could in no ways lay out mine obligations to free grace, but behoved, when I had babbled my fill, to seal up all with this, CHRIST IS MATCHLESS! O He is the wonder of the higher house! and will He not be your wonder and my wonder throughout the ages of lasting eternities? Come away then, let us labour to keep up that work now, wherein eternity will not weary us. We cannot now think rightly of Him, but we will get eternity to the work. His beauty and excellency is so ravishing, that a poor weak, daft-fond soul will be made to turn its dazzled eyes away from Him, when yet the heart will be melting in love's hand. O! but we be narrow vessels that can receive nothing; but hereafter we shall see Him as He is. O what is He? Angels cannot define Him, and we must be silent; yet this I must say, He is matchless: all perfection meets in Him, He is glorious, and He is the only best of choices. O! He is glorious in Himself, and manifests that in all His actings. His doings are like Himself, and carry large characters of all His attributes engraven upon them. Why are such confusions upon His church, but that

He may get occasion to make His wisdom conspicuous in bringing order out thereof? O! He will do it, and His carrying on a strange work of discovery is a pledge of it. His faithfulness is engaged to do it. Let us not fear, though enemies their cruelty and steppers aside their malice be more than formerly, yet His word shall stand sure. And poor mad fools, what are they doing, but crushing themselves, and setting up His throne?

Now, right honourable and dear Sir, there are many particulars which I would write, but I cannot get it done; howbeit I shall wait to catch some opportunity for it, our friend George having at the time given you a brief touch of some things. The Lord helps him to give many evidences of sincerity and stedfastness in the cause, and affection to such in all places who are most sorely shot at upon the cause's account. I thought to have written something unto you anent Tho. Linning, but George having spoken my mind, I shall forbear. Yet there is one thing which is your duty, and which is also my duty to mention unto you, and that is, that you would take pains upon John Tait to wear out that bad impression which James Russel hath given him of us. O, deal tenderly with him, for he is but young, yet (I hope) of zealous intentions. Be concerned with him in that strange place, for he is a child of many prayers. His relations bear a great affection to the cause, and to all who own the same; and your name is very savoury unto them. It is weighty to me, that James Russel hath insinuated himself so much upon him; for his being sent abroad was (in some measure) upon expectation that he and I should be together.

Now, right honourable and dear Sir, let not difficulties damp you. There is nothing that falls out but what is in kindness both to the remnant and to you. Regard not the reproaches of tongues. Are not these the badges of your honour? Our lot must not be thought strange, for the Lord's people heretofore have met with the like. Remember, "Ye have need of patience." We have enemies now upon all hands; and I must say, that man James Russel hath been a costly James Russel to the poor Church of Scotland. I shall say no more; but, as malice of opposites to the cause increases, let our love thereunto and to one another increase. I am your assured friend and servant in the Lord, and your unworthy brother in afflictions and reproaches for His name's sake,

JAMES RENWICK.

'*P.S.*'—My love and service to your dear sister and that banished family which is much upon my heart. Your desire anent Mr Brakell shall be obeyed.

The next letter is addressed to Mrs Jean Hamilton, at Leewarden.

LETTER XXX.

June 20, 1684.

Worthy Madam,—I received your letter, which unbosomed to me a troubled case, which in no small measure does affect my spirit. But as I am affected with the trouble of spirit which you express, so I am refreshed with my observing that you are not insensible of your case, your great complaint being of the want of light and life. But I am persuaded that a creature altogether wanting the one and the other cannot be troubled anent their apprehended want of either; for none miss that which doth not belong unto them. A horse hath no sense of his want of the wings of an eagle, because these are not proper to him; but if he want use of his feet he presently misseth the same when he is put to go. Those who never knew anything of light and life cannot miss the same. I grant indeed, many unregenerate have a missing of common influences, which flashes are far from that heart-feeling that the believer is acquainted with. However I conceive, that as common influences are not permanent,

and tend nothing to the changing of the heart, so, the
poor creature gets leave to rest upon them, seeking no
further, and, when missing them, is, chiefly, if not only
troubled, because external duty then is neither so easy
nor pleasant. There are depths here that I dare not
now launch out into, lest time will not allow me to
bring myself out again. But, O Madam! what shall
I say unto you? Let no less than Christ Himself satisfy
you. Study to dwell under the impression of His
preciousness, for the contemplation hereof fills the
heart with love unto Him; and love (you know) is a
most active and lively thing. And judge not your
state by what you find your case (as to your sense)
sometimes to be; for a very fruitful tree will bear
neither fruit nor leaves in the winter season, while as
much sap will be in the root. Spend not time in
debating, but in the sincere and serious use of those
means that you have of union and communion with
Christ. This is both the shortest and the surest way
to win to fixedness. Neither seek sense's satisfaction
for the present, but a well-grounded assurance for
the future. Look to the infinite power, and infinite
love of Christ; *there* is a two-edged sword to cut
asunder all your Gordian knots. Infinite power, what
can it not do? and infinite love, what will it not
do! Never seek any thing in yourself to commend you
to Christ, for that will keep you still staggering; so, to
His grace, who is able to perfect what concerneth you,
do I recommend you. But as to your troubled case, in
your not knowing well whether you be called to stay
where you are, or to come home, I confess, when I
ponder all circumstances, I find it very puzzling, and
I may say, it has given me some errands to God, and I
am in no small measure concerned therewith. But I
would desire you, without anxiety, to wait on a little;
for the Lord by His providential dispensations, or in
a more extraordinary way, will determine you. Some
concerned friends are also spoken to anent it, that they
would ponder the case before the Lord, and see whether

they will desire the babes to come home or not; and their mind (I think) will as soon be reported to your worthy brother, as this may come to your hand. So at the time, I can write the less anent it, and therefore leave you upon the Lord, who is all in all; begging, worthy Madam, that you would not forget the case that you know he is in, who remains your Ladyship's soul's wellwisher, sympathizer, and obedient servant in the Lord,   J. R.

'*P.S.*'—My love to all the sweet babes.

Two weeks later, we find him writing again to "The society of strangers at Leewarden."

Letter XXXI.

July 2, 1684.

Right Honourable and dearly Beloved in our Lord,— The report of the continuance of your sympathy with us, and of the increase of your zeal for the Lord of hosts, is greatly encouraging and refreshing to me; and which thing, together with the great uniteness of my heart unto you, impels me to presume upon the writing of a line unto you, though I be unapt to write unto such, and know not how to explicate myself. Now, that which I mainly desire is to commend unto the world the loveliness of Christ, the preciousness of His cause, the easiness of His yoke, and the sweetness of His cross, whereof I am sure you are not ignorant. But O, this is a work above the reach of poor sinning finite creatures !

Who can think, who can speak, or who can write of this ? The immeasurableness and freedom of the grace of Christ, the boundlessness of His power and infinite- ness of His love, are such a bottomless deep of joyful wonder, wherein those who are made perfect are everlastingly drowned. What can we in this falling tabernacle say or think, who but see in part and know in part? But O, let us take our eyes from beholding vanity, and feed them allenarlie* upon the fulness and all-sufficiency of precious and glorious Christ. What doubts and fears can we have, but enough is there to solve and answer them unto us. And I think if we poor creatures, whenever a fear or doubt did arise, presently turned our eyes to contemplate Christ's free all-sufficiency, we would find it immediately to vanish as dispelled smoke, indiscernible. But ah! our tempers are sinfully ready rather to pore upon our fears than to employ Christ for our help; and thereby the life which we might have of joyful praise is turned into a life of despondent anxiety. O they that see Christ to be theirs can find no want!

And what mad fools, idle persons, and foolish choosers are they who make it not their work to have Christ! But I confess Christ unto many (even that profess much) is as the ample world is to them, they have a passing view thereof, with little or nothing of possession. So many get a dissolving, transient view of Christ with the literal, illuminate eye of the mind, but have never a renewed heart to affect† Him only for Himself as the all-satisfying and enriching pearl of price. O these think they have a love to Him, but their desires are after that which is His and not after Himself. They desire liberation from the guilt and punishment of sin, and a possession in a heaven which they build up to themselves in their brain, but they care not though there were not such a thing as Jesus Christ. O what spurious love is this!

Can any in reason think but a suitor, whom a maid condescended to match with only upon the account of his estate and means without regard of his person, had good ground to refuse such base and spurious love? And how shall Christ regard the adulterate love of such self-seekers? And another sort of folk cover over their pride with a vizor of humility, and cry forth, Christ is a King, and they are sitting upon a dunghill.

* Only.   † Desire.

How can they consent to so great and high a match! If they were queens they would do it. But O that such would consider that while they seek anything in themselves to commend them to Christ, they will still stagger and stay away. But let them lay aside their coyness and once come to Him and match with Him, and He will make them queens and matches meet for Himself. Christ comes to woo His bride in the garments of condescendency. He took upon Him our nature, that He might say to the worms of the earth, "Ye are My brethren and My sisters." And O how glorious is He in those garments, being also clothed with the robes of ravishing majesty! How complete and how free a Saviour is He! Yea, how communicative a good; so that each of His own have Him—so as if not any other beside them had Him. Each of us hath as much of the sun as we would have, though there were no others on earth to partake with us. So is the enjoyment of that blessed Sun of Righteousness to all His chosen. Each one of them hath Him all.

O what a blessed enjoyment is this which each of His saints does enjoy without envying or wronging one another! What a blessed choice is Christ! What a lovely choice is He! O He is lovely—He is lovely! And all that choose Him will say that he is lovely, and that they have made a brave bargain. It was said of a heathen, Socrates, all that knew him loved him, and they that did not love him it was because they did not know him. Indeed, they that love not Christ it is because they know Him not. If He were known, what a great, gracious, powerful, loving, bountiful, and excellent One He is, the heart would be filled with love unto Him. If He were known—if He were known, the soul's outcry would be, "He is altogether matchless; who is like unto Him?" Love thinketh the beloved hath no parallel, and love loveth all that is the beloved's. Hence, as Christ is lovely to His own, so His cause is precious. It is precious—it is precious. It is His declarative glory. It is that whereby He maketh His name known.

How honourable is it to be an owner of the same! What badges of honour are reproaches and revilings upon that account! As love unto Him makes His cause precious, so where that is, nothing will be thought too costly to bestow upon the cause's account. What will love not undergo! What will love not forego for the beloved's honour! We need no more to commend this common cause unto us than this: It is Christ's cause. And, seeing His glory is concerned in it, it is our honour to be concerned with it. So also love to that lovely One, or an uptaking of His loveliness which cannot but beget love unto Him, maketh His yoke easy. Love is an oil to our wheels, to make them run swiftly and lightly the way of His commandments. O love makes obedience easy and pleasant work, for the command binds the conscience, and love gains the affections. So, when conscience and inclination go together, it must needs be an easy work. Christ's yoke was easy and pleasant unto David when He said (Ps. cxix. 127), "I love Thy commandments above gold; yea, above fine gold." And that which is greatly to be marked there is, as the world was casting off Christ's yoke, so David was taking it on more heartsomely. "They have made void Thy law, therefore I love Thy commandments, &c.," saith he. A mark of true love indeed. The more that Christ is rejected and despised by others, the more to be beloved by His own.

O what shall be said of love to Christ! Love is a resolute soldier for Him, love is a valiant champion in His lists. Love despises, yea, I may say, wishes for difficulties to get itself shown. Love sees not a spot upon all the cross. Love gets never a bitter cup put into its hand but the beloved frowns. It thinks not His cross bitter, but reads delightsomeness engraven upon it. Love will rejoice to cross the natural part of the will to please Christ. Love will not stand to venture upon the swellings of Jordan with Him and for Him. The heaps of great waters are nothing in love's eye. The deeper that love wades, it thinks it the sweeter. Losses, wanderings, tossings, deaths, and dangers, are nothing to love. Cant. viii. 6, 7 : "Love is strong as death ; jealousy is cruel as the grave ; the coals thereof are coals of fire, which hath a most vehement flame. Many waters cannot quench love, neither can the floods drown it : if a man would give all the substance of his house for love, it would utterly be contemned." O what shall I say? Let us love Christ. Let us love Him and exalt His grace. And they that do not, let them be Anathema Maranatha.

Now, right honourable and dearly beloved in our lovely Lord, ye have expressed greatly your love to wronged Christ and His precious cause by your standing still to condole and commiserate the case of His mournful and distressed people in this land. Ye have evidenced heart sympathy with us. Your hands have not been bound up from helping, strengthening, and encouraging us. Ye have been instruments to minister a refreshful cup of consolation unto us. Ye have stood with us when others have left us. O stand by truth and duty ; keep thereby, though all men should deny the one and forsake the other. Let this be your study, and our study. And so let us stand on with and for another. Let nothing damp you or mar your confidence. The cause is the Lord's. He shall prevail. He will overturn thrones and kingdoms, and get Himself a name. And amongst the rest the tribe of Levi must get a dash ; but go ye on. Let it be your only work to follow the Lord fully and seriously, and your latter end shall be peace. Thus committing you all unto the Lord for directing and upholding grace, for His making you in your places and stations, as hitherto He hath done in a great measure, brazen walls and iron pillars against all error and ungodliness, and for His enabling you by His grace to endure to the end, that so ye may everlastingly triumph with

Him in glory. So, hoping that I need not desire you
to be mindful of a poor, wrestling, bleeding, and
wronged Church, and of him whose life is a wading
through snares, discouragements, hazards, deaths, and
dangers, and who is, right honourable and dearly
beloved in the Lord, your real and constant friend and
servant in all Christian duty,

JAMES RENWICK.

LETTER XXXII.

July 9, 1684.

Right honourable and dear Sir,—Your letter which
I received was wonderfully sweet and refreshing to me,
and was made a means (in some measure) to prepare
me for what I was to meet with. For immediately thereafter I was involved in such trials as before I had
not been trysted with, but all indeed to manifest, in a
wonderful manner, the Lord's power and love to and for
His people. For, upon the Sabbath, after your letter
came to my hand, we met for public worship, near the
Whin-bog in the Monkland ; but that country having
generally apostatised into an open hostility against
the Lord, some went quickly away unto Glasgow, and
gave notice unto the enemy's forces. Howbeit we
heard thereof ere forenoon's sermon was ended, yet
continued until that part of the work was gone about.
Thereafter, we thought it fit to depart from that place,
and also that the armed men should keep together for
our better defence and safety ; which (through God's
goodness) was a means to keep the enemy from noticing
and pursuing after stragglers, they being stricken into
some quandary and terror, and keeping both their
horse and foot in one body. Yet they lodged all that
night (we not knowing of it) within a mile of some,
and two miles of others of us, intending to set forward
toward the houses where we were. But the Lord,
whose ways are wonderful, made use of a malignant

gentleman to detain them, he asserting that none of us went toward that airt. Notwithstanding, this wakened up the adversaries more; so that they kept up a pursuit and search, which proved very obstructive to our Convention, which was upon the Thursday thereafter. For, upon that very day, they came with horse and foot to search the moors where we were, and came here upon us ere we could get any thing concluded: which thing moved us (we suspecting that they, some way or other, had gotten notice of some of us being together) to remove from that place some way off into a little glen, where we resolved to keep ourselves obscure. But after we had rested and refreshed ourselves a little, we espied four of their foot marching toward us: whereupon it was thought fit to send out so many to meet them, who, when they came together fired upon one another. But the Lord's gracious providence so ordered it, that there was not the least scathe upon our side, there being one of the enemy so wounded that he died since. Howbeit the shots alarmed the rest of our enemies who were upon the hill, and, when we drew out to the open fields, we saw their foot not very far from us, and got present advertisement that the enemy was still upon the pursuit, and near unto us. We, in all haste, set forward through the moss, having no outward strength to fly unto, but by crossing the way of the adversary: whereupon we expected an encounter with them. Yet, committing ourselves into the Lord's hand, we went on, until we came unto another certain moss, where we staid until night, and got much of our business done. But in all this, the wonderful power of God was seen, in both inspiriting His people for that exigency, and preserving us from falling into the hands of the adversaries. Yea, though He shewed us wonders therein, yet He delighted to shew us more. For, upon the Saturday night thereafter, there was a competent number of us met in a barn for worship, and had not well begun until we heard both the drums and trumpets of the enemy; but we thought it most expedient to set watches without, and continue at our work until we saw further. Nevertheless, in all these tumults and dangers, the Lord's goodness was so manifested to His people, that He not only hid them under His wings, and preserved them, but He also kept their spirits from the least fear, confusion, or commotion ; yea, the very sight of some of them would have made resolute soldiers amongst us. So after this hazard was over, some of us thought it convenient to stay where we were (it being a woody place) until the Sabbath day was past. But, ere the middle of the day, we got an alarm that the enemy was within two miles or thereabout, coming toward that airt ; whereupon we went over the Clyde. But so soon as that was, we, being in number about six or seven, had almost encountered a party of the enemy's horse, who, at the crossing of our way, had inevitably met with us, if the Lord had not so ordered it, that a friend of ours had seen them ere they could see us ; who thereupon came running toward us with a white napkin (because conspicuous to us) flourishing in his hand : whereupon we halted, and when he came to us, we lurked among some bushes until the enemy passed by. Thereafter we setting forward by two and two upon our journey, which was intended to be but short, some two of us met with one of the adversary's number upon horseback, who presently fled with all his might toward Lanark, we being within three short miles thereof ; which forced us to take a desperate course, in running through that plenished country unto Darmead Moss, still expecting to foregather with that hostile town of Lanark, both horse and foot. But the Lord's power and goodness was such toward us, that we escaped all their hands ; which thing was great matter of admiration unto us all, and made me to wonder not a little ; that scripture, Psal. cxxvi. 2, 3, being my companion, "Then said they among the heathen, The Lord hath done great things for them. The Lord hath done great things for us ; whereof we are glad ;" and also that other Psalm (cxi. 6). "He hath shewed His people the power of His works, that He may give them the heritage of the heathen." O ! all those things that He did to us and for us, were matter of great rejoicing in Himself. But as I thought I saw them to be pledges of greater things, whereby His attributes might be more manifested, they were made matter of double and greater joy unto me. He hath given us proofs of what He can do for His people in the day of their strait ; and He gives us good cause to commit unto His faithfulness the management and raising up of His seemingly buried work, and the carrying through of His people. And ever since, it hath been my chief exercise, yea, and a while before that, the deep and abiding impression of His unexpected, sudden, and glorious appearing for His name and people.

I think we are like unto a poor, despicable, helpless, dead-like company, lying depressed in a valley ; and He, as it were, by His word and works discovering Himself upon a hill-top in our view, stretching out His arms, and all fluttering to be at us,—calling unto us that we would join our hearts and voices together, and cry Him down unto us, offering that His power and love meeting together shall tread down and dissipate unto nothing our dreaded obstructions of one sort or another. Yea, I say, if I know anything of the mind of the Lord, this is His special call unto all His sincere followers this day, Isa. lxii. 6, 7. "Ye that make mention of the Lord, keep not silence ; and give Him no rest, till He establish, and till He make Jerusalem a praise in the earth." O ! let us all join together in this exercise, and let us be sincere, fervent and constant in it. Let us be at no manner of ease while Zion is in trouble ; for though we should be content with our calamity, yet we should in no ways be content with our sin procuring the same, nor with the preservation of enemies in their insolence and rebellion against the Lord, whereby His name is daily blasphemed ; and this has been procured by our backsliding. I say, let us join

in this exercise, in crying to the Lord for His appearing.
His people's delivery shall be so glorious, that it shall
abundantly make up for all the cost, wrestling, and
suffering that they can be at ; and though many of them
with their bodily eyes may never see it, and though
some of those that, in their places and stations, are
employed about the building, may never see the cope-
stone put thereupon, for as short a work as the great
Master-builder will make of it, yet what's the matter ?
They are about their duty, and their delivery shall be
more complete and glorious.   For mine own part, though
the enemy should not get me reached, seemingly this
tabernacle of clay will soon fall ; for I am oftentimes
variously and greatly distempered in my body.   But
while the Lord hath anything to do with me, I shall
continue, and I desire to continue no longer ; though
many live longer than the Lord hath work for them.
Howbeit, I many times admire the Lord's kindness
toward me, for I never find any distemper of my body
but when I am so circumstanced, as, in many respects,
I may dispense with it ; and, through His grace, this is
all my desire to spend and be spent for Him in His
work, until my course be ended.   And for seeing better
days with my bodily eyes (though I am persuaded they
are near at hand) I am not in the least anxious, neither
was that desire either soon or late my exercise ; for
though they will be a happy people who will be so
privileged, yet I count them more happy who are altogether without fear, care, sinning or sorrowing.

As for other news, right honourable and dearly beloved in our Lord, very many of us, within these three
quarters of a year, have fallen amongst the enemies'
hands.   Some they executed upon scaffolds ; but the
Lord so owned and countenanced such, especially those
five at Glasgow, that the sight of them took great effect
upon the generality of the people, and raised such a
feeling amongst them, as was dreaded by the enemy.
Yea, and a grand persecutor, called Major Windram,
had three children, who within a little while of each other

died, one of them a very young boy, and two daughters
come to the years of discretion, who died very sweetly
and satisfyingly, declaring, that the Lord's hand was
stretched forth against them, because of the hand their
father had in shedding the blood of the saints, and
obtesting him before God, that he would quit the course
that he followed : which things had some, though no
promising, effect upon him. Whereupon, since the
enemy thought it most conducive to their purpose to
banish them all, so many who carried very stedfastly
were sent away, leaving faithful joint testimonies behind them : whereof one was subscribed by twenty-
two hands, twenty of them having carried honestly,
and the other two acknowledging their fainting, in
either seeking or consenting unto banishment. But, I
think, the Lord had a special end in the exile of such,
sending them away to be witnesses against the many
complying ministers and professors who are going to
that same place. May not we be content to want a
company of our friends out of our own land, that they
may be a testimony for the Lord in another place ?
Howbeit the enemies' hands are wonderfully bound up
now from shedding of blood. I do not know what may
be done, through the Lord's permission, by these new
created powers, the Earl of Perth being called chancellor ; but York's faction is discourted, there being a
variance, at least pretended, betwixt his brother and
him. But if real, I think it may be a means to shorten
some of their days. As for what we did at our last
General Meeting ; after we had resolved to answer your
desires, we laid it upon T. Linning to write his Testimony, and show it to the next meeting, which he
engaged to do. If the meeting be pleased therewith, I
think he will go abroad unto you. For my own part,
if his Testimony be satisfying, I can say nothing against
it ; for I think he is the most hopeful lad, by appearance, that we have, and hath kythed * much willingness
to serve the remnant any way. But at our last meeting

* Shown.

we got not Mr William Boyd spoken to, nor heard.
Nevertheless I am sadly afraid that he breed us work
yet; but I pray the Lord may disappoint my fears.

Now, right honourable and dearly beloved in our
sweet and precious Lord, what shall I say unto you? or
how shall I express myself? The incomparableness of
time's trials and sufferings with the loveliness of Christ,
and the glory that shall be revealed thereafter, makes
me sometimes that I see neither trouble nor danger,
mine eyes being shut thereat, and carried to behold a
small glimpse of that which is beyond tribulation's
reach; but in such a case silent wondering is most my
exercise. O! what a life will it be, when we shall
neither sin nor sorrow! when we shall lay down our
arms, and take up the palm of victory and triumph in
our hands, and follow the Lamb with songs of praise in
our mouths! Everlasting love and joy will be all the
work that is there. O! what manner of work is that
—the ardency of love, without abating or intermissions
and allayments, arising from the enjoyment of so
lovely and beloved an object—what manner of work
is that? They that get a sight of that will be made
to cry out, "We will spend no more labour for that
which satisfieth not." O! the full and sufficient satisfaction that is in the matchless pearl, Christ. He is
all things desirable. Let us bestow all our love, our
whole affections upon Him. And when we have done,
let us wonder that He should seek it, and take it off
our hands. While in these lists of jostling, let us put
all our weapons in love's hand. Love is a resolute
soldier; love is an undaunted champion; love's eye is
so much taken up with contemplating the Beloved,
that it cannot see dangers in the way, but runs blindly
upon them; and yet not blindly, it knoweth for whom,
and for what it so ventureth. Love will never turn the
weapons against the Beloved; yea, will never turn the
back upon the Beloved's quarrel. O! what a champion
is love! I confess good company, and abiding company, is much to be desired, and love is that. Faith

at length will vanish into sight, and hope into possession, but love is the Christian's continual companion,
and a brave companion it is ; for it is no burden to love
when there is the lasting enjoyment of the Beloved,
and the full and continual assurance of immeasurable
love again, as it is when love is made perfect.

Ah ! if time would stay, I would not weary to write
unto your Honour ; for, I do not know when, if ever, I
may have the occasion again. But while I am, I desire
to be concerned with you. O ! go on and fear not.
The Lord, I hope, will show you a token for good, that
they who hate you may see it and be ashamed. Dread
nothing in your intended journey,—the Lord will be
with you. I pray again and again that so it may be,
and that He may bless your labours, and make them
contribute to the procuring a uniformity amongst the
churches, that so He may be one, and His name one
amongst us. I hope I need not desire you to mind me,
a poor thing, who have much to do, and nothing in
myself to do with, and who remains, Honourable and
dear Sir, your real, constant sympathizing friend and
servant in the Lord,   JAMES RENWICK.

LETTER XXXIII.

August 12, 1684.

Right honourable and dear Sir,—I thought once that
your expectation of our letters should have been more
quickly answered than now it could be ; but the holy
and wise God, who doeth all things well, so ordered it
that it is fallen out otherwise. For upon the penult *
day of July, when I was going, in company with other
three, to the General Meeting, we espied two dragoons
meeting us, and not expecting any more to be following, we went forward not dreading them. But when
we came within word and shot, we saw a party of

* The last but one.

about twenty more very near upon us : whereupon, seeing there was no probability of resisting them, we turned up to a hill called Dungavel. But my three neighbours being upon foot and I upon horseback, they compassed about by the foot of the hill, but I took up to the height, being hotly pursued by many of that party ; some whereof were at my right hand to keep me from the mosses, and others behind, who always as they came within shot, discharged upon me. So, being near unto the top of the hill, and finding myself beset round about, and seeing no visible door of escape, I thought fit to quit the horse which I had, and wait till I saw what God did in it. But after I had lighted from the horse, I saw before me a piece of good equitable * ground, whereupon I essayed to mount again upon the horse, but the beast would not stand unto me ; whereupon I resolved to kill the horse, lest the enemy should be thereby strengthened. Howbeit, having but one shot, I thought fit to keep it for a greater extremity, and finding the beast such as would not stand still, I reached it with a shabble † which I had, conjecturing that possibly (the place being uninhabited) the beast might save my wallet and the papers, together with Mr Boyd's wallet. Thus I went up to the very top of the hill upon foot, and seeing myself so encompassed that I could not run from them, and that I was in no ways able to fight with them, I judged it my best to clap upon the ground. So I went into a cairn, which by situation was about six or seven paces of ground out of all their eyes, thinking to lie down upon it, all the hill being green and bare in that place, knowing that God could carry their sight over it. So coming to the top of it, I espied in it a pit, which, when I saw, it entered into my mind, that it was ordained of God for hiding me. Thus I lay down into it, winning by God's goodness, to a cheerful submission to death, torture, or whatsoever His will might be. But I was, in no small

* Level.　　　　† A kind of crooked sword.

measure, confident that no evil at that time could happen unto me, the Lord giving me that Scripture, Psal. vi. 8. "Depart," &c., which was so powerful, that I was made (I think) 100 times to repeat it over, ere I got myself stayed, together with that other Psalm (xci. 11) "For He shall," &c., which was such unto me, that I lifted up my head to see these angels; but, considering my folly in that particular, I was made to laugh at mine own witlessness. So I lay still until the sun set, sometimes praying and sometimes praising God, though, Oh! I can do neither to purpose. But all the joy that the Lord's works of wonder for me did afford was swallowed up in sorrow, because of what befel my dear brethren, who (all that were with me) fell into the enemies' hands, one of them receiving eleven wounds. Then, after all, when I thought upon drawing off the hill, not knowing the way to one friend's house in the whole country, I besought the Lord, that as He had hid me, so He would lead and guide me. Thus I set my face toward Clyde, and after I had travelled about four miles, I met with Windhill, with whom I stayed two days, and kept a meeting upon the second night, even while the militia were searching that side of the country; and twice that night I very wonderfully escaped, as it had been even out of their very paws. O! time would fail me to relate the Lord's works of wonder for poor unworthy me: for even since, in one day, I have escaped three or four signal hazards. O! what shall I say of the Lord's way with me? He will either have me taught, otherwise He will have me appear to be indocile. O for grace, grace to answer His pains taken upon me! And as for the present case of our land, it was never such; enemies have issued forth a proclamation, calling all the militia be-north Tay to be in readiness against the fifteenth of this month with fifteen days' provision, and it is thought to spread over the westland Shires. But the Lord knows what their purposes are. However, they have proclaimed, that all men in country habit, wherever they are seen, are to be challenged, and kept till it be known what they are. Now, the adversary is most cruel, and apprehends not only all men, but even the women whom they can get their hands upon, and uses them most barbarously. O what meaneth this hot furnace! surely it is not to consume, it is to purge and refine. O for grace, for grace to endure unto the end! I think Scotland is now like a woman in hard labour, who must either get a speedy help and delivery, else she will be in peril of dying in travail. But courage yet, for her sharpest hour is at the minute of her delivery. Die, die she will not, for the Lord is but hastening her through her travail. The more sore her pains be, the more joyful her delivery will be; yea, the Lord will make brave mirth at it, for He will have a feast of many a man's carcase at it. As for more particular news, T. L.* will give you an account. I have not seen his Testimony, but I think, he is a good honest lad. Rob. G.† hath carried always very stedfastly, and is now sentenced with banishment. A wonderful restraint upon enemies indeed.

I saw your Honour's last letters which you wrote home anent Mr F.'s ‡ business; and I cannot pass this, that I observed in the strain of them much trouble, if not discouragement to be held forth. O fy upon you, where is all your undaunted boldness and true magnanimity now? What fear you? What can he and his party do? they are incapable of doing harm here. They are but rendering themselves such, as their memories shall be written over with contempt and ignominy to all after generations.

Now, the Lord be with you, O my brother, and teach you to use your weapons rightly for Him in this day of rencounter. O cease not, cease not to pray for poor Scotland, now in travail, and for him who is your Honour's, as formerly,   J. R.

* Thomas Linning, mentioned in previous letter.

† Probably Robert Goodwin of Glasgow, referred to again in Letter lix.

‡ Mr Flint's.

'*P.S.*'—Lest advantage should be taken against the Cause by reason of suspicion in that head, I thought fit to tell you that that part of our reply to James Russel's information which related to myself was not at all penned or drawn up by me.

If time would permit, ilk day furnishes me both with sad and refreshful tidings to report unto your Honour; refreshful, for our prison houses are filled with songs of joy and praise, yea, they were never more refreshful, for they are palaces indeed. But our sad case otherwise still increases; for many are apprehended, yea women are sought after and incarcerated, and some of them banished, and men executed upon the very day when they receive the sentence of death.

From these letters it is obvious that the furnace of persecution was now being heated seven times. Besides, Renwick's fame as a preacher had already excited so much attention, that more strenuous efforts were now put forth by his enemies to get him into their hands. On August 30th, 1684, he was formally summoned at the Cross of Edinburgh, and the Pier of Leith, to appear before the Privy Council, and in the following month, letters of intercommuning were issued against him, in which he was described as a pretended preacher and a seditious vagabond, and all loyal subjects were prohibited from holding any intercourse with him or with his followers.

"We command and charge all and sundry our lieges and subjects," so runs this legal ocument, "that they nor none of them presume, nor take upon hand to reset, supply, or intercommune with the said Mr James Renwick, rebel aforesaid; nor furnish him with meat, drink, house, harbour, victual, nor no other thing useful

or comfortable to him ; or to have intelligence with him
by word, writ, or message, or any other manner of way
whatsoever, under the pain of being esteemed art and
part with him in the crimes foresaid, and pursued
therefor with all rigour to the terror of others. And
we hereby require all our sheriffs and other officers to
apprehend and commit to prison the person of the
said Mr James Renwick wherever they can find or
apprehend him."

This atrocious proclamation was speedily answered
by the United Societies, who, at a general meeting on
October 15, resolved " to warn intelligencers and bloody
Doegs of the wickedness of their ways, and to threaten
them (in case of persisting in malicious shedding of their
blood, or instigating thereto and assisting therein), that
they would not be so slack-handed in time coming to
revenge it." They therefore instructed Mr Renwick to
draw up a declaration for this purpose, which was afterwards affixed to several market crosses and church
doors, and was known as "the Apologetical Declaration and Admonitory Vindication of the true Presbyterians of the Church of Scotland, especially anent
intelligencers and informers."

In this public document, which produced a deep
impression, and was followed by important results,
the Covenanters testified their adherence to previous
declarations wherein they had disowned the authority of Charles Stuart, and declared war against him
and his accomplices. While expressing abhorrence
of the spirit and practice of revenge, they declared to
all that "whosoever stretched forth their hands against
them by shedding their blood either by authoritative
commanding as the justiciary, or actual doing as the
military, or searching out and delivering them up to

their enemies as the gentry, or informing against them wickedly and willingly as the viperous and malicious bishops and curates, or raising the hue and cry as the common intelligencers—they should repute them enemies to God and the covenanted work of Reformation, and punish them according to their power and the degree of their offence!" This Declaration, for a time, struck terror to the hearts of many of their enemies, though afterwards it was used as an instrument of torture by the persecutors, who framed a special Oath of Abjuration regarding it, which they pressed unmercifully on all suspected persons. To this Renwick refers in the following letter addressed to some friends :—

LETTER XXXIV.

Loving Friends,—According to your desire, and my promise, I shall write to you my thoughts (in weakness) of this fair faced though foul-hearted Oath, so violently pressed upon the consciences of young and old, lad and lass, by the wicked powers of the land, whereby many souls are catched in the snare, and fallen in the pit digged by them, not considering, or else not willing to see the hook under so fair a bait, nor the poison in the cup, although all their dainties be deceitful meat. And as this, upon the one hand, ought to be matter of deep sorrow, and mournful lamentation before the Lord, to all seriously concerned, and tender of the Lord's work and cause, against the wrongs and injuries done unto Him ; and that there should be so many (and that in a covenanted land) wearying of His sweet and easy yoke, as if He had been a barren wilderness, and a land of drought to them, who have now left His colours, and fled from His camp, and run unto Satan's (that great red dragon fighting against Michael and his angels) and lifted themselves under his banner, taking on his livery, and wreathing his yoke about their necks : O foolish people and un-wise, have they thus requited the Lord ? But as that yoke is a beggarly bondage, and an enslaving thraldom, so their wages (if free mercy prevent not) shall be well paid them, even to *drink of the wine of the wrath of God, which is poured out without mixture into the cup of His in-dignation,* Rev. xiv. 10.

So, upon the other hand, we have this as a ground of encouragement, and matter of praise before the Lord, that notwithstanding so many are rushing, as the horse into the battle, into enemies' camps, and receiving their mark in their right hand, or forehead, yet there are many in this land whom the Lord has helped, and honoured by His grace to follow Him, walking in His way, and He hath kept them at a distance from the pollutions and abominations of the times, and out of these destructive paths 'enabled them' yea, *to resist unto blood striving against sin.* And I am hopeful He will keep a Remnant, whom neither the wind of tempta-tion shall blow away, nor the flame of persecution burn, nor the fire of judgment consume ; but they shall be a holy seed, to do service to Him, as a teil tree, or oak, whose substance is in them, when the carcases of thousands shall dung the wilderness.

Having premised this, I shall next unbosom my thoughts of the sinfulness of the Oath by producing some reasons against the Oath itself, earnestly desiring any who shall be at the pains to look on this line, to read it seriously, singly and impartially, weighing the same in the balances of the sanctuary. And

1*st*, There can no oath be taken rightly, except the person taking it swear in truth, in judgment and in righteousness. But, O how can any think to take it, when the designs thereof (as shall be shown) are so evidently destructive to the interest of religion, that is now lying at the stake, and also, the persons imposing it are avowed enemies to God, and all righteousness, and are so lawfully and justly disowned, as having no right to govern for their perjury and murder, for their usurpation in things ecclesiastic, and tyranny in things civil.

2*dly*, All who answer the enemies' demand, in taking this oath, are guilty of complying with their hellish and wicked designs to root out, and raze to the foundation the Protestant interest (which, alas, is brought low by them already) that they may set up in its place their superstitious idolatry, and build their cursed Babel. For, to effectuate this, they fall upon this design, to have the hands, heads, and hearts of all tied up from doing any thing for the preservation of religion. Is not this evident from that oath, wherein they swear not to have war against, but peace with those whose designs are such? O dreadful and monstrous wickedness, to be guilty of rooting out the work of God, and laying the foundation of that cursed Babel again!

3*dly*, All the takers of this wretched oath cannot free themselves of being guilty of condemning all that our fore-fathers have done in the defence and preservation of our glorious work of Reformation, and in defence of themselves, against Papists, Prelates, and Malignants.

4*thly*, All the takers of this oath swear never to make war with these who are following their footsteps, yea, and worse than these who went before them. Yea, the taking thereof says that the enemies' opposition has been right, and that the Lord's people are wrong, and acted as fools, and suffered as such, which were blasphemy to assert. For the import and design of that Declaration, abjured by the oath, is nothing but to carry on and advance that glorious work of Reformation, and to defend themselves against all opposers (which nature allows), seeing their enemies had declared war against them, and their declaring war was but a repelling of violence. O wicked sin, to be guilty of condemning and burying of such a glorious work!

5*thly*, All who take this oath swear unto a lie, for it says that the Declaration is for killing all who serve his Majesty in church, state, army, or country; whereas it makes a plain distinction obvious to all, between the more moderate and the cruel and blood-thirsty, and makes the degree of punishment according to the degree of their offence. And doth not the taking of God (who is truth itself) to witness to such a lie, make the sin greatly heinous, and may not such expect that their bands will be made strong ?

6*thly*, The swearers of this oath make themselves guilty of that blasphemous supremacy, established by their law, in the person of a dying wretched mortal, over all persons, and in all causes, which properly belongs to Christ, as being head in and over His own church. And this they have twined into the oath in these words "all who serve his Majesty in Church and State." And as by this oath, the Prelates, Curates, and other officers of their church are said not to serve or be subject to Christ but to him, and he to be their head and fountain from whence they derive their power, so these who take this oath, may expect to meet with that same measure of wrath, if repentance prevent it not, with these who are actually guilty of robbing Christ of His royal prerogatives, when He arises as an incensed Mediator to reclaim His own rights and declarative glory, thus usurped and trode upon by the wicked.

7*thly*, By taking of this oath, they become guilty of perjury, a wicked and epidemic sin ; for in our Solemn League and Covenant, we are bound, to the utmost of our power, to extirpate popery, prelacy, and malignancy, &c. Now, how can any fulfil their engagements to God, when they swear not to have war, yea not so much as move their tongue (which they will interpret to be a declaring war) against the chief ringleaders, and promoters of popery and prelacy ? And O can any free this of perjury ? Shall they break the covenant and be delivered ? No, the Lord who is a swift witness against all false swearers will punish such.

8*thly*, By taking this oath they swear to have peace with the enemies of God, these *Amalekites* against whom He will have war, from generation to generation ; and we are commanded in Deut. xxiii. 6. not to seek their peace nor prosperity all our days for ever. And is not this swearing, not to have war against His enemies, a clear breach of that command given by God to His people? And likewise in our baptismal vows we are given away to the Lord, to fight under His banner, against the devil, the world, and the flesh. O let us not break our vows in making peace with any of them, lest we provoke Him to let us fall as a prey before them, and them to have dominion over us. And ought not this to make a tender-hearted Christian fear at it, because they have made it a discriminating sign, and token, between the good and the bad, to know who are on their side and who not, and that none are to buy, or sell, without they have the mark of the beast (the pass shewing they have taken the oath of peace) in their right hand, or fore-head?

9*thly*, The swearing of it is a wronging of justice, seeing by this oath they are not to have war with any that serve his Majesty, in church, state, army, or country, whereas many of them by their open and avowed murder, perjury, blasphemy, and idolatry, have forfeited their lives, and made themselves liable to the stroke and sword of justice; for the land that is defiled with blood cannot be cleansed, but by the blood of him who shed it. Numb. xxxv. 31, 32, 33.

10*thly*, These who take this wretched oath of peace will not be exempted from the next trial that cometh through. For although they have gone on in the whole steps of defection formerly, yet if they answer not the present demand of the enemies, all that they have done before will be to no purpose. Yea what may be expected next, but that the Whore of Rome spread her mantle of darkness over these covenanted lands? O happy souls, in that day, who shall be found near God, and far from the tents of these wicked men! For it is to be feared that these, who have gone on in the former steps of defection, will make but a step of this also, seeing (it hath been observed) that defection in this day hath grown by degrees, and gone on by little and little, till they have been one with open enemies. Not desiring to trouble you further, I remain yours at command in the Lord Jesus,

JAMES RENWICK.

But now we have come to what are generally known as "the killing times" in Scotland, when the powers of darkness were let loose in the land, and the blood of the martyrs flowed like water. We shall reserve what we have to say regarding this period for another chapter. Meanwhile let us see, in this young soldier of Jesus Christ,

" One who never turned his back but marched breast forward,
Never doubted clouds would break,
Never dreamed, though right were worsted, wrong would triumph,
Held we fall to rise, are baffled to fight better,
Sleep to wake."

CHAPTER VII.

THE KILLING TIME.

IN February 1685 Charles II. died, and his brother, the Duke of York, an avowed Papist, ascended the throne. This important change did not bring any immediate relief to the Covenanters, whose sufferings rather increased than diminished under the new king. In particular, as the author of "Faithful Contendings Displayed" informs us, the persecution against the Societies reached now its greatest height. Many were cruelly and inhumanly murdered in the open fields, others were hanged, many thrown into prison and tortured with fiendish cruelty. Great diligence was also shown in searching for the fugitives, who were reduced to the utmost straits and forced to seek shelter in the wildest and loneliest places. In a word, as this old chronicler expresses it, such was the enraged cruelty and furious hellish zeal of these bloody adversaries against these poor people whom they designed wholly to cut off, that they spared neither the young man for his youth nor the old man for his grey hair and stooping age: yea, women, and these both old and young, escaped not their bloody and barbarous hands, some being strangely murdered and many cast into prison.

One stormy night, probably about this very time, a step was heard at the door of a lonely cottage in an

upland district of Ayrshire, the abode of John Brown
of Priesthill, "the Christian carrier." His young wife
sat with her baby at her breast, and with her little
step-daughter waited and watched for her husband's
return. Hastily opening the door and seeing a stranger
there, the young girl started back with fear and surprise; but gathering confidence from her mother's face,
and probably also from the stranger's appearance and
manner, she took him by the hand and led him near
the fire. This kindly act on the part of one so young,
says the narrator of this touching incident, went to the
heart of the weary pilgrim, who, with a tear in his eye
and a lip quivering with emotion, exclaimed, "The
blessing of him that is ready to perish be upon thy
young head, dear child." The utterance and the look
at once dispelled the mother's fears, whose welcome
then became as warm and cordial as that of the tender-
hearted and less suspicious child: and soon John Brown
himself arrived and at once recognised in the stranger
"the boy Renwick," as his enemies contemptuously
called him. In pious converse and in prayer, with only
a brief interval of rest, the night was spent; and ere
the dawn of day Renwick had to be off and away before
the light could reveal him to those who were in search.
On the 1st of May 1685 this cottage became the scene
of one of the bloodiest tragedies that have ever been
recorded. Early that morning Graham of Claverhouse,
who, as the Ettrick Shepherd truly says, "had the
nature of a wolf if he had the bravery of a bull dog,"
had come suddenly upon John while he was engaged in
cutting turf on the hill above the house. Having
brought him down to his own door, and put to him the
usual ensnaring questions as to the supremacy of the
king and the oath of abjuration, he then ordered him

to say his prayers and prepare for immediate death. Kneeling down and praying in such a strain that even the troopers were impressed, this martyr then kissed his weeping wife and children, and turning his face to heaven, earnestly besought that "all promised and purchased blessings might be multiplied upon them." Claverhouse having ordered six of his men to fire, and seeing them hesitate, drew his own pistol and fired it at the good man's head, turning at the same time to the newly made widow, and brutally asking, "What thinkest thou of thy husband now, woman?" "I ever thought much good of him," she nobly answered, "but more *now* than ever." "It were but justice to lay thee beside him," exclaimed the murderer. "If you were permitted," she bravely replied, "I doubt not but your cruelty would go that length: but how will you answer for this morning's work?" "To man I can be answerable," said this cruel monster, "and as for God, I will take Him in my own hands." Such was the man who has been described as a model soldier, a gentleman and a hero, but who is still more truly known in many parts of our land as the "bloody Clavers," and whose career was brought to a tragic close, four years after the scene we have described, in the Pass of Killiecrankie.

Scenes of a similar kind to that of Priesthill were, during this terrible period, enacted in other parts of our land. Thus, on the 11th of May 1685, Margaret M'Lauchlan, an old woman of upwards of sixty years of age, and Margaret Wilson, a girl of eighteen, were bound to stakes on the sands near Wigtown and drowned by the rising tide. "What see you yonder?" said their murderers, as they directed the attention of the younger of the two to her fellow-confessor who was staked farther out and who was then in the suffocating agonies of a protracted death. Firmly the brave and noble girl replied, "I see Christ suffering in one of His own members." About the same time four men were returning from Galloway, where they had been to hear James Renwick preach, when they were overtaken by a company of soldiers at Crossgellioch near Cumnock, and of the four three were shot there in cold blood, while one managed to escape. When a monument was being erected to their memory in 1827, the three bodies were found lying side by side only a little way beneath the surface, looking as if they had only been buried yesterday, the antiseptic properties of the black peat moss in which they were buried having doubtless preserved them fresh and undecayed.

> " A relic shown with miser care,
> A treasured lock of auburn hair,
> Was kept by those the stone that reared,
> Struck all with breathless wonder,
> When, as if yesterday interred,
> Those martyrs to their gaze appeared,
> Short space the moss-turf under.
>
> Ah ! who shall tell what hearts were wrung
> For those lone sleepers fair and young !
> What high wrought hopes, what breathings fond,
> In those dark days and olden,
> Were drowned in tears for him that owned
> That ringlet soft and golden ! "

These instances, chosen from multitudes of a similar kind, may suffice to explain why this year became afterwards known as the killing time in Scotland. The furnace of persecution was indeed heated sevenfold, and "nothing less was intended," says the eloquent author of the 'Fifty Years' Struggle of the Scottish Covenanters,' "than to consume and destroy every individual member of the detested sect. To all the usual appliances—fines, imprisonments, forfeitures, spoiling of goods, banishment, tortures, executions on the scaffold, military quarterings and ravages—there were now added other and more deadly means to ensure the extirpation of the Cameronians. *Extirpation!* that was now the word of the powers of darkness who ruled the country. The execution of the laws was committed wholly and absolutely to the soldiers. They had no limited instructions : they had powers and express orders to go through the whole country and kill ; kill in the house, kill in the field, kill one or many, as they should meet them ; kill with full indemnity against consequences, kill at their own discretion, and kill instantly and upon the spot. These times are still named with a shudder, 'The killing times of Scotland.'"

Great and constant, however, as was the danger to which Renwick was exposed, his courage never cooled because his faith never wavered. On the 28th of May 1685, with about two hundred men, he rode into the town of Sanquhar, and there, after praise and prayer, read and affixed to the market-cross a Declaration of their principles, similar to one which had been published by Richard Cameron at the same place about five years before. This second Declaration would probably have occasioned more trouble than the first, both because it was published with much more pomp and circumstance, and because it contained even a stronger protest against the reigning dynasty : but the attention of the Government was meanwhile occupied with two other serious attacks upon their authority—the one in England under the Duke of Monmouth, and the other in Scotland under the Earl of Argyle.

Ardent and intrepid on the field of battle, Monmouth, who was a natural son of Charles II., was everywhere else irresolute and unreliable. His descent upon the West of England, followed by his disastrous defeat and execution and the horrible atrocities subsequently inflicted on multitudes by Judge Jeffreys of unhappy memory, is familiar to all readers of History, and has recently been described by Conan Doyle in "Micah Clarke."

Archibald, ninth Earl of Argyle, though obnoxious to the Government, and finding it necessary to reside in Holland, had not been always friendly to the Covenanters. According to Macaulay, "his compliances in Ecclesiastical matters had given scandal to rigid Presbyterians : and so far had he been from showing any inclination to resistance that, when the Covenanters had been persecuted into insurrection, he had brought into the field a large body of his dependents to support the Government." During his exile on the Continent, his views on religious questions had undergone a great change, and henceforth he became very zealous for the cause of liberty and religion. Among the exiled Scots, however, there was a faction not friendly to him, including Sir Patrick Hume of Polwarth and Sir John Cochran, second son of the Earl of Dundonald, and to the disputes which subsequently arose among his officers was largely to be ascribed the failure of his expedition. From the time he landed in Scotland until his army was dispersed not many weeks elapsed, and after a hasty trial he was condemned to death and beheaded on the 30th June 1685. According to Macaulay, only a single acrimonious expression escaped him on the scaffold. One of the Episcopal clergymen who attended him called out in a loud voice—" My Lord dies a Protestant." "Yes," said the Earl, stepping forward, " and not only a Protestant, but with a heart hatred of Popery, of Prelacy, and of all superstition."

For reasons which appeared cogent to himself and his immediate followers, Renwick refused to join the ill-fated expedition of Argyle, which fact, however, did not prevent him from sharing in some of its unhappy consequences. According to one who lived at that time, and was himself a sufferer for Christ, "all the forces, foot, horse, dragoons, militia troops, and companies of Lowlanders were poured in upon all the western and southern shires, to range through all the rocks, woods, muirs, and mountains, pursuing the chase with indefatigable travel, and saying, *They had now gotten away with Monmouth and Argyle, they must now fall on with Renwick and the old regiment.* . . . Moreover, the latter had little sympathy except from those who could give little succour. Yet all these things did not move him from, nor mar him in his work, but under all these afflictions he was confirmed more and more that the work was the Lord's, and that He would own it; and by the grace and goodness of God he was still the more animated and enlarged in spirit, and enabled in body to increase his diligence in preaching, baptising, and exercising every week, once at least."

We now introduce several letters belonging to this period. The first, addressed to Sir Robert Hamilton, was written soon after the death of the King, to whom evidently Renwick refers in the words "He hath houghed off our antagonist's chief factor.'

Letter XXXV.

Feb. 28, 1685.

Right Honourable and dear Sir,—I received your letter, which was many ways refreshing unto me, as also the way of its coming to my hand; for when I was upon my travels, about the setting forth of my master's wares, there arose such a storm of weather, which forced me to turn off my journey a little, to the nearest great inn, and there I got your letter, and also my wares better received off my hand than ever before in that place. Hence I am made to see, that divine providence is a mysterious thing, and that I never lose a whit the more of a storm. Also there is one thing in your letter which made me not a little admire,* to wit, your apprehension that I was sorely sick, that there was a great skaith † amongst traders, and that my sickness was a mean of my preservation— a leal guess indeed. In reference hereunto, I must tell you a pretty passage. Upon a certain night, after the dismission of a market, there went about forty of our merchants forward a little before me, upon the way that I was going, with whom I trysted to meet the night following. But after a little sleep, sickness so possessed me that I was not able to keep my tryst. Whereupon I sent away some merchants that were with me to go forward with the rest about their business, who, upon the day following, were assaulted with a great multitude of our antagonists, who were six for one, so that our merchants were not able to stand ; whereupon they took the retreat, and outstripped their antagonists without any skaith, save the loss of one. Now before this came to pass I dreaded it. But what think you of my sickness and your guess? For if I had been with the rest I had been taken from all trading ; for my body is so weakened with much travel, that though I travel more than any, yet I cannot come so good speed as others, when need requireth. Also, within two days my sickness left me. Now, I leave all this to your thoughts, for it would be tedious for me to write mine ; and I think you may guess at them, as you did at that which was more dark. But to come to the substance of your letter, you have opened up the mystery of our trade abroad, which I

* Wonder. † Scarcity or loss.

dreaded, yet I understood it not; but I agree with
your advice, as to these men's subscribing of our principal accounts. But my master is taking the wisest
way in it, for now he hath houghed off our antagonist's
chief factor. So that, I think, all merchants will now
shortly side themselves, and when at the push they declare themselves willingly whose trade they are for, it
will speak forth the most ingenuity, and we will know
the better what to think of them. So we need not be
rash in our proposals, till we see how these men settle;
for now they must settle some way or other. This is
my poor advice at the time, but I have not as yet met
with any number of our merchants to consult with
anent it. However, the same mystery from abroad is
also at home with us; but I find all our merchants
pretty steadfast, for all sorts are most earnest that we
should trade with them, and they with us. But I judge,
they respect not the advantage of our trade therein,
but of their own. Nevertheless, what think you makes
them so earnest to trade with us? Our wares go as
well off our hands at home; this is part of the reason
of it. Our merchants daily increase, this is another
part. But I judge the chief reason to be this, they look
upon us as venturous merchants, that dow not abide
dealing with naughty commodities, but set out aye for
wholesale; and that we are resolute, so that no storm
will keep us back from our intended voyage. Whereupon they think, if we would trade with them, they
would get us set upon all desperate traffic, and if we
did win, it would be to their hand, and if we lost, we
would but lose ourselves, which the most part of them
would not regard much. Here, I think, lies the knack.

But, worthy Sir, for your further satisfaction and
information anent our trade at home, these few things
I think fit to tell you that I observe, (1.) That the
great part of the country give their approbation to
our trade, and the way thereof, though they have not
hearts to give their gold and money for our wares.
(2.) That very many think our wares so worthy, that

they spare not to bestow either gold or money upon them. (3.) That very many, who, I thought, would not have looked us in the face, resort to our markets in all places. (4.) Very many are seeking to be in our incorporations, who, I think, are downright for our trade; but I fear some of them be seeking rather that we should have a great stock, and that they should share with us, than that my master should get credit; whereas He respects His credit more than He doth all the gold and money in the world. (5.) None are received in amongst us, who either leave us, or rue their trading with us. (6.) Our merchants are all fearless, as if they could not lose any thing. (7.) They are resolute,—they will not slip a market for a foul day, or lie in the harbour because of a storm. (8.) The waiters are so angry at our goods, that ordinarily they do not bring them (when they catch them) to public roupings, or to be burnt by the hands of the common hangman, but destroy them where they may find them. This is occasioned partly by the resoluteness of our merchants, who will not let the waiters carry away our goods,—so they come to be destroyed when the waiters are the strongest party; and partly by the maliciousness of the waiters, who, unless our merchants renounce their trade, presently destroy their goods. I may say, my master hath gotten us some brave resolute merchants, whom a hasty proposal never surpriseth. (9.) The waiters have gotten many of the best of our goods destroyed; yea, they have captured more from us within these two years, than I thought then we had; and the more they take, we have the more behind. But this is only through the wit of my master; yea, He is so wise, that ere He want wares He will make stones give silver. (10.) There is some difference amongst our own merchants anent the manner of seeking in our debts of the last accounts, which we gave in against our antagonists; but I do not fear that my master will suffer a break to be among us upon that head, for we all agree in the matter.

Now, to come to what is your desire in your memorandum sent unto me.

1. As to that information anent Mr Lap.,* I got it from young Mr Fisher, who had it from his brother at London. As also, I know that his brother had left off trading with the leading merchants at London, save with Mr Fife, with whom I hear not that he tradeth much.

2. As to correspondence with Groemvezyh (by whom I understand Mr Br.†), there hath been more since his flitting; and as for any letters betwixt him and Mr Fisher, elder, is a thing unknown to me; neither have I any distinct notion of his seeking to trade with us, save by the apprentice you sent over.

3. As to our late accounts, we shall see to get it unto you; as also how that money may be received off your hand.

Now, Right honourable Sir, at the time I shall trouble you no further, not knowing well how to get this conveyed unto your hand. But I leave you to my master's direction and counsel, who, I know, can make known unto you the secrets of our trade, and the engines of our opposers. My love to all friends who wish us a good market, and show them I forget them not. I am, yours to serve you to my power in my master's employment, JA. BRUCE.

' P.S.'—I do not know what you understand by M. B. in your letter.

LETTER XXXVI.

This letter is addressed to Mrs Jean Hamilton, and has reference to her conscientious scruples about attending church in Holland.

---

* Perhaps George Lapsley of Linlithgow, whose case is somewhat fully described by Woodrow. He escaped from prison, and lived in Edinburgh for many years after the Revolution.

† Mr Brakell.

March 2, 1685.

Worthy Madam,—Your letter was long in coming to my hand, and it hath been longer in answering ; but I had never the expectation of any occasion before this, as also your case was troublesome to me, and I knew not well what to say anent it. And the most that I can say yet is, that I desire earnestly to sympathise with you, and to mind you before the Lord, for I know your burdens. However, as to what is a cause of part of your trouble, to wit, your unclearness anent hearing, I dare not advise you to it :

1. Because of the many corruptions, which, I fear, are not so burdensome to them now, as once I apprehended they were to some of them.

2. Because of your own unclearness anent it. I say this, not that I make our clearness a sufficient warrant either to do or not do, for then the Scriptures would not be the rule ; yet who esteemeth any thing to be unclean, to him it is unclean. As also, I think, your unclearness is not groundless. But here arise two difficulties :

(1.) How shall this be reconciled with your worthy brother's practice ? Yet I do not see them jostle together ; for though he heareth, yet I know he withdraweth from what is corrupt, which you could not get so handsomely done.

(2.) How shall this be reconciled with the ordination ? Yet neither is there any contradiction here ; for in the ordination they came to us, and acted according to Scotland's reformation, and if those, whom you were to hear, would do so in all points of worship, you need not have any scruple.

But as to your coming home with the children, I see not how you can resolve upon it as yet ; for though your case be sad there, as to many things, it would be more sad here. Therefore my poor advice is, that you would contentedly stay a little, till you see what the Lord doth, and wrestle through your difficulties the best way you can ; for we are expecting strange things suddenly at home. Yet if you saw a general calamity coming upon that place, better to come home and share in Scotland's calamity, in whose sin we have all shared, than to share in the calamity of another place.

Now, dear Madam, my dear and worthy friend, look to the Lord Himself for your direction, upholding, encouragement, comfort, and upmaking : for come what will, it shall be well with the righteous, and all shall end in a public testimony of divine favour to those who wait upon the Lord. For though He should shake heaven and earth, yet He will be the hope of His people, and the strength of the children of Israel, Joel iii. 16. Now, to the word of His grace I commend you, remaining your Ladyship's undoubted and sympathising friend in the Lord,   JAMES BRUCE.

' P.S.'—My love to all the dear babes.

The next two letters are addressed to Sir Robert Hamilton, and are without signature. Public affairs are evidently in a very critical condition, and the necessity for concealment has increased.

LETTER XXXVII.

EDIN., May 13, 1685.

Right Honourable and dear Sir,—I have met with our friend Robert, and got some account of affairs, which hath made me to wonder not a little ; but Andrew Cameron his information makes me to wonder more. For I would not have believed that policy could mask over temporal designs with such fair colours and pretences. Whereupon, we have great need of the wisdom of the serpent, as well as the harmlessness of the dove. I find, Andrew Cameron's drift is to get us to join with A.*; but to me his arguments are more dissuasive than persuasive. But I dread Mr—— greatly, having seen a paper

* Argyle.

from his hand, where he yields to all their desire. I fear the hand of Joab hath been in it; and he would, forsooth, have it published in our name. But (through grace) I will oppose it with my whole strength. I am likewise afraid of some others amongst us, but of none save of such as I had former jealousies, but could not bottom sufficient reasons against them. I have seen also your animadversions upon the Association, which I agree with; for I look upon it as a Cromwellian and Bothwellian compound. But as to your animadversions on our Declaration, I think, the commentaries of politics have made you look upon it after another sort than otherwise you would have done. For we require it to be taken alongst jointly with our other testimonies and actings, and so the door is no wider than it was: neither can any show any thing in that Declaration but what I think may easily be reconciled with our former proceedings. So, I think it a thing below you or me to trouble ourselves with the various expositions that persons, for their own ends, put upon it. For some represent it as the strictest thing that ever came from our hands, thereby to make us odious. Some again, as the laxest that thereupon they may get a door to enter. But there is none opened, and our wall is so well cemented, that through our camp-master, they will not break it through. If some shall leap over it, and go out from us, yet our wall shall stand inviolable. Therefore trouble not yourself (O right honourable) with Logomachies, for our practice will comment upon it.

Now hoping to meet with friends shortly, I will be in a capacity to inform you fully; and, praying that the Lord may give light and life, I am, Right Honourable, yours as formerly.

Letter XXXVIII.

July 9, 1685.

Right Honourable Sir,—If I durst have ventured it with the post, or could have had another occasion, I

would have written to you ere this time; for, I know,
you will be anxious to hear how it is with us. But it
would take a great volume, and require an accurate
observing capacity to write our case. Howbeit this is
no small comfort and encouragement, that the Lord so
visibly takes our matters in His own guiding. For,
before Argyle brake, many of our friends were greatly
puzzled, whether the Lord was calling them to follow
their former methods, or to draw altogether by themselves, and to emit a declaration of their own. Whereupon, there was a meeting appointed to consider the
matter, and also a day for prayer. But the Lord disappointed our meetings, one after another, until Argyle
was apprehended and his party scattered; so this was
put out of our heads. Yet our snares since have been
greater than they were before; for Mr Barclay and Mr
Langlands pass up and down the country, and have got
themselves too much insinuated upon several of our
wanderers, pretending no difference from us, but a
willingness to join with us. Howbeit, I met with Mr
Langlands, and found him no otherwise than when I
was in Holland. He owned his writing of that letter
to Mr Brakell, but would grant with no wrong therein.
So the main thing that they drive at is, to have us to
lay aside our challenges, and they would be silent.
But it is clear to me, that the Lord doth not send
them; for, if He did, they would not cover their
iniquity. Also, their need, and not our need, hath
moved them; but if they shall (in such a strain)
step to the fields with public preaching, I think they
will not keep them long, for the Lord hath taken
possession of our high places until He return to our
temple again. Howbeit, if it were the Lord's will that
you were amongst us, I think that might (through the
Lord's assistance) be instrumental of very much good.
But for my soul, I dare not advise you to come, considering what hazards you may run in your coming.
Yet you may lay it out before the Lord; but if He do
not open a door for your journey, do not venture upon

it, for, I hope, He is reserving you for some great work. O be not anxious, for the Lord will make a stroke clear our controversies.

As for our news, Argyle's party is wholly dissipated, for they disagreed among themselves, not upon the stating of their quarrel, but upon their way of prosecuting it. No conditions made to them were kept, and this rendered them very dissatisfied. Argyle is beheaded, Rumbold executed, after the manner of worthy Rathillet, Sir John Cochran apprehended, and his son, with several others. But Monmouth is still busied in England, whereupon the Scottish forces are marched right to the border, which animates William Cleland, &c., to make a new stir, and so our difficulties are as formerly. As for your brother William, he was lieutenant to Rumbold. He is yet alive, with some of his friends. I resolve to speer him out, and inform him. I have seen John Nisbet, who saith he is with us in all things, and that he came only with Argyle for passage, being under no engagements, and taking no place from them. Andrew Cameron is a great agent for them, and not simple in their business; he refuseth joining with any ministers who were not actually indulged, or defenders of such. Geo. Hill and David Steel are well; but Rob. Spear cannot find an open door to come unto you. M. B. is like to die in prison. Mr Alexander Shields seems to be of a right stamp. Now, I hope your Honour will pardon my confusion, occasioned by my hasty pen. I cannot express my thoughts unto you; but I say again, the Lord will take our matters in His own hand. O! let us be busy with Himself, and commit all unto Him who hath the government upon His shoulders. Scotland's day is coming. Happy those who are in their chambers. My love and service to all friends with you, foreigners and others. The blessing of Him who is in the burning bush be with you. I am, Honourable Sir, yours as formerly.

And now, if we may judge from internal evidence, this seems to be the right place for another letter bearing Renwick's initials but without date, which also is addressed to Sir Robert Hamilton, and reveals not only the sufferings of the persecuted but their compensating joy and peace. It contains an interesting statement regarding the Rev. Alexander Shields, who has been referred to in the previous letter as a man "of a right stamp." Here mention is made of "a foul fall," of which, however, he has truly repented. From other sources we learn that on March 6th of this year while under examination by the Judges, he disowned the Sanquhar Declaration, and a few months afterwards signed the Oath of Abjuration. As, however, we are further informed that he was sent under a guard to the Bass, we are prepared for Renwick's allusions to his repentance and to the delight with which his former companions welcomed him again to their fellowship. After his escape from prison in October 1686, he was closely associated with Renwick, an account of whose life and labours and sufferings he afterwards published to the world.

Letter XXXIX.

Right Honourable and dear Sir,—I received yours, and was refreshed to see a line from your hand again. Yet I am not a little troubled that our converse by letters should not be more frequent; but continual hurrying and tossing stops it on my part, together with such a multitude of business, that sometimes I would put a greater price upon an hour of time than upon much riches. O Sir! who know my work, if they had not hearts harder than adamants, they would be affected with commiseration; but why should I say thus, for who knew the Lord's kindness to worm unworthy me

I

would make me the object of their envy. I may say this indeed, that the Lord suffers not my work, however insupportable to flesh and blood, to be burdensome unto me ; for, though the world thinketh my case most miserable, yet, I think, it is so happy that I know not a man this day, upon the face of the earth, with whom I would exchange my lot. O ! it is more sweet and pleasant to be swimming in the swellings of Jordan for Christ and with Christ, than to swatter in the pleasures of sin, and delights of the flesh. Yea, though Christians had not a heaven hereafter, I cannot but judge their case (even here) happy beyond all others ; as the Psalmist saith,—"Thou hast put gladness in my heart, more than in the time when their corn and their wine increased," Psal. iv. 7. And when the world frowns most, I know, it is the time wherein the Lord smiles most upon His own. O therefore, let none of them fear a suffering lot. Enemies think themselves satisfied that we are put to wander in dark and stormy nights through mosses and mountains ; but if they knew how we are feasted, when others are sleeping, they would gnash their teeth for anger. O ! I cannot express, how sweet times I have had when the curtains of Heaven have been drawn, when the quietness of all things, in the silent watches of the night, has brought to my mind the duty of admiring the deep, silent, and inexpressible ocean of joy and wonder, wherein the whole family of the higher house are everlastingly drowned, each star leading me out to wonder what He must be who is the Star of Jacob, the bright and morning Star, who maketh all His own to shine as stars of the firmament. Indeed (if I may term it so) I am meikle obliged to enemies; for, though they purpose my misery, yet they are instrumental in covering many a fat table to me ; and while they are pining away in dusky envy and pale fear, I am feeding in peace and joy. O poor fools ! what can they do ? The greatest wrong that they can do to us is, to be instruments in bringing a chariot to carry us to that higher house ;

and should we not think this the greatest favour? Let enemies never think that they can make the people of God's case miserable, while He lives and reigns; and I wot well, He hath that to give, and will give that which will sweeten all the sours of His followers. And I may say this to His praise, that I have found so much of His kindness and supply in setting about His work in such hard circumstances, that though the prevailing of a body of death sometimes, and a desire to be with Himself, make me long for dissolution; yet, I think, I could be content to dwell if it were 1000 years in this infirm and weakened body of clay, with continual toil and hazard, to carry His name to His people.

Now Right Honourable, as to news here, know, that the Lord is still increasing His people in number and spiritual strength, and many a sacrifice He is taking off their hands; for there are not many days wherein His truths are not sealed with blood, and that in all places, so that, I think, within a little, there shall not be a moss or mountain in the West of Scotland which shall not be flowered with martyrs. Enemies have brought down the Highlanders upon us, and they with the forces do run through the country (Lord give direction and strength), and kill all whom they meet with, if they do not say whatsoever they bid them. We are fearing massacres; here is a massacre indeed. Oh that my head were waters, and mine eyes rivers of tears, that I might weep without intermission, "for the slain of the daughter of my people." Also, they have given out, by Act of Parliament and open proclamation, that all ministers and hearers, who are found in the fields, are to be killed presently; and, found in houses, the minister is to be killed, and the people fined. The devil now is come down in great wrath, because he knoweth his time to be but short. Mr A. Peden is come to Scotland of purpose (as I hear) to join with us, and is said to be clear in all things; but I have not yet seen him: howbeit I do not dread him as to any hostile draught. Mr Alexander Shields is yet alive, and seems aye to be more and more right. He indeed hath made a foul fall, but I think he is duly sensible : it hath cost him many an hour's bitter exercise, and many a bitter outcry. All the rest of our prisoners are very well encouraged. I have of late made a hasty journey into England, the length of Newcastle, and (blessed be the Lord) with much more nor expected encouragement and success. But as to your desire in your letter, I cannot at this instant answer it; but I shall keep your memorandum till I get it done, for I have been these eight days so hurried and chased with continual alarms, that I could not get settled to write any, and the Lord, to manifest His power, gave me a most remarkable delivery.

Now, dear Sir, begging it of you and of all friends, that you will be busy and instant with God, that He may be with us in this day of our extremity, and commending you all to the Grace of God, with my love and service to yourself and them of whose con-cernedness with the Lord's cause we are all sensible, and that they are most strengthening to you against all your antagonists, particularly to Euph. Van Heerma, Huysvrow B. Pearson, Euph. Catarina Earl, to whom I purpose (God willing) to write, I am ever, as formerly,

J. R.

'P.S.'—Know also that Mr Flint's business is crushed here : for I have met with some in Fife with whom I was well pleased and they with me, and I am hopeful of them all excepting John Henderson. Likewise there were about forty-eight of his hearers apprehended, some discovering the rest, who are a company of poor, ignorant, swearing bodies, all of them, and do anything with the enemy.

Letter XL.

This letter is addressed to Robert Spear whose name occurs in Letter 38.

October 23, 1685.

Dear friend,—What passed at our last meeting, time will not allow me to inform you of, neither need I be careful about the same ; for I know that the bearer can do it as distinctly as I. However, I thought fit to write unto you, showing that the meeting are no ways discontent with your purpose of going abroad at this time. And as to what I have written to my honourable and dear friend, which I did let you see, though I judged it not fit to communicate the same to other friends, as I was telling you by words, so I desire that you would signify unto him, that he must take it only as my thoughts at that time, which (in a great measure) were undigested, and through the multitude of business and contendings, and various weights upon my spirit, not a little confused. Also, as I was telling you my mind more fully anent these things than I have written it, so I desire that you would speak with him concerning the same, showing my thoughts more conspicuously than my letter doth. Moreover, if I have written any thing which is unseasonable, or not right and equal, I am content to be informed and instructed by him : but it is my desire (if he will agree therewith), that after his reading and considering the same, it may be destroyed, for I think it not any advantage to the cause to keep any letters from friends, but what is written as their fixed and deliberate thoughts about matters.

Now, for your coming home, I think you have seen many depths of mercy and judgment manifested to the poor church of Scotland. You have seen the afflicted remnant brought unto and through many difficulties, you have seen much matter of joy and sorrow, so, I hope, your travels hither have not been without fruit. So, praying that the Lord may make His own hand appear at His own work, and establish a remnant in His own way, in the midst of snares and damping difficulties, and, commending you to His direction, assistance, protection, and provision, I am, your assured friend and servant in the Lord   J. R.

LETTER XLI.

To Mrs Jean Hamilton.

Nov. 18, 1685.

Worthy Madam, — You doubtless think my long silence strange, and it is far contrary to my own resolution; but the abounding of inward care, and the continuing of outward tossing block me up from doing many things which I would. It is no great wonder that a man, under such variety of providences as I am, cannot be master of his own purposes. Howbeit, I may say, your case, and the case of the family, lie in such a measure upon my heart, that I cannot get the same forgotten; and though this be an insignificant thing, and of little purpose to your Ladyship, yet I own it is my duty. I never look upon your case but I think it is in some things singular. Your lot is cast in a strange land, separated from your friends and acquaintances. But communion and fellowship with God will make your lot sweet and pleasant unto you, and furnish you with abundance of joy in every outward condition; and this, I hope, you are sometimes sensibly tasting. Also, I doubt not but the company of your worthy brother, and of some dear foreigners, is not a little refreshful to you. Moreover, when I consider your circumstances, Ruth's cleaving to Naomi is still brought before me. Without the least of flattery I say it, I think what you have done for your dear sister's family (coming from sincerity, of which, charity, which is not blind, will not let me doubt) is as acceptable before God, and as much to be praised amongst men. But knowing that this is a subject, which, though I could not pass, yet you, Madam, desire not to be treated upon; therefore, I shall forbear it, and shall show you some of my thoughts (indistinct and insignificant as they are) anent our poor Scotland.

1. I think we are not yet entered our Jordan; for though we have come through a miry and thorny wil-

derness, yet our Jordan is before us, and it will be very deep, but it will not be very broad. When the ark of God enters it, it shall be like to drown, but it shall suddenly and admirably win to the other side.

2. I think safety shall only be to those who have their hands nearest the ark. Oh then! many a woe to the ministers and professors whose hands have been drawn back from the work, and to those whose malice is against the burden-bearers. It shall be as is said, Isa. xxvi. 11, "Lord, when thy hand is lifted up, they will not see: but they shall see, and be ashamed for their envy at the people; yea, the fire of thine enemies shall devour them."

3. I think that Scotland shall be made a waste land, ere God's controversy against it be ended. He will sell the heritages of earls, lords, and others, yea, and their carcases good cheap.

4. I think the Lord (until He raise His work again) will guide and manage it more by providences than by instruments. This is, that His hand may be alone seen in it, and that He may get the glory;—what is most glorifying to Him, should it not be most pleasant and rejoicing to us?

5. I think that when the Lord returns to us again, it will be with such a measure and outpouring of His Spirit, that the remnant that shall be left shall have a very heaven upon earth, and our land shall be made the joy of all lands.

But as to those, or such like, I shall say no more, knowing that you are both really and distinctly exercised anent our case. What is for us this day, but that we make Christ sure for ourselves, and spend our days here below in admiring the loveliness and condescension of our Beloved, and our own happiness in enjoying such a portion? But this is a great work,—time is not equal for it,—therefore we shall get eternity for it. O let us study the increase of the beauty of holiness, for happiness is inferior unto it. It is by holiness we are made like unto God, and is not this true nobility?

O ! what is like unto it ! If we knew more of this study and attainment, desertion would be less of our exercise, and we should enjoy more of the smilings of His sweet countenance, and of the breathings of His Spirit. Also, while in this our pilgrimage, let His will be ours in all things ; whatever He may carve out for us, or any that we are concerned in, let us say amen to it, for, if He will it, it is enough for us. Yea, let us lay our account with the worst of it, that whatever come we may not be surprised.

Now, not to trouble your Ladyship further, praying that the all-sufficiency which is in Christ may be forthcoming for you, that so you may finish your course with His honour, and your own true joy, with the testimony of a conscience kept void of offence towards God, and towards all men, and that you may suck of the breasts of His consolations here, until you come to drink abundantly of the rivers of pleasure at His right hand, I am, Worthy Madam, your obliged and assured friend, and sympathising servant in our sweet Lord,

JAMES RENWICK.

In letter thirty-eight mention was made of two ministers, viz.—Mr Barclay and Mr Langlands who had accompanied the Earl of Argyle on his expedition into Scotland, and afterwards remained and created no little dissension among the Covenanters. From the Societies' minutes we learn that frequent conferences were held with these brethren, and many matters discussed, though with little satisfactory result. We now introduce a letter which Renwick wrote in reply to one from Mr Langlands to Mr Gavin Wotherspoon, asking you to notice the beautiful spirit which animates the writer from first to last, and particularly the earnest longing to which near the close he gives utterance for union among brethren.

Letter XLII.

December 13, 1685.

Sir,---I have seen your letter which you wrote to Gavin Wotherspoon, and it doth not a little trouble me, that ye have and exprest so great mistakes of us. Many are the wormwoods and bitter ingredients in our cup, and, I think, our sad and wide breaches (together with the various spiritual plagues that have seized upon our spirits) are amongst the bitterest. But until the Lord heal our backslidings (by taking away the guilt thereof, and breaking the power thereof, and removing the spiritual judgments, which are the saddest consequences thereof) and pour down the Spirit from on high, it will never be otherwise with us. Our ruptures will never be truly and safely removed, until our sins be confessed, mourned over and forsaken, and the unclean spirits of self-prejudice and mistakes be made to pass out of the land. For mine own part, union in the Lord would be a most rejoicing, pleasant, and desirable thing : I say, *that* union that is bottomed upon the truth and cemented with love, for *any* kind of union would be but a conspiracy and not union. O for that soul-ravishing day, when we shall have union rightly qualified ! I think that would be the Church of Scotland's restoration.

But to come to your foresaid letter : There are some things there, Sir, which (I say) are not a little astonishing to me. I shall not now enter into the list of the debate, but I desire, in the fear of the Lord, that ye would look otherwise upon our matters. Ye say, "that we have overturned Presbyterian Government even to the foundation, and put in its room a popular confusion :" And to prove this ye instance a paper of ours in reply to James Russel, his libel against us ; whence ye draw, that we commit to persons, that are not church officers, the trial both of the degree of scandals, and the degree of censures to be inflicted for the same. But in this ye wrong our paper very sadly, for it does not at all speak of censures, or the measure thereof committed to these persons, but only the trying and searching out the measure of the scandal. And by trying and searching there, we do not understand a judicial trying and searching, but only private and popular, by way of information ; not that we might judge or censure the person, if scandalous, but that we might have a judgment of our own duty, how to carry towards him, and if the measure of the scandal would bear the weight of our withdrawing from him. *Non per modum specialis delegationis sed per modum communis charitatis*, 'not by way of special delegation, but by way of common charity,' which is no act of the keys. And this is very clear, seeing our paper makes no mention of censure, though ye allege the same upon it. Also charity, which thinketh no evil, would put this construction upon our words, seeing they can so well bear it. Again, the word (try) is taken in this sense, 1 John iv. 1. "Try the spirits," which epistle is not written to church guides only. Rutherford, in his Peaceable Plea for Presbytery, chap. i. page 83, disclaims a representative church in a common sense, which is a number sent by a community to give laws absolutely trying : as if believers should say, we resign our faith and conscience to you, to hold good whatsoever you determine, without repeal, or trial. Now, doth not this make it clear, that our words will bear this sense ? All that we understand and express by them is also competent to professors of the faith ; as Acts xvii. 11 : " These of Berea received the word with all readiness of mind, and searched the Scriptures daily, whether these things were so." Now, these were the believers in Berea, and not the church guides, as is clear from the 12th verse, where it is spoken of women, who are not admitted to bear any office in the church. Moreover, Acts xi. "These of the circumcision contended with Peter," for an alleged scandal, for "eating with the uncircum-

cised:" and he rehearses the matter from the beginning, and expounds it in order to them. From this
I do not draw (with the Independents) that the power
of censuring church guides is in the hands of the
people as in their argument from the forecited place :
but I hold what holy and learned Rutherford saith in
answer thereunto, in his Peaceable Plea, chap. iv. p.
51, 52, (to wit) That Peter, or any church guide, is
to purge himself before any one brother of a scandal.
Yea, the necessity of his salvation, and so the law of
nature forbids to offend the weak, and willeth him to
purge himself, if he were a Pope, saith Occom. If
Peter had done wrong, he was obliged to confess his
scandal before one offended brother, and also, before
all the church : but that proveth not jurisdiction in
the believer. Lastly, If this belong not unto people,
they have nothing but a blind implicit faith; and
what better are they than Papists, who must believe as the church believes? Yea, hath not every
private Christian a judgment of discretion, even in
reference to the actions of others? seeing they are
to do nothing doubtingly but to be fully persuaded
in their own minds, Rom. xiv. 5, 23. But some
(I know) say, that withdrawing from a scandalous
person is a censuring of a scandalous person, and
to withdraw from a scandalous minister is to depose
him, and make him no minister. But this I deny;
for simple withdrawing is not the inflicting of a
censure, but only the believers testifying their sense,
that the censure should be inflicted (to wit) by such
as are competent : and this is warranted by Scripture, Rom. xiv. 17, Eph. v. 11, 2 Thess. iii. 14, and
many such like places. Also, Rutherford saith, in his
Peaceable Plea, chap. iv. p. 25, "that the law of
nature will warrant a popular and private subtrac-
tion and separation from the ministry of a known
wolf and seducer," and alloweth what Parker saith,
from Saravia, *Licet tutela inculpata uti si malus rector
ab ecclesia deponi nequit* 'it is lawful to use that

blameless and just defence, if the bad church-guide
cannot be deposed.' Any private persons may take
that care for the safety of their souls, that they may
do for the safety of their bodies. For a son may defend
himself, by flying from his distracted father coming to
kill him ; and none will call this an act judicial of
authority, but only an act natural. Now, I say private
separation from scandalous persons is not depriving
of them, if they be pastors ; nor excommunicating of
them, if they be professors. For the latter is an act
of authority, belonging to those to whom Christ hath
given the keys ; but the former is an act natural,
belonging to every believer. Likewise, if withdrawing
from a scandalous person be a censuring of scandalous
persons, then the professors, who withdraw from the
curates, do censure the curates, which I hope no sound
presbyterian will say. Howbeit, I distinguish betwixt
a person scandalous really, and a person scandalous
judicially ; and between a church in a settled state,
and a church in a broken state. So, I say, when a
church is in a settled state, a person really scandalous
cannot be withdrawn from, until (at least) he be
judicially, by two or three witnesses, convicted, before
the church, Rutherford's Peaceable Plea, chap. ix. p. 171.
seeing that the brethren offended have church judicatories to appeal unto, for taking order with offenders.
But when the church is in a broken state, and "every
man (as the children of Israel, when they wanted
Governors) "doing that which is right in his own eyes,"
there may and should be withdrawing from a person
scandalous really, though he be not scandalous judicially;
because then ecclesiastic judicatories, for censuring of
him, cannot be had. Otherwise, all must go into a
mixed confusion together, the faithful must become
partakers of other men's sins, private and popular
means of reclaiming offending brethren shall be stopped,
and the testimonies of the faithful shall fall to the
ground. But (mark it) I am not, even in this case, for
a rude off-hand withdrawing, until private admonition

(according to Christ's method) once and again, prove
ineffectual, and the offender declare his obstinacy.
Now, I beg that ye would consider how heavy a charge
ye have laid upon us, by asserting, "That we have
overturned presbyterian government even to the
foundation, and put in its room popular confusion,"
seeing your grounds are bottomless. And as to this
I shall no more. But ye have a way, Sir, of drawing
stretched consequences from words and sentences
(which I cannot join with) as ye have done from
the foresaid words in our foresaid reply, as to all
unprejudiced persons may be manifest. As also,
from that word [treacherous] in our protestation
against the Scottish congregation at Rotterdam, asserting and writing that the foresaid word [treacherous]
imports a design to betray. But for my own part, I
could never see that it imported more than a practical
deserting of duty, or betraying of trust, abstracting
from the person's design ; and I never knew another
commentary upon it. And I desire to know, what way
treacherous (expressed Zeph. iii. 4.) will bear your
sense. Also, great Mr Durham, in his treatise upon
scandal, doth say, "That the term, malicious, is not to
be referred to the design of the person, though malicious
be still taken in as bad a sense as treacherous." Ah !
the Lord behold our case. James Russell spreads of
us, that we went off at the left hand, by admitting
scandalous persons amongst us : and ye write of us,
that we went off at the right hand, by devolving the
church power upon the shoulders of the people ; so
we are beat upon both hands. The Lord help us !

Secondly, Ye say, "We have most unhappily thrust in
ourselves into the Magistrate's room, and taken to us
the Civil Government." Wherefrom do ye draw this ?
From our declining the Magistrates, because tyrants ?
Then every man declining a prelate, because a church
officer not of Christ's appointment, thrusts himself into
the prelate's room, and takes unto himself the ecclesiastic government ; and what great absurdity will be

here? But mistake me not; for I will not misinterpret your words. Ye say, "That if every man of us, for himself, had said, he could not own the Magistrates and the present Government, because tyrants and tyrannical, there had been little to be said, especially if we had done as we said, striving like men to cast off the yoke." But, granting it had been so, there would have been something to be said; for little to be said imports something to be said, and I know many said very much even against the matter of the dead. Also, we could have said more than that we, every man for himself, could not own the Government, because tyrannical, and the Magistrates, because tyrants. For we could have said, we, for ourselves and all our adherents and all these by whom we were sent and commissionated for that deed, could not own the fore-saids; and that the law of God, the law of nature, and the fundamental laws of our land, and our covenants, did oblige all the subjects of our kingdom (especially these who yet profess adherence to our covenants) to do, as we have done. And this is all that I understand, by any words in our Declaration, about which ye make so much matter of debate. Also, how can it be instructed, that we have acted as a convention of estates? The mere disowning of the present government and governors doth it not, for that is an act radical and natural. And as for the expression itself, in our Lanark Declaration (used in the historical relation of the Sanquhar Declaration preceding), to wit, convention of estates, what needeth so much fighting about it, seeing ye know our mind? Famous Mr Rutherford saith, in his Peaceable Plea, chap. ix. p. 107, "that he lists not to strive about names." We crave only that right that God and nature have given us; and come in behind us, or go out before us who will, let us have our own place. Howbeit, as to me, these words that ye fight so much against in our Declaration may bear a safe sense, though I disown the sense ye put upon them. For,

as to convention of estates, I understand it not in a
formal and proper sense, extending itself judicially
over the whole land (although all were obliged to
have concurred with us, by reason of the duty of
the action) but in an improper and figurative sense;
yea, may it not be said by synecdoche? the better
part getting the domination of the whole; the acting
jointly, by common consent, and explicit commission,
for that effect, from several honest sufferers, in several
corners of the land, in the name of all their adherents;
and founding upon the law of nature, the fundamental
laws of the kingdom, and our laudable constitutions.
And as to the other expressions, in our Lanark Declaration, to wit, "In our name and authority," I understand
it not as importing the authority of the judge, but the
authority of the law, which certainly they had, they
keeping by the fundamental laws of the land.

And as to that in our first Declaration at Sanquhar,
viz. "Representatives of church and covenanted nation,"
what absurdity is there in saying, that these elders,
who keep closest by the lawful constitutions of a church,
are the representatives thereof, and people of a covenanted nation, who keep closest by their covenants (even
though they were never so few), are the representatives
thereof, as it is covenanted, though not in an authoritative and nomothetical, yet in a material and principal
sense, as it hath a relation to the word from whence it
is derived, that is, *representatives*, not, as it is strictly
taken, for those who are clothed with formal authority,
but, as it is largely taken, for those who do represent
or are in the place of others, doing that which all, whom
they represent, are obliged unto, from the nature of the
thing? But I do not hold, that these Declarations were
emitted by a formal judicatory, as having the authority
of any judge; for as yet I see not how some persons, as
having ecclesiastic authority, and others, as having
civil authority, could authoritatively concur in one
action. I leave this to the tyrant's council, which is
made up of lords spiritual and temporal, as they call

them. So I look upon the Declarations to be emitted by the publishers, as free subjects, for themselves, and these, from whom they are commissionated, for that effect, and all others their adherents. And, for mine own part, I wish that these words had been otherwise expressed, that so they might not have admitted of such various senses. Nevertheless, I still think, where there is a cordial agreeing with the matter and intent of these papers, there would not be any such inveighing against these expressions; especially seeing the minds of the owners thereof are found (even anent the same) and their meaning good. And I wonder greatly how ye can exclaim so much against the foresaid names, seeing we told you many times, in our conferences together, our judgment concerning them, that we owned them not in the sense that ye put upon them; and that, rather than that debate should be kept up, upon such a head merely, though we could not resile from them in any safe and sound sense, wherein we our-selves could take them, yet, for union's sake in the Lord, we would be content to lay them aside, desiring no more of any who would join with us (as to that head) than their cordial agreement with the matter and intent of our foresaid Declarations. Yet, not-withstanding of all this, ye often recurred upon these words at our meeting, and now have written, that "we have most unhappily thrust ourselves into the Magis-trates' room," and that "we continue most unhappily to manage civil affairs." Seeing that ye know our minds, Sir, why will ye make men such offenders for words? Suppose they could bear no safe sense at all, will such a spirit be helpful to the healing of our breaches? And how comes it, that in the relation which ye give of our conferences, ye say, "that we have disowned such things," and in this your letter, ye say the contrary, asserting, that "we continue yet most unhappily to manage civil affairs"; and where, as ye say, "there would have been little to be said, especially if we had done as we said, striving like men to cast off the yoke." We have done as the Lord gave us spirit and ability; and He hath assisted many of us, (O praise be to Him alone for it) to wrestle to our utmost breath, and to leave our blood both on scaffolds and fields, in testimony against the wrongs done to our Lord Jesus, by that tyrannical government. And I think people should not speak much of our doing little, until they do more themselves. And for my own part, I wish the Lord might polish and raise up a party, whose zealous, Christian, and manly actions might obscure all ours. For the glory is only due to the Lord, and not to any creature; and a self-denied Christian would desire, that all instruments' hands may be hid, to the end that the Lord's hand may the more appear; so that, He may get all the praise of the work. Now, from this, I wish ye may see how groundless your accusation is.

Thirdly, You say "that we have imposed most unhappy restrictions upon ministers, in the exercise of their ministry." I think, this poor mistaken remnant never in the least intended any restrictions on ministers, but only desire that they may declare unto them the mind of God faithfully, both anent the sins and duties of our day. They would have ministers taking a liberty to preach up all duties, and down all sins. This is no restriction, neither is it any imposition, neither is it a prescribing rules to ministers; for the Word of God hath prescribed this rule, Isa. lviii. 1. "Shew my people their transgressions, and the house of Jacob their sins." Jer. xv. 19, "If thou take forth the precious from the vile, thou shalt be as my mouth." But this is a "pleading with our mother," Hos. ii. 2; and a saying to Archippus, "Take heed to the ministry which thou hast received of the Lord, that thou fulfil it." And this the Scriptures do allow, and this I hope ye will not deny. But to prove your assertion, I know ye will instance the first call given to the ministers which ye did see yourself long before I saw it. Yet what needs this? seeing it was so frequently told in public, that that call was not owned by us, as to all especially the lesser things in it, for *pudor est nemini in meliora transire* 'it is a shame for no man to mend the least thing that is amiss.' Should not every Christian (in whatsoever capacity) be still stepping forward unto better? seeing there is neither perfection nor infallibility here. I must say, that more tenderness should be used towards a poor wasted bleeding people, chased by a cruel enemy, as partridges in the wilderness, their blood spilt in great measure; yea, and left in the dark by their leaders. Especially seeing they are so willing to receive instruction, and to take with any thing that ever looked like the least wrong among them. Which thing I have not yet seen in others; for they defend even their gross scandals, and will not acknowledge any offence, in particular among themselves, through the whole tract of our defections.

Further, ye wrong us when ye say, "that because they preach upon such and such terms, we call them silent and unfaithful, and require disowning of them." For, before even these terms were offered to them, by the suffering party, which I wish had been yet undone, we were in the same case and circumstances as to them, that we are in to this day. And as for the question put to these, who are admitted to sit in our general meeting, &c., it is anent "the joining with the complying, silent, and unfaithful ministers of the time." It is not my concern now, to descend in application to particular persons; yet I ask, 1*st*, Whether or not are there any such in Scotland? 2*ndly*, If there be any such, whether or not should they be joined with? 3*dly*, If they are to be joined with, what mean such Scripture precepts, Rom. xvi. 17; 2 Thess. iii. 14? And what mean our General Assemblies to decree, "that complying ministers with the adversaries, and silent and unfaithful ministers anent the sins of the time (if persisting in them) ought to be deposed"? And, 4*thly*, Whether or not that, which will bear the weight of deposition, will bear the weight of withdrawing, when deposition cannot be had, the ministers persisting in their offensive courses? Now, I hold, that people are not to judge ministers, yet they are to have a judgment of their own duty, how to carry towards ministers. I am against people's desiring any thing of ministers but what is divinely bound upon them by the Word of God, and ecclesiastically by our national and solemn Covenants, and Acts of our General Assemblies; so this is not the people's imposition, restriction, or binding, but what is bound by the authority of God and the church. And if these ties were regarded, as they should be, honest people would be satisfied themselves, and otherwise constructed by others; and there would not be such differences, when we would descend into particulars.

Now, I desire from real charity towards you, that ye would weigh matters in the balance of the sanctuary, which is even and impartial, and forbear your far-fetched and sickly consequences, which ye draw from honest actions.

Also, I thought fit to insinuate unto you here, that there are some things in the relation of what past at our conference as it was resumed by you before our general meeting, which I can sufficiently prove, to be in a great part, misrepresented; as afterwards (if need be) may be made manifest. But as to what ye have said, in your letter, of me in particular, I heartily forgive you, and shall be very brief in my reply.

Ye say, *First*, that I have written in a letter to a friend in Ireland, "that there is not a minister in Scotland, England, or Ireland, faithful, save one." I humbly and kindly desire, that ye would consider upon what grounds ye have said such a thing. For the charge I deny; and the expression (yes, such a thought) would savour so much of the basest of self (which, though it be as our skin, wherein our flesh and bones are enchambered, and so nature is most tender of one penny breadth of it) that therefore I would abhor it.

If I have written any thing of the unfaithfulness of ministers indefinitely, yet it is a wire-drawing of words, or a wrong drawn consequence, to infer, that I have said, "There is none faithful in Britain or Ireland save one;" for it is not unusual in the scriptures to speak indefinitely of a plurality that which is to be instanced of any of that sort. See learned Mr David Dickson upon Matth. xxvii. 44. I shall say no more as to this, but, God pardon the unfaithfulness of ministers; and let their deeds prove who hath been faithful, and who not.

Secondly, Ye say, "that by my own confession, I am not a minister of this church;" which I altogether deny. For that which I said was, that I am a minister in that place wherever I have a call from the people, and do embrace it. And if your assertion will follow from this truly, I see not well; but I am short-sighted always. There are several other things in your letter, anent which I was thinking to have written unto you; but I being loathe to trouble you, and the things themselves not so material, I shall forbear, only desiring, that what I have said ye would not take in ill part. For, so far as I can see into mine own heart, it is neither self, nor prejudice, that hath moved me unto it; but merely, that truth may be cleared, and that the actings of the poor wounded suffering party may not be so sadly misrepresented, to the great detriment of the cause of Christ. Also, I beg, ye would not give ear to busy-bodies, and tale-bearers their whispering in your ears; for such have had no small hand in widening of our breaches. I wish they may have pardon of God for what they have done. O that the Lord's elect were agreeing in truth! O that all these that shall agree in heaven, were agreeing upon earth! I think if my blood could be a means to procure it, I could willingly offer it up, upon that account. But I speak as a fool. O that all the Lord's people were searching out their sins, taking with their guilt, mourning for, and forsaking their iniquities! This would be yet some branch of hope. But that is coming, which will make many change their thoughts. For I write it, and abide by it, That the Lord is coming with a flood of His anger upon Scotland; and ere His controversies be ended, He will work a strange work in the land. For (Micah vii. 11, 12, 13) although "in the days that her walls are to be built, the decree shall be far removed, and they shall come to her from sea to sea, and from mountain to mountain, notwithstanding the land shall be desolate, because of them that dwell therein, for the fruit of their doings." O happy are they who are going into their chambers, and closing door and windows about them, that wrath may have no entry in! O happy they who are sighing and crying for all the abominations that are done in the earth! But in the meantime, it doth not a little quiet and comfort me that Christ hath told, that the government is upon his shoulders, and He knoweth how to erect a glorious fabric out of a mass of confusion; and I believe, He will make the succeeding generation to reap a glorious fruit of the sad sufferings and contendings, that have been in our day. Not to trouble you further, I wish peace and truth may be your companions.—I am, Sir, your soul's wellwisher, and friend in Jesus Christ,   JAMES RENWICK.

CHAPTER VIII.

A LULL IN THE STORM.

HE year 1686 was chiefly remarkable for repeated attempts, on the part of the King, to obtain relief for his Roman Catholic subjects from the legal penalties and disabilities their religion imposed on them. Unfortunately, however, for their success, these attempts were accompanied by an avowed determination to enforce the existing laws on the poor Covenanters, and also to prepare the way for the establishment of Popery in the land. Already at the beginning of the year, some of the principal offices under the Crown were held by Papists, while a Popish Chapel was fitted up in the Chancellor's house, where mass was regularly said. Notwithstanding the low state of morality and religion among the governing classes, there was still a sufficient amount of patriotism and piety to resist the King's demands. Hence, on the 29th of April, when the Parliament met at Edinburgh, and a letter from the King was read, exhorting the Estates to give relief to his Roman Catholic subjects, and offering in return free trade with England and an amnesty for political offences, the request was courteously but firmly refused. James, however, persisted in urging his demands. Affirming that he had been only too gracious when he had condescended to ask the assent of the Scottish Estates to his wishes, he claimed, in the exercise of the royal prerogative, to admit Papists in crowds to all kinds of offices and honours. In a letter to the Privy Council he announced his intention to fit up a Roman Catholic Chapel in Holyrood Palace, and gave orders that the Judges should treat all the laws against Papists as null and void, on pain of his high displeasure. At the same time, he comforted the Episcopalians with the assurance, that, though he was determined to protect the Roman Catholic Church against them, he was equally determined to protect them against any encroachment on the part of the Presbyterians.

From various expressions in Renwick's letters it is obvious, that while these negotiations were in progress, he and his followers were allowed to breathe more freely. Still, nothing was further from the King's intention than to relax the violent measures which had been in operation against the Societies. Hence, at the close of the year, on December 9th, a proclamation was issued against Renwick, offering a reward of a hundred pounds sterling to any who should bring him in, dead or alive. The following were the terms of this Proclamation:—"Forasmuch as one Mr James Renwick, a flagitious and scandalous person, has presumed and taken upon hand, these several years bygone, to congregate together members of our unwary and ignorant commons to house and field conventicles, which our law so justly terms the nurseries of sedition and rendezvous of rebellion— we, out of our royal care and tenderness to our people, being desirous to deliver all our loving subjects from the malign influence of such a wretched impostor, have therefore prohibited and discharged all our subjects that none of them offer, or presume to harbour, reset, supply, &c., but do their utmost endeavour to pursue him as the worst of traitors. And if, in the pursuit of the said Mr James Renwick, he or any of his rebellious associates resisting to be taken, any of our subjects shall happen to kill or mutilate him, or any of them, we hereby declare that they, nor none assisting them shall ever be called in question, and that their doing thereof shall be reputed good and acceptable service to us. And for the better encouragement to such as shall apprehend and bring in the person of the said Mr James Renwick, traitor foresaid, dead or alive, he or they shall have the reward of One Hundred Pounds Sterling money, to be instantly paid to him by the Commissioners of our treasury."

We now introduce two letters which are without date, but which from a study of their contents we have assigned to this period. The first is addressed to the prisoners in the Canongate Tolbooth, the other to the prisoners in the Tolbooths of Edinburgh, Glasgow, and elsewhere in Scotland.

Letter XLIII.

Dearly beloved in our Lord, and much honoured sufferers for His name,—I hear that men have passed sentence of banishment against you ; but I hope what man can do is no surprisal to you, you having counted all cost that you may be put to. Howbeit, as no created power can banish you from your God, or your God from you, so I hope, what men have now done against you shall, by God's blessing, be a means to chase you nearer unto your rest. Yea, moreover, you do not know but that it is to hide you from the approaching calamity, which the Lord is immediately to bring on this land; I say, immediately, for He is hastening His work, ay, He is working fast. One step of His now cannot stay upon another, for He is coming post-haste unto us; and now He must come, for our mother is in her pangs, and now she must either get help and be delivered, or else she will die in travail. But die she will not, though she be in hard labour, for the greatness of her pain will only tend to make her delivery the more joyful. O joyful! O joyful delivery! and, to make it so, our Lord must have a singular feast at it. Yea, He will have such a feast in Scotland, that proclamation shall go forth from the one end of heaven to the other, inviting all the fowls of the heavens, and the beasts of the earth to come unto the Lord's feast;—a feast of the carcases of the in-habitants of Scotland, great and small. Neither their wit nor their might will deliver them in that day. O happy is the man or the woman that is removed from hearing the very report of what is coming on this land! Yea, the earth shall be made to tremble, ears to tingle, hearts to melt, bowels to sound, and knees to smite one upon another, at the report of Scotland's judgments. They shall in that day be thought to have sped well, who have got away out of the way of these things. Yet I cannot look upon this, but I must cast a view upon what is beyond it. Mercies, mercies, mercies are swimming toward the Lord's people. O they are strange mercies, and He will make them singular people who will be privileged with them.

Now, as for your parts, remember, "the earth is the Lord's and the fulness thereof." Wherever you may be cast, study always to be in your duty, and let the Lord be "your Portion in the land of the living." That He may make up all your wants in Himself shall be the prayer of him, who is your real and constant sympathiser, in all your sufferings for Christ,

JAMES RENWICK.

LETTER XLIV.

Much respected and beloved in the Lord,—The most
holy and wise God hath seen it fit to place His people,
in this our day, in very strange circumstances, they
having both the subtlety and cruelty of stated enemies,
and also of pretended declining friends to grapple with.
Yea, I think, there never was a generation who had
such snares strewed in their way, yea, so many
stumbling-blocks laid before them as we have.   Is
not this to be seen, that enemies to God and His truths
have much more prevailed, by their hidden snares,
their subtile plots against the work and people of
God veiled and masked over with a pretence of favour,
than by their cruel outrages, virulent and violent
persecutions, screwed up to the highest pitch of their
bounded power? This consideration, together with a
desire to respect the advantage of the public work of
God, and the welfare of the souls of people, and that
we may be wise at the last (considering that we have
been made to know by sad experience the sin and
danger of accepting their pretended favours, and are
called to be mindful of the many bonds and obligations
that lie upon us from the Lord, and to discharge my
duty and exonerate my conscience as in His sight)
hath moved me to presume to write to you, my
dear friends in bonds for Christ, my poor advice
anent your duty under your present trials and sufferings, especially in reference to that late indemnity
of the date of Feb. 26th, 1685, given out by the Duke
of York, under the name of King James VII. I
think all pretended favours, that come from the hands
of such enemies, may justly be suspected by us, considering how great skaith and damage heretofore the
work and people of God have endured thereby, as
witness by that Indulgence before and after Bothwell.
I hope, in the Lord's goodness, that this present snare
shall not have such prevalency, and particularly that
you, whose soul's welfare I tender very much, and in

whose trials and sufferings I desire to be a burden
bearer and co-partner, may be guarded the more
against it.

In all friendliness and humility, I call you to consider these few among many other evils, in the foresaid indemnity.   As (1.) That those who accept of
that indemnity do most directly homologate the pretended authority of James Duke of York, which is
far contrary to our covenants, whereby we are sworn,
in our stations, and to the utmost of our power to
extirpate such, and do say, that it was lawful, just,
and legal, to proclaim him the King of Scotland, &c.,
whereupon that indemnity is granted.   (2.) Those
who accept of that indemnity do take with the
name of wicked and seditious subjects and rebels,
which the enemies in their proclamation put upon
them ; yea, they call themselves transgressors, for an
indemnity or pardon is only extended toward such,
and those who accept of it do palpably acknowledge
a crime.   (3.)   Those who accept of that indemnity do
most grossly comply with the granters of it, who require
that fugitives, in sign (mark it,) of their acceptance
of the same, do either take the Oath of Allegiance, or
else find caution to transport themselves out of the
three kingdoms of Scotland, England, and Ireland, and
never to return again without license, under pain of
death.   Now, seeing these enemies require such gross
compliance, in sign and token of the acceptance of that
indemnity, what must they hold the acceptance of itself
to be ?   There are only two things, which they propose
to the acceptors thereof to make choice of, and these
are, 1st.   The oath of allegiance ; but of this I shall not
speak, judging that none, who have not surrendered
altogether their consciences, and renounced their covenants, will swear allegiance to such enemies, especially
to Papists, who are discerned by Acts of Parliament to
be punished as idolaters, as enemies to the true religion,
and all Christian government, and whom we have, with
uplifted hands to the most high God, many times sworn

to extirpate ; which is inconsistent with any allegiance.
The 2d. is, They must find caution to transport themselves (as is said) out of these three kingdoms, and not
to return without license, under the pain of death.
This may prove ensnaring to some ; but it should not,
neither will it, if they consider what it implies. For
they cannot make that choice, without acknowledging
and taking with such gross transgressions and malver-
sations, as make them justly to forfeit all right of
subjects in these three kingdoms. O ! I hope, no true
sons of the Church of Scotland will so renounce their
interest in Scotland's cause, covenants, and contendings.
Yea, moreover, they cannot make such a choice, unless
they engage to these enemies, for their peaceable
behaviour ; which is to be understood as, in their sense,
a renouncing of duty, and a complying with their
impositions, in that time, whatsoever, betwixt the
publication of the foresaid indemnity, and the 20th of
May, which is the time appointed for their transporta-
tion. (4.) Those who accept of that indemnity do
greatly transgress and sin against those who are excepted
out of it, such as ministers, heritors, &c. For thereby
they expose the foresaids to be the butt of the
adversary's malice and fury, and do deny to be any more
sufferers with them for the interest of Christ. (5.)
Those who accept of that indemnity do comply with the
purposes of the enemies in general and particular, which
are to ruin the work and people of God, by breaking and
dividing them, and cheating some of them out of their
consciences. As we are to consider them as following
the same purposes in their granting of pretended
favours, and in persecutions and bloodshed, so we
are to suspect and dread their favours as the height of
cruelty, and this the more, because they are veiled and
masked over with fair pretences ; like unto those who
should make a bed to repose themselves in, and lay
therein a naked knife or dagger with the point upward.
As it is said in Obadiah ver. 7, "They that eat thy bread
have laid a wound under thee ;" whereupon, he is

declared to " be of no understanding," because he yielded
himself to them, and was brought over by the subtlety
of his confederates, and those that "were at peace"
with him. (6.) Those who accept of that indemnity, do
help forward that purpose of enemies in particular in
granting of it, which is, that they may get the better
course taken with the more faithful, who trouble their
kingdom most, and such as they are most mad against.
For, as they say in their proclamation, they grant the
said indemnity, before they determine their pleasure
concerning such, which, say they, they hope to attain
in a very short time. But as the hope of hypocrites,
so the hope of enemies perisheth ; for Zion is a burdensome stone, Zech. xii. 3, and their backs shall be
broken with lifting it up. (7.) Those who accept of
that indemnity do palpably break their covenant with
the most high God ; for therein we are sworn not to be
divided and broken off from our blessed union, either
directly or indirectly by terror or persuasion. Now,
that indemnity doth manifestly break off those who are
excepted out of it, and those included who do take it,
from either acting in, or suffering for their duty together. (8.) Those who accept of that indemnity do
bind up their hands from acting any more for God, or
against His enemies. For as in accepting of it they
take with a transgression, so, upon the matter, they
engage not to transgress again ; yea, do not the conditions of that pardon hold out very formally so much ?
And is not here a most direct breach of covenant, yea,
a receding from the sum thereof ? (9.) It should be
considered that that indemnity is no indemnity, but,
under that name, a subtile and masked traducing of
people to a compliance ; for it is granted upon such and
such conditions, and that in sign and token of acceptance thereof. O then ! is not the granter a liberal
churl ?

Now, dear friends, as to this purpose, I hope I need
say no more unto you, having spoken these things for
your confirmation, judging that you are clear of them

already. Let enemies paint over their seeming favours as they will, yet considering the hand that reacheth them, we may justly dread them, and suspect them. "Do men gather grapes of thorns, or figs of thistles?" Can any drink clean water out of a corrupt fountain? Shall Zion ever expect any thing but a poisonable herb out of Babylon's garden? Or will ever an enemy do a favour? What hold shall we lay on Papists, whose principles lead them neither to give faith to, nor keep faith with heretics, as they term us? If you would keep near God, keep far from enemies both within and without, and make it your work to be acquainted with the exercise of real religion. You have a noble opportunity for this study, for the Lord hath blocked you up from many worldly cares and outward disturbances; and why hath He done this, but that He may get you taken up only with Himself? I have heard it of prisoners, that God made Himself much more known to them in bonds, than ever He did when they were at liberty; and I hope that it is so with not a few of you. O the wisdom of God who can make enemies instruments of so much good to His people! O take Him for your all, who is a non-such portion. In the supposed enjoyment of all created things there are still wants, but in the enjoyment of Him there is nothing wanting; yea, more than a soul can desire, and than all created capacities are able to comprehend, is to be found in Him, for He is all in all. He is that treasure of which enemies cannot rob you, though they be permitted to come and bereave you of life, and all created comforts. Is not this a part of His excellency? O then make Him your choice, and according to His promise, "He will go through fire and water with you." He will be with you in prison, in torture, in bonds, in banishment, and in death. Is not His presence enough? Yea, all your trials "shall work together for your good," as He hath said. Therefore rejoice, not only in them, but because of them; and, in all your seekings, seek to have His image more and more renewed in you. O employ

the power and efficacy of His grace for carrying on in
you a progress in holiness, for, the more of this you attain to, the more of His special manifestations you shall
enjoy. It is His own image that the Lord delighteth
to smile and breathe upon, and to converse with. O
holiness! is it not many ways preferable to happiness?
Albeit man's nature doth more affect happiness than
holiness, because he desires more that which is more
pleasant, than that which is more excellent, yet without holiness there can be no happiness; for what is it
that maketh heaven to be heaven, but because there is
there the full enjoyment of God, and perfect immunity
and freedom from all sin?

As for the work and people of God, though I leave
you to the Lord's free Spirit, for His exercising you
always suitably anent their present case, yet there are
these things, which I think you should be much in
wrestling for with God on their behalf;—that He may
give grace to His people to guide rightly their present
case, for it is very hard to be guided, in respect of the
many mercies and judgments that are in their cup.
Also they are now, as it were, at some push and extremity, the work being, if I may express it so, between
the losing and the winning. But it is in His hand, with
whom nothing can miscarry. Let us leave it there, and
be about our duty. Let us plead that He may give direction to His people, for extreme difficulties put people
to the greatest puzzle to know what to do; also a wrong
step now will do very much skaith, but His name is
Counsellor. Let us ask that He may give them grace
to persevere and endure to the end, for I think we may
expect the sharpest of our trials to be yet to come, but
His grace is sufficient. O! as they will be sharp, pray
that they may be short, for the elect's sake, as the
Lord hath said.

As to your own imprisonment, O my dear friends,
wait upon the Lord for your outgate. You know
not what He may do: He can make prison-houses
hiding-places. As I believe there is mercy in your

lot, so there may be more than either you or others can see. Believe that the best may be, and yet prepare for the worst. Put a blank in the Lord's hand, and resolve upon the worst that men can do unto you ; for that is the safest, and it shall not fare the worse with you, even as to outward matters. Withal, I say, do not misbelieve; for God, who hath hitherto restrained enemies, can bind them yet up from executing their purposes against you.

Now the multitude of business, and the shortness of time force me to be but brief, which, I hope, your charity will cover with the mantle of a favourable construction. I shall detain you no further ; but unto the Lord's grace I leave you, praying that you may be kept faithful in this hour of temptation, that you may be helped always to make a right choice in every condition, that you may be so enabled to war against the world, the devil, and the flesh, as that you may not put a stain upon the honour of that holy name by which you are called, and that you may be still fed with the fatness of that land afar off, until you come to the complete and full enjoyment of Him. Begging the help of your prayers, I am, dear friends, your assured sympathising friend in your tribulation, and your servant in our Lord Christ,   JAMES RENWICK.

The next letter is addressed to the honourable Society of strangers at Leewarden in Friesland.

LETTER XLV.

Feb. 18, 1686.

Honourable and dearly beloved in our sweet Lord,— I have had often blushes with myself, when I thought upon my omitting to write unto you, but, I may say, my delay was neither voluntary nor wilful, but a matter of necessity : for a man, under such various exigencies of providence as I am, cannot be master of his own purposes. Besides that I am daily looking

out, either to be presently killed, where I may be
found, or else dragged into a prison or scaffold, various
weighty and perplexing occurrences, day by day,
come inevitably in my way, which take up my
thoughts, filling my spirit with care and my hands
with business. But if I had proven as forgetful of
you, as I have been blocked up from saluting you
with a line from my hand, I had been far out of my
duty before the Lord, and grossly ungrateful toward
you. Howbeit, right honourable and dearly beloved,
I need not insist in apologising for myself with you,
for I know you have such a feeling of our burdens,
that you commiserate our case, and pity our perplexities : therefore I'll break off this, and go on in
what the Lord gives me to say.

There is no rational creature which doth not set some
one thing or other before its eyes as its main end, and
chief good ; and, according to the various predominants,
in sensual and mad men, are their various main ends.
Hence it is, that there did result so many different
opinions among Heathen philosophers about man's
chief good. But here is the great mistake with foolish
vain men, that, whatever they seek after, it is but
few who bend toward the true chief good, which is
God Himself. There are indeed gods many and lords
many, for whatever any fixeth his desires upon, and
aimeth in all his actions at the obtaining and enjoying
thereof, is his lord and his god, whether it be honour
or riches, or some object or other of vile concupiscence ;
yet there is but one God who is truly and only desire-
worthy, love-worthy, and honour-worthy. This One
hath not a match, nor a parallel ; for what can equal
Him ? yea, what in any worth can come the length
of the latchet of His shoes ? He is that inestimable
jewel, invaluable treasure, and incomparable pearl of
price, that only worthy Desire of all nations. O ! take
a look of Him as He is the Being of beings, having
being of Himself independent of all other beings, and
upon whom all other things depend in their being and

L

operations. "In Him we live, in Him we move, and
of Him we have our being." Do not all the pieces of
the creation,—heaven, earth, and sea, sun, moon, and
stars,—the commonest and unworthiest creature that
moveth upon the earth,—bear large characters of His
wisdom, power, and goodness? Doth not His mysterious common providence, making the sharpest sighted
of His creatures hide their faces, and become silent
before Him, declare Him to be God, and that He is "of
one mind, and who can turn Him?" Do not the various
instruments that execute His will, signified by four
chariots (Zech. vi. 1) bringing about various dispensations, which are pointed out by the different colours of
the horses; whether calamities of war, signified by the
red; or other doleful miseries, signified by the black;
mixed dispensations, black and white so to speak, of
mercy and judgment, signified by the grizzled and bay;
or dispensations of mercy, signified by the white—I
say, do not all these come forth from between the two
mountains of brass? The one mountain signifieth His
unalterable decree, and the other His effectual providence, which watcheth and waiteth that instruments
bring nothing to the birth but what has been conceived
in the womb of His eternal purpose. O take a look of
Him in His perfection. He is without measure and
limits, without beginning and ending. He is one and
the same in His nature, in His counsels, and in His
love. He perfectly knoweth Himself, and all things
that are possible. He can do all things that do not
imply a contradiction, and argue imperfection. He is
good, and doeth good. He is righteous in Himself, and
equal in all His ways of dealing with His creatures. He
is true without any dissimulation. He is holy and
delighteth in His own holiness, and in every resemblance
of it, in His angels, and in His saints. O! who can
think of Him, and who can speak of Him aright? He
is infinite in all His attributes, and every perfection
hath a perfect meeting in Him. Albeit some of His
attributes are in some degree communicable to His

creatures, yet they are in Him in an altogether incom-
municable manner and measure. There is nothing in
God, but what is God, for this is His name, "I am that
I am." Again, I say, who can think of Him, and who can
speak of Him aright? Who can comprehend Him, or
compass Him about? Who by understanding can search
out God? Humble and believing ignorance is better
than curious and prying knowledge: for all that we can
know of Him is, to know that we cannot know Him.

Let us yet come a little nearer, and take a look of
Him as He is our Saviour, in His condescendency, love,
power, faithfulness, and other properties. O! how condescending He is! Though He is that high and lofty
One, the Father's equal, yet He stooped so low as to
take upon Him the nature of man, and all the sinless
infirmities that attend it. He became "flesh of our
flesh, and bone of our bone," and that in the lowly condition of a servant. He seeks the creature's affection
as if it were of some worth, and seeks men and women
to match with Him. O how loving is He! It is a
strong love that He beareth to the seed of Abraham.
Doth not all this shine in all that He hath done? He
emptied Himself that they might become full. He made
Himself poor, though Maker and Possessor of heaven
and earth, that they might become rich. He fulfilled
the law for them, that He might purchase for them life
and happiness. He made Himself a sacrifice unto the
death, that He might satisfy offended justice, and make
reconciliation for them. O such a death! so cursed!
so shameful! so painful! and so lingering! But above
all He had the full weight of the wrath of God to bear,
which all the strength of angels and men could not
have endured: but He, being God, could not fall
under it. O what manner of love is this! In effect He
did not care what He suffered. Let justice charge home
upon Him with all its rigour and severity, seeing He
was to gain His point, and purchase a part of mankind
from Satan to Himself, from sin to holiness, from misery
to happiness, so that man, however unworthy, base,

sinful, and miserable, yet is the centre of His love. O! how powerful is He! He is mighty to save, able to save to the uttermost; all the strong-holds of the soul cannot hold out against Him. His power is irresistible; by this He can do what He will; and by His love He will do what we need. Again, He is so faithful, that what He saith He doeth. He will not retract one promise that is gone out of His mouth, neither will He fail in fulfilling all His threatenings.

Much might be said of these things, but not the thousandth part of the truth can be told. When we win to His house above, and see Him as He is, we will be ashamed of all our babblings about Him. They that have been most ravished with His love, and most eloquent to speak forth the praise of His comeliness and properties, will see that they have been, but at best, babes learning to speak. O what shall I say! He is the wonderful, matchless, and glorious inestimable jewel, and incomparable pearl of price. O who would not choose Him! Who would not give away themselves to Him! Let man look through heaven and earth, and seek a portion where he will, he shall not find the like of Christ. O then! let us be altogether His, and nothing our own. Our time let it be His, our understanding let it be His, our will let it be His, our affections let them be His, the travail of our souls let it be His, our strength let it be His, our names, lives, and enjoyments let them all be His; let us be fully surrendered and entirely consecrated unto Him. This is a comprehensive matter indeed. But what else should we be taken up with, but with the improvement of this resignation, always travelling through His properties, viewing them as our riches, delighting to improve our interest in Him, by receiving from His hand what we need, and desiring that He improve His interest in us, by doing with us, and taking from us, what He pleaseth? Let us see Him, and observe, and say, "What have we to do any more with our idols?" Oh! that vanity should get so much as one look from me! I think, He never took pains upon any but that they might be emptied of all things beside Himself, and not have a will of their own, nor affection to any other thing ; and yet, ah ! the bad entertainment He gets from my hand. I can neither esteem Him myself, nor commend Him to others ; though my work be to trumpet aloud His praise, and be an under-suiter to gain the bride's consent to the lovely Bridegroom, I can do nothing in it, and little can angels do in it to any purpose. Yet, I can tell this unto all, that my Master infinitely passeth my commendations. He is so excellent, that it would but be an obscuring His excellency, for me to babble about it.

O right honourable and dear friends, are you not longing for the full enjoyment of Him, looking out for the breaking of the day, and the fleeing away of the shadows, that you may no more see Him darkly as through a glass, but may behold Him as He is, and enjoy Him perfectly and constantly? This, O this ! what a happiness is it! What shall I say more? For you know more of Him than I can tell you, and all that I can say is but, as it were, to bring Him to remembrance. I thank God on your behalf, that your zeal is heard of in many places. You have become companions with us in our afflictions. Your sympathy with the persecuted party is evident to us all, and we hear that we have a great room in your prayers. Man cannot repay your kindness to us, but I know you look not to man in it, but that you do it out of love to the Lord, for you have no outward encouragement to it. O that the Lord, who hath joined together a few in Leewarden and a party in Scotland in such oneness of mind and affection, may, when He returns to us again, join Scotland and Friesland in covenant together, to serve the Lord their God.

And you, O beloved, grow in grace, and endure to the end. I doubt not but you have laid your all at Christ's feet. O take nothing back again. Be resolute in His cause, and valiant in His matters. When His kingdom is so low, let Him want none of your help that is competent for you, and He shall help you. *Own Him, and*

He will own you. Stand with Him, and He will stand with you, and make you victorious. Whoever shall fight against you, you shall overcome. It is good fighting in Christ's camp, for all His soldiers shall certainly prevail. O look to your Captain and His encouragements, that you faint not. I apprehend that you meet with sore blows and bickerings ; yea, I think, you scarcely want any conflict that we have, save only that you are not as yet in such hazard of your lives. But, as nothing more than this doth endear you unto us, so no external condition will more draw out God's heart towards you. But this I will say, be well resolved against whatever man can do unto you. I think, no Christian ought now to be secure. The Man of sin is plotting and strengthening his force what he can, and he will not be content with part of Christ's kingdom : his aim is it all. He stirs himself now so fast in his saddle, that, I think, it is not long to his fall. However, many lands may look for strange plagues ; though Britain and Ireland shall be made the centre of His judgments, yet His indignation shall not be contained within their limits. O ! judgments, sudden and sore wasting judgments, are coming on Britain and Ireland. Christ mounted on the red horse of severity will ride through the breadth and length of these lands. The appearance of some parties did so fill me with temporal expectations, but they did not make some change their thoughts. As they knew little of God's way, who looked for such good from such hands, so I thought them fools who conjectured, that a deliverance should come before a desolation. I say again, be resolved against what man can do unto you, *for there are no more Christians than there are martyrs in resolution and affection.* "The kingdom of heaven must be taken by violence, and the violent take it by force." The more and greater difficulties be in the way, a right sight of the kingdom makes the way the more pleasant. O fear not difficulties ; for many trials that when looked upon at a distance seem big and mounting, yet, when they and you meet, you shall find them nothing. *If I could commend anything besides Christ, it would be the cross of Christ.* Those things, which make carnal onlookers think my condition hard and miserable, make me think it sweet and pleasant. I have found hazards, reproaches, contempt, weariness, cold, night-wanderings, stormy tempests, and deserts so desirable, that it is a greater difficulty to me, not to be ambitious of these things, than to submit unto them. O rejoice in the cross, for it is all paved with love. The fewer that will bear it, it is your greater honour to be friends to it. Follow Christ with the cross upon your backs, and set none else before you as your leader, for man is a poor fallible changeable creature. Let it be your care not to fall upon the stumbling-blocks cast in your way. Woe to the world because of offences. Though you have your own share of the revilings of this time, yet be not reproached with reproachers ; though the sourness of others grieve you, yet let it not infect you. *Let zeal be accompanied with meekness, that you may be free from passion and prejudice ;* and *let meekness be backed with zeal, that you may be free of lukewarmness and indifference.* Let meekness be extended toward all persons, and zeal against all sins ; and, if you would not lose your ground, be positive against sin in the first proposal and motion thereof. You will not get it shifted by, and yourselves kept free of it by hurting yourselves, and not appearing freely against it, though there may be an unwillingness unto it. I conceive that Aaron had no will to make the golden calf, and he thought to have put it out of the Israelites' minds, by bidding them break off their golden ear-rings, and bring them unto him. But this simple shift would not do it,—the saint of God is pitifully ensnared ; and, if he was simple in opposing that abomination, he got as silly an excuse for himself. It would not have been thought that a child would have said, "there came out this calf."

Now, commit your cause unto the Lord, for judgment and righteousness shall yet meet together again upon the earth. The Lord is interested in His own work; therefore He can neither forget it nor forsake it, and such as wait for Him shall never be put to shame. But, O long and cry for His appearance, that He may right wrongs, and rule for Himself, and claim His own right of possession; that the promised day may come when this shall be voiced along the heavens "The kingdoms of the world are become the kingdom of our Lord, and of His Christ." He is busy in order to this. He is carrying on a discovery of all sorts of folk, enemies and others. I thought His discovery had been near through Scotland before this, but He lets me see myself a fool for so judging. He sees many things to be discovered that man sees not. But happy are they who are sincere and entire; they need not fear, for "when they are tried, they shall come forth as gold."

Now, as to our present case, I wot not well what to say anent it, there are so many mercies and judgments in it to be spoken of. God hath taken this last year many from us, by banishment, and by death on scaffolds, especially on the fields, where none (for the most part) were to see them die, but the executioners; and yet God fills up their rooms again. Neither are these things permitted to damp such as are left. Some have, which is more sad, fallen off from us, and yet God is filling up their places also, and making others more stedfast; and notwithstanding both of persecutions and reproaches, the Lord hath opened doors for me in several places of Scotland, where there used to be no such access before, and hath multiplied my work so upon my hands (I speak it to His praise) that I have observed my work, I say, to be now in some shires threefold, and, in some, fourfold more than it was. O that God would send forth labourers! There seems to be much ado in Scotland with them. Also, it is almost incredible to tell what zeal, what tenderness, what painfulness in duty, what circumspectness of walk, in many young ones of ten, eleven, twelve and fourteen years of age, in many places of Scotland, which I look upon as one of the visible and greatest tokens for good that we have.

But, right honourable and dearly beloved, not to detain you further, I acknowledge myself your debtor while I live, for your many prayers put up for this poor distressed church, whereof I know I have had a share; for your sympathy and kindness otherwise manifested to us; for your care of that family with you, wherein we are all concerned; and particularly for your encouraging, strengthening of, and kindness to my dear and worthy friend, our right honourable delegate. I bless the Lord who hath given you zeal for Himself, and hath helped you to stand with a poor despised party in making stours * for His interest. I commend you to Him, that He may make His rich grace abound in you, that He may perfect what concerns you, and make you persevere unto the end, and Himself be your exceeding rich reward. I hope I need not desire you to pray for me. I am, honourable and dearly beloved, your obliged friend, and obedient servant in the Lord,   JAMES RENWICK.

LETTER XLVI.

From this letter it appears that Renwick is now very busy, taking full advantage of the larger amount of liberty at present allowed for preaching. Enemies, however, are busy too, bringing mischievous and malignant charges against him and his friend Sir Robert Hamilton, to whom he now writes as follows :—

May 3, 1686.

Honourable and dear Sir,—I have seen your letter to your dear and worthy sisters. As it speaks forth your sore bickerings and hot encounters, it maketh me sad; but again I rejoice that your lot is squared

---

* Efforts or struggles, occasioning much dust and confusion.

out so like the case of the Lord's work this day. Oh! though your travels be through many deeps, and the floods seem to be waxing upon you, yet, when your feet shall be established upon Canaan's banks, you shall forget the same. Though now you be standing in the swellings of Jordan, yet these shall pass away from you, and you shall be lifted up, and be set before the throne of the Lamb of God, clothed with the robes of righteousness, crowned with the crown of glory, with the palm of victory and triumph in your hand, with the song of Moses and of the Lamb in your mouth, singing hallelujahs for ever and ever. O what will you think of yourself then ? O what will you think of that posture ? Let your eyes be still upon these, and glory in your present tribulation. Rejoice in your light affliction which is but for a moment. Count your antagonists your greatest friends, for what are they doing by all the storms they raise against you, but contributing to the mass of your glory ? O fear them not, but keep your Captain-general upon your right hand, and then cry to them to shoot their fill.

I had written to your Honour far sooner, but my work keepeth me busy, so much of it lies in the remote corners of the land, as Galloway, Nithsdale, Annandale, &c. I have not been near Edinburgh since the 16th of October 1685, and I have travelled since through Clydesdale, Eskdale, some of the Forest, Annandale, some of Galloway, Kyle and Cunningham ; and in all these places I examined the Societies as I passed through, several other persons coming to hear, and I found my work greater this last journey than ever before. Also in lower Cunningham, where there had never been any field-preachers, I got kindly acceptance, and great multitudes came to hear ; and I have had several calls since from that country-side. Such like have I found through Renfrew. Moreover, the Lord hath wrought a great change upon the barony of Sanquhar, the parish of Kirkconnel, and these dark corners. Generally they come to hear the gospel and are quitting many of the defections of the time ; yea, I may say (to the Lord's praise) that our meetings were never so numerous, and the work did never thrive more than since man opposed it so much. As for Mr Langlands and my agreeing with him, there is little appearance of it; for I am where I was, and he is rather farther off than nearer hand. As for disowning the Lanark Declaration, I think you look upon it as so false, that I need say nothing ; and as for the ministers, they wot not what to do anent us, for, so far as I can know, they cannot two of them agree (for the most part) intent upon one thing. I heard of none of them coming forth to the country yet, but Mr Langlands and Mr Alcorn ; and they travelled through some of Kyle, through Carrick, and some of the shire of Galloway, and some of Clydesdale, and their preachings were kept, in a great measure, obscure. And as for such as are gone off from us, they are the most bitter against us. Alexander Gordon went into the Bass and Blackness with an information against us, containing many charges, wherewith, I hear, the ministers of Edinburgh are displeased, he having done it without their advice. Howbeit, we have written about six sheets of paper in answer to it, and we are to meet within two days about the concluding of it. However, we will do nothing in it rashly, for every word in such a matter ought to be well weighed and considered. But there are none gone off from us, but those who at that party's appearance in summer went off. Also, we have had some conference with some of them, an account whereof I shall send you with some other papers. I have written a letter to the sweet Societies at Leewarden, and will send it with the rest of the papers, and some other letters that I am to write. Moreover, I thought fit to acquaint you, that M. S. hath a purpose to go over again to Groningen. I desire you may be concerned with it, and lay it out before the Lord. O dear Sir, cry, cry for labourers to God's vineyard in Scotland, for I cannot express how much need there is of them,—great is the work that is here for them. If an honest way of sending forth T. could be had, I would gladly have it embraced, for I do not dread the young man; he is not of a dangerous spirit. O lay it out before the Lord.

Now, go on resolutely in the strength of our God, and regard not your opposers. Hold fast what is right, but be not reviling unto a reviler, nor scoffing unto a scoffer. Let zeal and meekness be your companions, the one in your one hand, and the other in your other hand, and wait on the Lord, and He shall give testimony for you.

Now, my love to the honourable sweet Society, your dear sister, and all the sweet family. I am, honourable and dear Sir, yours, as formerly,   JAMES RENWICK.

LETTER XLVII.

This letter is addressed to the two ladies Van Heermaen, referred to on page 52.

May 8, 1686.

Right honourable Ladies, dearly beloved in the Lord,—Multiplied confusions, and not forgetfulness of you, have so long hindered my writing unto you; but being confident of your constructing favourably of me as to this, I shall add no more for my apology, and what else can I say which you know not? You have learned both from the Bible and experience, that the Christian's way to the kingdom is through much tribulation; and I hope you have laid your account for all that can come in your way. Our natures would have the way so squared that we might travel without a rub, but it lieth through many an encounter. We would have it through a valley of roses, but it lieth through a valley of tears. We would have it so as to be travelled sleeping, but it must be travelled waking, and watching, and fighting. We would have it to be travelled laughing, but it must be travelled with weeping. But, whatever folks do think, when great necessity for and advantage by every difficulty is seen, the more that they meet with the way is more pleasant to believers, and a sight of the recompence of reward maketh bold and resolute to pass through every opposition. If they were possible, ten thousand deaths, ten thousand hells would seem nothing to a soul, who gets a sight of Christ at the other side of all these. O Christ is precious, Christ is your up-making! O what think you of that noble exchange, to embrace Christ entirely, and quit self entirely? Is not that receiving new wares for old? Is not that a receiving of gold, yea, of gold more precious than the gold of Sheba, and a quitting of dust more vile than the dust of the earth? O lovely soul that hath embraced lovely Christ,—rich and happy that hath embraced precious Christ! But woe unto them that would divide Him, and not take Him in all His offices, for they have not yet learned Him. Woe unto them that think they have no need of Christ, for they know not themselves. Woe to them that think they can close with Him when they please, for they are ignorant of grace. Woe to them that would have Christ and their own something beside, for they have neither loved nor conceived rightly of Him. Woe to them that make excuse for their not following of Him, for they know not their folly. Woe to them that will not close with all the crosses and the inconveniences that they meet with for Christ, for they are rebellious fools that look only to the cost, and not to the advantages of religion. They scar at it, and give this answer to Christ's call, His sayings are hard and who can bear them? None do account so of His yoke, but they who have not taken it on; for it is "easy and His burden is light." Those who will not believe His word for it, nor the experience of many saints and martyrs, let them take a trial of it themselves, and, if they get leave to weary, let them cast it off again. But, I am sure, there was never one that fully engaged with Him, that ever could find a heart to quit Him again.

O! that folks would not stand at such a distance, but come near and take a view of Him, and they would see that which would inevitably win their hearts. There are two things at which I cannot wonder enough, and these are, the invaluableness of Christ, and the low value which the children of men put upon Him. Judas sold Him for thirty pieces of silver, but many now-a-days sell Him for less; and, though they could get ten thousand worlds for Him, they but make a mad and foolish bargain, who would quit Him for these. Yea, suppose that it were possible one person could possess ten thousand worlds, and that everlastingly, he could not have, in the use thereof, so much contentment by far, as the smallest part Christ can give. Yea, one half-hour's enjoyment of Him would far surpass all the satisfaction in the supposed case. O then! what must the eternal and full enjoyment of Him be!

Now, dearly beloved, you who have made choice of Christ, what think you of your choice? O! admire His excellency, and wonder at your own happiness, and bend all your love towards Him, who hath made you so happy. Seek to shed abroad the savour of His sweet ointments, by a holy and spiritual walk, and improve dispensations to His glory and your own good, and lean upon Him in your travel through the wilderness; and though there be fiery serpents and drought in it, yet solace yourselves with His company, who hath said, that "He will never leave you, nor forsake you." Regard not losses, regard not reproaches, for He is your exceeding rich reward. I doubt not but you meet with your own measure of reproaches and contempt at the hands of this generation, for the great kindness you have shown to a wounded and wronged wrestling party in the furnace of affliction. But as this doth endear our affections unto you so much the more, so, I hope, you are better fixed than that that should prove a stumbling-block unto you. The parties, that we have to contend with, discover so much of a spirit of lying and prejudice, for the most part of them, that none of tenderness, who know them, will be in great hazard to be taken away with them. I am confident God will stain their pride, and silence their boasting, and that suddenly. I may say, I am sorry for what I see coming upon them. But, O worthy Ladies, keep you near God, and go on in your zeal, and persist in your stedfastness, and in the close of the day you shall be made to rejoice.

Now, I cannot express how much we are obliged unto you, for your tender care of our family that is with you, and the great encouragement that you are to our dear and honourable delegate. The Lord be your reward, and keep not back His hand from helping you in the time of your need.

No more at the time, but, taking my leave of you in the words of the Apostle, 1 Cor. xvi. 23, 24. "The grace of our Lord Jesus Christ be with you. My love be with you all in Christ Jesus." I am, Right honourable Ladies, your assured and obliged friend and servant in our sweet Lord, JAMES RENWICK.

LETTER XLVIII.

This letter is addressed to the Lady E. B., of whom we know nothing, except that she was another of those distinguished persons in Holland, who at this time befriended the cause of liberty and of the Gospel.

May 13, 1686.

Right honourable Lady, — Dearly beloved in the Lord, My insufficiency being in part known to me doth make me stand in awe to write to you ; but if I had the tongue of the learned, and the pen of a ready writer, I would employ them both in speaking well of the name of Christ, and commending His way. O ! His name is as ointment poured forth, and whoso gets a smell thereof cannot but love Him. And His

way is so lovely, that a poor soul that once gets his
foot upon it, and the eye looking forward, cannot
but choose to tread in those paths, though rubs and
crosses from enemies, both from within and without,
should be ever so multiplied. And no wonder; for,
when the children of God begin by grace to turn
their backs upon their old lovers, and to shake
off their weights, they get in hand the hundred-
fold, ten thousand times told, and are made to say,
as Psal. iv. 7, "Thou hast put gladness in my
heart, more than in the time that their corn and
their wine are increased." Many a time I think *they
can have no pleasant life who have not the Christian's
life*. Whatever the world think, yet the believer gets
that in time, which may sufficiently engage him to
go through, if it were possible, a thousand deaths in
obedience to the Lord. O then! since the imperfect
and inconstant enjoyment of Christ is such a thing,
what must the full and eternal enjoyment of Him be!
Of this it may be said, "Eye hath not seen, nor ear
heard, neither hath it entered into the heart of man to
conceive the things which God hath prepared for them
that love Him." The believer cannot but have a happy
life, when he has four things which the Scripture
calls precious, viz.: the precious redemption of the
soul, a precious faith, a precious Christ, and precious
promises. And the redemption of the soul, which is
precious, is by a precious faith, laying hold on a precious
Christ, held forth in precious promises. But when their
happiness shall be completed, then shall faith evanish
into sight, by the entire fulfilling of the promises, and
the soul be drowned in the bottomless ocean of the love
of precious Christ, and, bursting up with love, continu-
ally flaming toward Him again. O what a life must a
life of love be! And what inconceivable joy will it
yield! Christ will rejoice over His own spouse when
He hath taken her home to His own house, made with
His own hand, and hath clothed her with robes of His
own making, and entertained her with a banquet of His

own dressing. The invitation-word of the Giver of that banquet will be this, Song 'of Solomon' v. 1, "Eat, O friends ; drink, yea, drink abundantly, O beloved." That table will never be drawn, and the dainties will never wear tasteless ; for, as our Lord saith, Matt. xxvi. 29, "the wine there is new," and it never groweth old ; and His spouse's stomach will never suffocate, nor her appetite be satisfied. So, in heaven there is a continual eating and drinking, and a continual hungering and thirsting, a continual resting, and yet a never resting. Then shall the spouse rejoice in her Husband. All her love shall be bent towards Him, and her joy shall arise from her enjoying Him. Her love shall be full and constant, not admitting of intermissions or variableness ; her joy full and perpetual, not admitting of defect or changeableness. That which is a great part of the Christian's exercise here, to wit, his doubting of Christ's love, and his complaining of coldrifeness of love to him again, shall then be wholly removed ; and, instead of grief, at least mixtures of sorrow with his joy, he shall then have inconceivable joy. Is not Christ fully enjoyed, a match to love, and a prize to rejoice in ? Now, long for this, and seek after the abiding assurance of Christ's love, and more and more love communications thereof in your heart, until you arrive at this. Separate yourself more and more from every unclean thing, that cannot enter the gates of the city, where all this is to be enjoyed. And seeing such rich upmaking is to be had in Christ, especially seeing He is so worthy, regard not what you may be called to undergo in your owning of Him. I hope you have studied to let yourself, your name, your enjoyments, and your all, lie at Christ's feet, so as you can say of these, they are not your own. The more you do prove that they are His, by His calling for them, and making use of them, the more of His love He evidenceth towards you, and the more honour He putteth upon you. I think, men and women are for no use, but so far as they are for Christ. Whatever errands He

M

calls you to run, fear not skaith nor hazard, for it is
He that rideth these ways upon you, and so you shall
not stumble. He hath promised, Psal. cxxi. 3, "He
shall not suffer thy foot to be moved." Let the low
state of the Church of Scotland, and the dangerous
case of the Church in other lands, lie near your heart,
for ah! we may say at this day, "The house of David
is waxing weaker and weaker, and the house of Saul
waxing stronger and stronger." I fear a sad and
general stroke before it will be better with the
churches, for few are valiant for the truth upon the
earth. Nothing brings a church more low, and a
readier destruction upon a land, than regardlessness
of Christ's matters, and silly and shameful slipping
from them. This is that which hath occasioned our
breaches, and bred all our divisions in this church.
Because some of our worthies in our day, who have
gone before us, have been honoured and helped to
hold what our worthy fathers did conquer with their
blood, and bind over upon us by holy covenants, and
we are endeavouring to do the same, they and we have
been reproached as followers of new ways; but
"wisdom shall be justified of her own children."
Seeing our way-marks in the Scriptures, and our never-
to-be-forgotten Reformation, and the cloud of witnesses
walking in the same paths, we are not to regard much
what men say; but it were good for our reproachers
to be sober, for a little time will silence their boasting,
and make them change their thoughts, when they shall
not get space to amend them.

Now, dear and worthy Lady, I cannot express the
sense that I even have of the many obligations which
we are all under unto you, for your bowels have not
been shut up, nor your hands shortened towards us.
For your benefits towards us in this land, and those of
us who are amongst you, have been large indeed; but
we are not so refreshed with what we enjoy thereby, as
that these things are demonstrations of your love to
God, and respect to His work. What further shall

I say, but go on in the way and strength of the Lord. Be watchful, diligent, and spiritual; grow in grace, and persevere therein to the end. The God of all peace be with you! I am, Right honourable Lady, your assured friend, and obliged servant in the Lord,

JAMES RENWICK.

LETTERS XLIX.—LIII.

These are all addressed to Sir Robert Hamilton, against whom serious charges had been brought, from which he defended himself in a long letter to the Societies, of date Dec. 7th, 1685, which appears in "Faithful Contendings Displayed." To this defence Renwick refers in a somewhat qualified way, admiring the courage it evinced but questioning the wisdom of some of its statements.

LETTER XLIX.

May 22, 1686.

Honoured and dear Sir,—I have written to you a brief account of our affairs in another letter, but I know not if it be away yet. Howbeit, I hope it shall come to your hand; therefore, I shall now be the more short in what I have to say. As for news, there are not many. Only York hath written to his parliament for a liberty to the Papists, commending them in his own way very highly, as those who have been faithful to the crown upon all hazards. So the parliamentarians are consulting about rescinding the penal statutes against Papists, but are not like entirely to agree about the same. However, they have written back, that they will yield so far to his desire in that as their consciences will allow, and have offered a bond themselves to oppose all who may rise against him upon any pretext whatsoever. But a great many folk are gaping for a dissension between the Popish and Prelatic parties; which if it be, there will be an uncouth hotch-potch, for the most part of old traders (to wit, Argyle's party) will strike in with the latter. Kersland and Mr Boyd were both of some purpose to go to Holland when I last parted with them, but as to the time I am uncertain.

In my other letter, I spoke of sending you some papers; but now, the shortness of time will not allow me to get them transcribed, but I purpose to do it afterwards. Also there is a rude draught of a Vindica-tion, six sheets long or thereabouts, drawn up chiefly by Mr B. in answer to what charges are cast upon us, in which are many things very useful. However as it is not likely to have passage for the Linning, I durst not propose it to friends that they should send for it without being stamped;* but this is my humble advice unto you, that if you can get it stamped, and think that it will do good service, to essay it. If you have any exceptions against the stamping of it, our merchants will not press for it; but if you have no exceptions, but only fears, which may say something to yourself, but would not bear weight before men, then I would have these no more spoken of than necessity calls for, and not made mention of in the Linning's not being stamped. It will be fitter that you propose to our merchants the sending for the Linning than I, because I am rather for wrest-ling under a heavy burden, than to have an ill neigh-bour. Some apprehend that I am for no help at all, but it would be most fit that the Linning should speak, and signify to our merchants the case, and so you and I both would come under the less suspicion, for we have a strange generation to deal with. As for K.'s carriage here, so far as we can learn, he seems not to design the introducing of other parties, for he neither speaks nor acts in their favour. As for your Honour, I can hear of nothing that he speaks against you, relative to the public cause; but to some he hath

* The allusion here is to Mr Linning's ordination.

said, that you have not carried right towards their
family. And as for Mr Flint, he is married by Thomas
Russel to one Mrs Moor, who had been one with
J. Gibb.

Now, to be free with you about your letter, it
hath, indeed, gained the end of it, in clearing you of
what you were charged with, and satisfied friends as to
that. But many take it very ill, some saying that it
hath too much bitterness towards antagonists, and
that it adduceth personal failings : and some, that it
insinuates too much of a commendation of yourself,
holding forth that you are almost alone in all your
actions : and some, that it seems to flatter this party
by too much commending them. But for mine own
part, I could take it all in good part, and not miscon-
strue your intentions ; but what you write to the whole
I would have you so to write as to men, some of whom
may be your greatest reproachers the next day, and so
may be seeking all imaginable advantages against you.
But let the world say what they will, I must say this,—
and I say it without vanity or flattery,—that a little
of Robert Hamilton's spirit, in such a day as this, is
very much worth. Also, I think fit to intimate unto
you my purpose of rescribing my Testimony ; not that
I am resiling from any article thereof, but that I would
have the same more wisely and yet as plainly and as
freely expressed, and more confirmed and corroborated,
and also I would have my mind anent some other
exigencies and controversies inserted. Moreover, I
know not a man under whose name and patronage I
would commend it to the following generations,
but to despised, and yet much honoured Robert
Hamilton.

Now, I shall say no more ; only, take such a wise
way with foreigners, as that truth may get no loss, and
as they may be kept as much upon your side as can
be. For they come under another consideration than
those that are under the same bond of a covenant
with ourselves, and have the same word of testimony,

and whose profession imports not an opposite party, such as Independents, Anabaptists, &c.

So, Worthy and dear Sir, go on in the name and strength of your God, and quit not your confidence, though probability be against you, for it is a change-able rule. As for those who win not to judge by another rule, I never look for stedfastness at their hand. Wait upon the Lord, who will guide all matters aright, and bring forth advantage to His work out of every opposition, and that as universal as the opposition hath been made. Pray for him, who is, your Honour's most endeared friend, and servant in the Lord,   JAMES RENWICK.

LETTER L.

Aug. 13, 1686.

Hon. and dear Sir,—I have not many news to write to you at this time, yet I thought it my duty to acquaint you with some things. Our condition is in some measure changed in this respect, that the enemies for this year have not been so hotly pursuing after us as they were. Whatever it may flow from upon the enemies' part, whether from the Popish party being so busied in their contrivances, and other grand persecu-tors discourted, or from some other thing, yet, we can see the Lord's restraining hand in it, and that He "stays His rough wind in the day of His east wind." We are so taken up with other things, that, I think, it shall be a plague to the generation in making them carnal and secure.

I have been for a season in England, where, by the good hand of the Lord, we kept our Sabbath meetings all except one day in the fields, without any disturbance, but upon other days of the week they were kept in the night time. In that land, I got some discoveries of the Sectaries; for, at one preach-ing, where there were many Anabaptists hearing, because I asserted the divine right of infant-baptism from Scripture, clearing the same from the testimony of

some ancient authors, they who before had seemed to
have much love and affection would not afterwards
carry themselves civil, and told us that they had been
always willing to do, and had done for Scottish sufferers,
and that other Scottish ministers had not fallen upon such
heads. Such an upcast was a little troublesome unto
me, but by it I perceived, as also I expressed, that their
hospitality to Scottish ministers and sufferers had both
done the ministers and themselves ill, for it stopped the
ministers' mouths from declaring the counsel of God,
and made themselves lay weight upon such deeds, and
look upon Scottish ministers as so much obliged to them,
that they behoved to tolerate them. But this I say,
that they that deal freely with them will not get long
their countenance. Howbeit, at my coming away, one
of them told me, that they were resolved to collect for
me, but were informed that I would not accept thereof. Whereupon I told him that they were my friends
that informed so rightly, for I went not thither for
necessity, neither to seek theirs, but them. Also, at the
desire of friends in Scotland, some of us went to converse with a Presbyterian minister, whom we heard to
be well affected toward this party, and found him, as
we thought, to be a very humble tender man, much
exercised with that Church's case. After information,
he did agree with us in the word of our testimony, only
he was not so straight as to some matters of England as
we would desire ; but this is not to be thought strange
considering that he hath none either to go before
him nor with him in these things.

Since we came to Scotland, I hear that some of
these ministers, particularly Mr Barclay, Mr Langlands, and one Mr Bay are travelling in different
places through the country. I hear not tell of much
breaking among friends. But some of the other party
are going through with as gross slanders as can be
invented. One thing they are saying is, that they can
prove that I was with the Chancellor at Edinburgh ;
and they most partly profess, that in their travels they

are in a continual fear of us, that we will deliver them up to the enemy.

Now, what shall I say? Our case is singular. It is matter of great concernedness. The Lord hath seen that our furnace, by that inquisition and torture of the common enemies, hath not been searching enough, therefore He must prepare another kind of furnace to try us better. Blessed are they who shall come forth as gold. God will arise, and dispel these present mists and confusions, and let it be seen what great need there hath been of all that comes to pass. Oh, faith is a brave interpreter of dispensations, and never carries bad tidings.

O dear Sir, you are called forth to sail through a raging and rough sea; but trust to your pilot, and He will bring you to your harbour. O fear not,—He will not let the waves overwhelm you, and, the rougher the sea, the sweeter will your harbour be. Think it not strange of that stumbling dispensation that has fallen to you, for God hath a mind to let a generation stumble, whom He thinks worthy of no other thing. It speaks out anger towards us, but more anger to them that stumble at it. God is taking pains to purify, refine, and purge us; and He says He will have a pure people in Scotland, else He shall have none at all. That dispensation seems to be so immediately from God's hand, that we should say, "It is the Lord, let Him do what seemeth Him good." Our study should be to make a right use of it.

As for the papers you received from N. N., I sent you them, and left them unclosed, that in his passage he might let some friends see them, especially that those at Newcastle might see them. I desire to know your thoughts of the reply to Mr Robert Langland's letter, which I wrote, mostly for the behoof of some that seem to be godly and exercised, whose affections are towards us, but through various informations they are perplexed about some of our matters. So I laboured to take that away in it which I thought might be most convincing, and for their advantage, without truth's prejudice. As to the Vindication we are about, it is not yet perfected, neither in it will we do anything rashly; our friends have concluded, that you and I shall see it before it go forth.

Concerning Mr Boyd's business, friends (except a very few) were against giving him a certificate for ordination, but yet did give it. The occasion of a fast-day upon his account was to prevent disagreement that was like to be amongst friends anent his business. As for that affair concerning you and J. H., I bless the Lord that He hath helped you to lay it aside. I think it is according to His will, and I hope you will have much peace in it. She was with us few days, and was pretty free with us anent several things, particularly the trials of their family, and their being puzzled whether or not to come home to Scotland, if so be their brother would not stay abroad, but I would not advise them to one thing or another in that. As to your own coming home or staying abroad, I apprehend that friends would easily consent to your staying, or yet call you home, but I cannot well advise them to either of these, till I know upon what grounds to do it from yourself. It is likely that you and the family both will be necessitated through straitenedness in living in that land to come home. But if it come to that, I would have you to acquaint me, that you might be called, which may be a means to stop the insulting of many ; or if it were better to stay there, and if a little supply from our hand could keep you there, we would be content to give it. But man's malice is so much against you, that I am afraid of you in staying, and I am afraid of you in your voyage hither, and I am afraid of you in your being here. But if the Lord bring you home, I think you and I must not part, till the Lord by death, or some signal way, do it.

Now, dear Sir, what shall I say? The Lord hath carved out your lot after a strange sort. O study to get good by all His dispensations toward you, that you may bring forth the more fruit,—for "every branch that beareth fruit He purgeth it that it may bring forth more fruit." Let your burdens all lie upon the Lord. His back is strong enough. Is not His all-sufficiency your portion? Are you not then rich enough? and what can you want? O rejoice in reproaches, rejoice in ignominy, rejoice in wants, in perils, and in sufferings, for His name. The more of these you are called to endure, the more true honour is put upon you, and seek you the more to honour and glorify Him. Fight not against the world with the world's weapons of the flesh, viz., pride, passion, prejudice, lies, and contempt; but let yours be the weapons of the Spirit, viz., zeal, meekness, patience, and prayer to God, that He would either pity them and heal them, or else draw them out of the way. Whatever you write unto friends, write as unto men, who are for you to-day, and may be against you to-morrow.

Now, I pray that the Lord may be with you and that poor and sweet family, that He may give you enlargement in your distresses, and, when your sorrows abound, He may make your consolations to superabound. My love to your dear and worthy sister, the sweet children F. and R., the worthy ladies V. Heer., and any other of your strengtheners in the Lord. I am, Honourable and dear Sir, ever as formerly,

JAMES RENWICK.

LETTER LI.

October 23, 1686.

Hon. and dear Sir,—I received your letters, and they were very refreshing unto me. Your encounters are fierce, and you stand in the stour; but I hope you look upon your condition rather to be envied than pitied. O can you not say, that the fat feast of a peaceable conscience, and the enjoyment of the light of the Lord's countenance, is the hundredth fold a thousand

times told? "Light is sown for the righteous, and gladness for the upright in heart," Psal. xcvii. 11. O read
that psalm, and meditate upon it, and when you mind
it remember me, for it is a golden Scripture unto me.
What would you and I have more than that, "The
Lord reigneth, let us rejoice. Righteousness and judgment are the habitation of His throne?" But O who
can take Him up? who can behold His glory? Therefore He casteth "clouds round about Him. Let us be
glad because of His judgments. A fire goeth before
Him, to burn up His enemies."

As to what you write about my Testimony, I am refreshed; yet, when I look back upon the frame that I
was then in, I have much peace in my ingenuity, and,
though weakly, yet I think it hath the right state of
the cause in it, and I hope never to resile from it.
Also, its having your name doth the more commend it
unto me. When I shall write (which I have been
hitherto diverted from) it will be but an enlargement
upon, and confirmation of the foresaid Testimony, with
reasons, together with some additions as to what hath
fallen out since. As for my changing my method in
dealing with the parents of children to be baptized, I declare them to be misinformers who have so said unto
you. Those persons, that have complied with one
thing or other, I do not admit to present their children,
unless they have evidenced a right sense and practical
reformation, by standing out against the temptation
unto these things that they have been chargeable with,
and their engagement to give due satisfaction when
lawfully called for. Or else we have the attestation of
some acquainted with their case, that, in the judgment
of charity, they appear to be convinced of, and humbled
for their sin, and they engage to forbear their sin, and
give satisfaction in manner foresaid. But when compliers and persons guilty of defection come, who have
not as yet desisted from their offensive courses, I do not
let them present their children. Neither will or do I
let other persons present their children, lest the parents

should be hardened in their sin thereby, unless they engage to forbear, and give satisfaction as said is; and some prove true and some prove false. Further, when the parents are guilty of very gross compliance, even though they have given evidences of a right sense thereof, I do not admit them, but suffer another to present their children, for fear of reproach, albeit I might do it lawfully.

But, dear Sir, my difficulty upon this head is often times very great. The different cases of persons put me sometimes to a nonplus. This I think strange, that now when the ministers are passing through the country, many persons who are involved in the courses of defection scruple to take their children unto them.

In answer to what you write concerning Kersland,* I know him to be nothing the better of the company of some, and I resolve that he shall be dealt with, both freely and tenderly, at the next General Meeting. As for Mr Boyd, I used freedom with him, in a line, before he went away; but the reports that I have heard of him, since I saw him, have been both troublesome and displeasing unto me. I know not upon what grounds he can express his hope of union, for I see no way as yet how it shall be obtained in the Lord. Yea, as matters now stand, I hold myself obliged to resent that information of his, for it puts such as are coming forward to stand still. For mine own part, though I should be left alone, and branded with singularity, while they continue as they are, I resolve not to unite *dum spiritus hos regit artus;*† and there is little hope of their growing better. Neither will Mr Boyd find that party amongst us, who are inclined to hear those, so strong as he expects; but, after pains for information and admonition, we shall then show how we will carry towards them. Let me be mistaken, as men please to say, this is my study not to partake in other men's

---

* Mentioned in Letter 49. Probably this was a son of Robert Ker of Kersland, who suffered much and died in Holland in 1680.

† While life lasts.

sins, neither to cover them. But, considering the confusions of this time, and the weakness of poor people,
I hold it my duty to be a help and a prop, as I can,
to those that are staggering, and to carry so forward
such as will go off, as that their stumbling, neither in law,
nor in my own conscience, may be charged upon me.
This is like unto my Master, who hath promised to
save them that halt, and gather them that are driven
out. As for the Vindication which Mr B. did let you
see, I need not speak any thing, for we have altered it,
and sent unto you a transcript of the present draft,
which is not yet condescended upon, until you and our
Societies see it. So let it not trouble you, neither the
certificate that was granted unto him ; for though the
most part were dissatisfied with some things in him, and
had their jealousies anent him, yet, considering what
he left behind him written with his own hand, and that
he was not fully discovered, they thought that they
could not deny such a certificate unto him. If he
should make a bad use of it against us, he will be a
man most ungrateful, and will contradict what he hath
left under his own hand amongst us, and, if so, I wish
it had never been granted unto him. Your cousin Mrs
J. K. was with us some days, and we were pretty free
with her ; but, you know, she is ordinarily reserved.
As for what you wrote about the laying aside of that
business, I bless the Lord that He hath helped you unto
it, for many considerations called for it.

Now, Right Honourable and very dear Sir, I remit
you to the bearer for news amongst us. He can give
you an account of my progress in England, and also
of Colin's * going to Ireland. But I think fit to shew
you, that, at the last Correspondence, friends judged it
convenient to send one to Mr Thomas Douglas to converse with him, and know where he stands, which this
bearer is resolved, according to their conclusion, to set
about. When they asked my concurrence and consent,
I answered that I could not actively concur therewith,

* Colin Alison, referred to in Letter 53.

because I knew not what to expect by it, yet I should not oppose their sending any of their number to confer with him, for I thought the thing in itself could not well be denied to them. I am (with many) under the suspicion, that I desire no help, though the persons were never so right; whereas, the Lord is my witness, it would be my greatest rejoicing this day, to have some ministers to concur with me, for it would be a great advantage to the work, and a great ease to me. For, notwithstanding of all breakings, my business multiplies still upon my hand, and people are more earnest now than ever I knew them after the gospel. O that the Lord would send forth labourers! As for this bearer, I am glad that he hath come unto you, for he hath his own dissatisfaction with you, whereupon he and I have had some bickerings; but I do not know him to have vented himself to your prejudice. Also, he is very honest toward the cause, and singularly useful; therefore you may be free with, and tender of him, for I expect he will be free with you.

Now, dear and Honourable Sir, being in haste, and also disturbed yesternight from writing, by an alarm of the enemy, I shall add no further, but desire to know your mind anent a particular, which is like to break us more than any thing that the ministers can do. It is the joining of children, servants, and others, in the family exercise of their parents, masters and others, who are compliers. Thus, committing you, your sister and the sweet family unto the Lord, I am, Honourable and dear Sir, ever as formerly,   JAMES RENWICK.

LETTER LII.

Jan. 10, 1687.

Honoured and dear Sir,—I received yours, and am greatly refreshed with it, both in respect of its coming from you, and in respect of the strain of it, for I perceive in it a zeal for the right carrying of the ark of

God through this howling wilderness. It would be to me matter of joy to observe this spirit in any who bear the ark, and in all who profess to follow it, for I am persuaded, that the wrong way of bearing and handling the ark will keep it longer in the wilderness, but will never carry it through Jordan and settle it in the land of Canaan. For mine own part, I see it so difficult a thing to move one step rightly forward with it, that I am in a continual fear anent what I do. I wish I were more in the exercise of that fear, for it would put me to look more unto the Lord, whom I desire and aim to set before mine eyes at all times. If I shall give the ark a wrong touch, I may say (so far as I can see into mine own heart) it will be through blindness and not through biasness. O to be framed for the work of the day, for there is none fit for it but such as have honest hearts, ingenuous spirits, and the faces of lions. They will be a strange sort of folk whom the Lord will make any singular use of. As for the case of our Societies, I am in some consternation of spirit when I reflect upon it. There is a choice handful amongst them, whom, I hope, the Lord will not forsake; but some are not so fixed and resolute as they ought to be, and others, I fear, have little principle, but follow example. Several others are little exercised with their soul's case, and the Lord is hiding His face in some measure from the whole, which some are sensible of, and groaning under. Wherefore, I look for a more narrow sieve which we must yet go through, and that the Lord will lay aside many. O that fanning and winnowing that is coming ! But the least good grain shall not fall to the ground. Yea, I do not look that the Lord's work shall be delivered till this generation of His wrath be hurled out of the way, and, I think, they are blind who see not a desolation coming upon the land. "In mine ears, said the Lord of hosts, of a truth many houses shall be desolate, even great and fair without inhabitant ;" Isa. v. 9. "But he that is left in Zion, and he that remaineth in Jerusalem, shall be called holy, even every one that is written among the living in Jerusalem ;" Isaiah iv. 3. For mine own part, I apprehend, that that dark hour is now very near at hand, which shall come upon the church before the fall of Antichrist, and the Lord's glorious appearing for His church, which shall be in the last days. O blessed shall they be who wait for the Lord "in the way of His judgments," and who are of "the righteous nation which keeps the truth," for the gates shall be opened unto them, Isa. xxvi. 2, 8. I am, your Honour's sympathising friend and servant in the Lord,

JAMES RENWICK.

LETTER LIII.

Jan. 11, 1687.

Honoured and dear Sir,—I conceive it is both to your loss and our loss, yea, to the disadvantage of the cause, that you hear so seldom from us, and how matters are amongst us. For my part, I cannot help it, having always such throng of weighty business, continual travel through many a vast wilderness, and sometimes bad accommodation ; so that it is a rare thing for me to get a spare hour.

However, considering the importance of what was done at the last General Meeting, I judge it necessary to give you a true account thereof. There came two ministers to the last meeting, December 22, 1686, viz., Mr David Houston, and Mr Alexander Shields. But I shall first give you an account of our carrying toward the said Mr David, and toward the foresaid Mr Alexander. When I was in England the last summer, the General Meeting of our Societies being informed that Mr David Houston refused concurrence with, and subjection to the ministers in Ireland because of their defections, and that he preached faithfully against all the sins of the times, did send unto him Colin Alison and William Nairn to know the verity thereof. These, after

full and free communing with the said Mr David anent
all the heads of our present Testimony, received great
satisfaction. He also signified unto them his resolution
of coming unto us. Before we sent any unto him
again, we did convocate all our friends who had been
living any time in Ireland, and had now come over to
us, that we might inform ourselves anent what they
knew of the said Mr David. They could not relate any
difference in his principles from us, but they gave in
some accusation against him which they had by report,
and which were all *personalia*. All which accusations
were drawn up and delivered to James Boyle, who was
sent to Ireland to get the verity or falsehood of every
one of these things instructed ; and, on finding them to
be but calumnies, he was to conduct the foresaid Mr
David to us, according to his own resolution. So the
said James laying out search for information anent
these reports, conferring with some of Mr David's
accusers, bringing him some of them face to face,
likewise conferring with some of his neighbours and
ordinary hearers, and finding no ground for the foresaid
accusations, did conduct Mr David unto us, that we
might satisfy ourselves anent him in a free communing
with himself.

Wherefore, Mr David came to our last General
Meeting, which was upon December 22, 1686, being
accompanied by one James Kinloch, who was particularly sent by some societies in Ireland to our Correspondence, and who also testified before us all for Mr
David's honesty and innocency of the aforesaid allegations. After which, we did read over in Mr David's
hearing the introduction to our Vindication, wherein
are summarily comprehended some signal steps of our
church's defection, and a brief declaration of our present testimony, both as to what we own and disown,
together with the fifth head of the same Vindication,
containing (among other things) ten grounds, every one
of which we judge sufficient for withdrawing from
ministers of this covenanted and reformed church to

whom they are applicable, in this broken and declining state. Then we asked Mr David's judgment of what he had heard, and whether or not he was of one mind with us as to every part of our present testimony; to which he replied, that as to some matters of fact he was ignorant, but he agreed with our judgment and principles in all that he had heard, adding that it was foretold by Luther, That before Christ's glorious appearance for His church in the last days, the controversy should be stated and rid about ministry and magistracy. So Mr David being desired to remove, we gave in our minds about his answer, and it was sustained as satisfying in that point. After this, we consulted among ourselves what was necessary to desire for our further satisfaction anent him, and, having heard from himself that he had some papers with him which would tend to our information and clearing, concerning his carriage for many years, we called him to us again, and desired to hear these papers. So, there was read in our hearing, first his license, then his ordination, which was to the parish of ——, a little before the Restoration, next (as I remember) a paper which he had drawn up himself, and given to the ministers in Ireland, containing his reasons wherefore he would not be subordinate unto, nor concur with them, whereof their opposition to the suffering party in Scotland was one. Afterward were read some certificates, from the people in the respective places in Ireland where he had exercised his ministry, some whereof were of a very late date, and one of them bearing, that they had been greatly refreshed and edified with his preaching the gospel amongst them, but that he had denied them other privileges for reasons satisfying to himself; by which he declared they understood his refusing to baptise their children, because of their paying exactions to the enemy, and this we looked upon as the greater testimony. Further, we enquired how long he had kept a meeting-house in Ireland, and upon what terms. We then declared that the terms of his holding were not sinful, for he was settled by the ministers upon the call of the people. Whensoever he knew of any transaction of the said ministers with the so-called magistrate, he forsook his meeting-house, and refused subordination to these ministers, which was a little after Bothwell. Moreover he declared, and James Kinloch witnessed the same, that at the incoming of the associators, Anno 1685, he gave a plain and public testimony against that hotch-potch confederacy. Now, Mr David being desired to remove again, we communed together anent what we had heard from his papers and from his own mouth, and found a great measure of satisfaction therefrom. Howbeit, to remove scruples yet further, we called him again to us, and dealt freely with him in telling him what was reported, by some, of him, desiring to hear what he had to say to these things himself. All which allegations he heard very patiently, and answered to them one by one, as they were given in, very pleasantly ; and thus he gave very demonstrative evidences of his innocence.

Now, from all the foresaids, we being in such a measure satisfied in our consciences, concerning the said Mr David, our Societies did both call him, and hear him preach for further trial, whereunto I gave my consent, seeing no reason wherefore I could deny it. But he is not as yet settled amongst us as our minister by a formal and a solemn call to that effect. Howbeit, for the time, I know not of any ground that will be for excepting against it, for I hear that he preaches very zealously and faithfully wherever he goes, and carries strictly in administering the sacrament of baptism. For mine own part, from his expressing himself at our Correspondence, I thought he seemed to have a right state of the cause, and a right impression of the case of the church, and to be tender-hearted and zealous in the frame of his spirit, particularly for the royalties of Christ, and against the idol of the Lord's jealousy, the ecclesiastic supremacy and civil tyranny.

As for our carriage towards the foresaid Mr Alexander Shields, he, having by the providence of God made his escape out of prison, after a little space of time (without seeking after any party of ministers against whom we have exceptions) came to the country, unto this contending and suffering party. At length upon the 5th of December, 1686, he came to a meeting which we had in Galloway, in the wood of Earlston, for preaching. Going alongst with me from thence, upon the day following, I told him, albeit I had some satisfaction concerning him from what I had seen under his own hand, and albeit I expected more by further converse with him, yet I thought it most rational in itself, most conducive to the preservation of union amongst us, and also according to the conclusion of our General Meeting, that nothing which concerns the whole should be done without acquainting them therewith. I said, moreover, that he should not be employed in the public work until he came to the General Correspondence, that all might be satisfied anent him ; which he did take very well, and desired us to take that method with him which we would do with any backslidden minister, if God should touch his heart and bring him out from his defections unto the public work. Howbeit, we thought fit to employ him sometimes to go about family exercise, not seeing any reason why this should be forborne, for thereby we might attain to more clearness anent him. And, indeed, in a certain family, where some neighbours (as in ordinary) were gathered unto the worship, I was greatly refreshed with what he spake from Rom. xii. 12, especially with what he had in prayer, with a heavy lamentation to this purpose ; "I cannot longer contain, but I must confess unto the Lord before this people, I am ashamed to offer my body a living sacrifice to Thee, yet I must do it ; for I, a prisoner and a preacher, might have been a martyr, and in glory with Thee and Thy glorified martyrs above, but I sinfully and shamefully saved my life with disowning thy friends and owning thy

enemies, and it will be a wonder if ever Thou put
such an honourable opportunity in my hand again."
Very seldom did he go about exercise, but, either in
prayer, or in speaking from the scripture, he brake
forth into heavy lamentations, confessing particularly
his defections. So, at the time of our General Meeting
coming, which was December 22, as said is, the foresaid Mr Alexander came to the same, and we did read
over in his hearing (he being present with Mr David)
the introduction to our Vindication, wherein are comprehended some special steps of our church's defection,
and a brief declaration of our present testimony, both
as to what we own and disown, together with the fifth
head of the same Vindication, containing among other
things ten grounds, every one of which we judge sufficient for withdrawing from ministers of this covenanted
and reformed church to whom they are applicable, in
this broken and declining state. Then we asked
Mr Alexander's judgment concerning what he had
heard, and whether or not he was of one mind with us
as to every part of our present testimony. To which
he replied, that he agreed cordially with us in all that
he had heard, and particularly in the foresaid ten
grounds, judging every one of them to bear a solidity
and sufficiency in point of withdrawing. But, said he,
there are some things there testified against, whereof I
am guilty, and I will take a little time to unbosom myself unto you anent the same. So he began his confession with some pre-occupying cautions, desiring
that none might think he was moved to what he now
was about to do, from the affection of applause from
any man, or, that he might be in with a party (for he
knew he would not want alluring employment if he
had freedom to embrace it) but only that he might
give God the glory, vindicate the cause, exonerate his
own conscience, and satisfy offended brethren. In-
timating, also, that he looked not upon the Societies as
competent for handling ecclesiastic matters, and that he
knew they did not assume the same unto themselves,

though they were falsely branded therewith, yet he held himself bound in duty, to declare with sorrow before them, wherein he had denied any part of the testimony which they did own. Then he proceeded to the particulars of his confession, and acknowledged,—

1. That he had involved himself in the guilt of owning the (so-called) authority of James VII. showing the exceeding sinfulness of it, and taking shame unto himself.

2. He acknowledged himself guilty of taking the oath of Abjuration, and of relapsing into the same iniquity, the sinfulness whereof he held out at great length, making it appear, that by that oath many orthodox principles, which concern us greatly to contend for, are abjured. He declared the occasion of his being inveigled in these transgressions was the entering into an accommodation with the enemy; for he could propose nothing unto them but they still added and yielded to it, until they got him a silly fish catched in their angle. Howbeit, hereby (as he said) he did not extenuate or excuse his sin, for albeit he had as much to say for himself as any man could have, who had declared in such a measure, yet he would neither stifle his own conscience, nor blind the eyes of others, wherefore he showed both the sin and danger of entering upon any accommodation whatsoever with the enemy.

Now he spoke largely to all these particulars, discovering such heinous and manifold sin therein, that, I think, none could have done it, unless they had known the terrors of the Lord. He showed also the aggravation thereof, desiring every one to look upon his sin with the aggravating circumstances that he can see in it. And he expressed so much sense and ingenuousness, that none, I think, could require more of him; and I know not who would not have been satisfied as to the foresaids, who had heard him express himself so fully, so plainly, so freely, and with so much sense, grief, and self-condemning. I thought it both singular and promising, to see a clergyman come forth with such a confession of his own defections, when so few of that set are seen in our age to be honoured with the like.

So Mr Alexander being desired to remove, we communed together about what we heard, and all declared they found themselves satisfied as to the foresaids. After this, it was consulted amongst us what was necessary to desire for our further satisfaction anent him, and we judged it expedient to enquire how and by whom he was licensed to preach. Whereupon, I having conferred with him before thereanent gave a brief account thereof, and signified that, a considerable while ago, I saw it under his own hand, that if the business of his licence were to be done yet, he would neither take it from such persons, neither would they give it him, and that of late he said unto myself that he knew not one of those who had granted it that now he could concur with. However, we thought it convenient to call himself, that he might give an account thereof before us all, which he did, showing that he went to London with an intention to be an amanuensis to Dr Owen, or some of their great doctors who were writing books for the press, and that he had a letter of recommendation to one Mr Blackie, a Scottish minister, who trysted him to speak with him a certain season, and had several ministers convened, unknown to Mr Alexander, who did press and enjoin him to take licence. So, being carried unto it in that sudden and surprising way, he accepted it from the hands of Scottish ministers then in London, but without any impositions or sinful restrictions. However, a little after, the oath of allegiance becoming the trial of that place, the foresaid Mr Alexander studied, as he had occasion in preaching, plainly and satisfyingly to discover the sin of it, which was so ill taken by the ministers by whom he was licensed, that they threatened and sought to stop his mouth, but he refused to submit unto them.

Now, to this very purpose was the relation that Mr Alexander himself gave. So, considering what is before related, the Societies for themselves, and I, with the concurrence of some elders then present, did call him to officiate in preaching the word to the suffering remnant of this church. Wherefore, upon the Sabbath following, he and I did preach together, he having his text 2 Cor. v. 11, in these words, in the former part of the verse, viz. :—"Knowing, therefore, the terror of the Lord, we persuade men"; in which preaching, I may say, he particularly asserted every part of our present testimony, both as to non-compliance with enemies, non-concurrence with defective parties, and disowning the pretended authority of James VII., and also doctrinally confessed his own particular defections, and cried out, that "knowing the terror of the Lord" in these things he "persuaded men." Having appointed a fast upon the Thursday following, I briefly drew up about the number of forty-four causes of humiliation, omitting no piece of defection of old or of late, that I knew or could remember, which causes he cordially agreed with, and expressed the same publicly in his preaching before the congregation, declaring every one of them to be a great cause of humiliation. He confessed again his own defections, holding forth the sin thereof to be very heinous, with much sorrow and regret. So I find Mr Alexander to be one with us in our present testimony. I look upon him as having the zeal of God in his spirit, and the poor remnant have much of his heart; and, I think, the Lord is with him, and that he cannot be challenged as deficient in the application of his doctrine. For mine own part, I have been refreshed with hearing him, and have been animated to zeal by his preaching and discourse.

But there was a certain offence given by some, wherein Mr Alexander was a partaker, and wherewith I was dissatisfied, and that was their deserting of the testimony which some eminent worthies at Utrecht keep up against Mr Fleming, minister to the Scottish congregation at Rotterdam, in withdrawing from him for his manifest scandal ; which testimony I cordially (as heretofore) agree with, and look upon it (according as I know) as the first clear stating of our testimony in our later times, against the daubers and plasterers of defection. Wherefore I did speak with Mr Alexander anent the same : he knows my mind well enough in that affair. I expressed my dissatisfaction, and apprehended him to be sensible of the evils of that breach. As we were occasionally speaking of it at another time, he called their withdrawing, their testimony against Mr Fleming. Howbeit, considering that Mr Alexander's partaking in the foresaid offence was very little known in Scotland, and so they not being the persons offended ; considering his giving a practical testimony in that affair, by discountenancing the foresaid congregation, whatever time since that he hath been in Holland ; considering his present strictness, and cordial agreement with us in all our present controversies, and not knowing how to manage that affair to the edification of the Societies, I say upon these and such considerations it was not brought before the General Correspondence.

Now, Right Honourable and dear Sir, I have given you a true and full account of our carriage toward Mr Alexander Shields. If you were with him now, I think you would say as much for him as I have said ; for he doth not carry as a mids-man betwixt us and other parties, or one who endeavours to obscure and cast dirt upon our contendings, to jostle us off our feet and pervert us from the right ways of the Lord, but he hath taken the defence of every part of our present testimony. When I was telling him in discourse that the famous Mr Cameron had said in a sermon, that the Sanquhar Declaration would shake the throne of Britain, Mr Alexander replied, Yea, and the thrones of the kingdoms throughout the world. He hath a high esteem of the Queensferry papers,* and expressed his dissatisfaction that they were not more valued ; all which spoke forth his zeal and cordial

* Found on the person of Henry Hall of Haughhead (June 3, 1680), and generally attributed to Cargill.

agreement with the honest state of the cause, in hearing whereof I was not a little refreshed. I think, the Lord hath suffered him to fall into the hands of the enemies and to fall before them, for laying him low in humility, and raising him up in zeal. So, whatever may come to pass afterward, in the meantime I am made to look upon both Mr David's and his coming forth in such a manner, as a mercy to the poor church of Scotland. It hath been a means to wipe away some of our reproach from among men, and to put some dash upon the confidence of our oppressors, who, for ought I can hear, do look upon them both, as upon those whom they judge most obstinate among us. Howbeit, I shall be glad to have your thoughts anent what I have written, for I do reverence you and your judgment as much as ever.

Right Honourable and dear Sir, I know your bicker-ings are hot, and your encounters are fierce, and these multiplied upon you. You are hated and despised of men for your faithfulness and jealousy for your God. Yea, I am in great fear of your being in continual hazard of your life from Scottish men, or through their indignation ; the consideration of all which fills my heart with sorrow, when it comes before me, and sometimes draws water from mine eyes. But again, when I remember what a feast you have of peace of conscience and joy in the Lord, together what you have in hope, I am made to rejoice in the midst of my sorrow, and to account you a blessed man. O go on in the strength of the Lord. Fear not the anti-christian enemies. Grace is sufficient for you, victory is certain, and the prize waits for you.

Now, I leave the work upon Him, upon Whose shoulders the government is laid. I am apprehensive that the dark hour is now near at hand, which will come upon the church before Christ's glorious appear-ance in the last days. But He will rise and make a dispersion of His enemies, and he who endureth to the end shall be saved. I am, Right Honourable, yours as formerly, JAMES RENWICK.

P.S.—I am sometimes very much exercised in my thoughts about your coming to Scotland, but, considering what strange things may come out of it, and what hazard you will run, I dare not be peremptory in desiring you, until I see a weighty and urgent call unto it. But if matters be so with you as to determine positively, let me know, and a handful will call you, who will be your brethren and servants in tribulation for Christ.

JAMES RENWICK.

CHAPTER IX.

A NEW DEPARTURE.

OON after this a new departure was made by the King in his relations to his Scottish subjects. Forced at length to see that he could not obtain entire liberty for Roman Catholics and yet maintain the laws against Protestant Dissenters, at the beginning of 1687 James made his first hesitating and ungracious concessions to the Presbyterians. On the 12th of February, he published a Proclamation at Edinburgh, granting them permission to meet for worship in their own houses, but forbidding them to use a barn or out-house for religious exercises, and distinctly notifying that if they dared to hold conventicles in the open air the law which denounced death against both preachers and hearers should be enforced without mercy. This Proclamation was followed by two others of a similar import, on the 28th of June and the 5th October, the latter declaring that all persons, preachers, and hearers, present at any meeting in the open fields, shall be prosecuted with the utmost rigour of the law. Thus, while those, who accepted the indulgence and complied with its conditions, enjoyed a certain measure of liberty which had formerly been denied them, others, like Renwick, who for conscientious reasons rejected it, were more than ever exposed to suspicion and active hostilities. While the indulged ministers and people regarded these as troublers in Israel, the concentrated force of the enemy was directed against them. More particularly was this the case with Renwick, on whose shoulders the whole burden of the Covenanting struggle now rested. Shields and Houston, his former associates, had both left the country, the one for Holland, the other for Ireland, so that, alone and unassisted, he had to conduct the business of the United Societies, besides answering the numerous calls which were made upon him from different parts of the country, in his ministerial and pastoral character. Naturally of a delicate constitution, he was now often so prostrated with physical weakness and suffering that he had to be carried from place to place on the shoulders of his devoted followers or supported when on horseback. In Letter 54, which is addressed to Sir Alexander Gordon of Earlston, at this time a prisoner in the Bass, he refers specially to his work in the South of Scotland, knowing that this would interest him most.

LETTER LIV.

Jan. 27, 1687.

Honoured and dear Sir,--I have not been forgetful of you, though I have long delayed to write. The real occasion of my so long delay was the throng of business, (having so much to do, I being in continual travel) together with a designed forbearance, until I had this course finished in Galloway, that I might give you an account of the present case of this country. I had great access in it to preach the gospel, the Lord wonderfully restraining enemies, and drawing out very many to hear, and moving them to give great outward encouragement. We kept thirteen field meetings, whereof four were in the daylight, and I studied quickly to declare and assert in its own place every part of our present testimony. We had also nine meetings for examination of the Societies, calling the most adjacent together into one meeting for that effect. And I hope, through the Lord's blessing, that that small piece of labour shall not want its fruit. But upon the other hand, I met with no small opposition in Galloway. I went to that shire, and preached there; a great many were vexed, and did their utmost to oppose it. When I came to Kirkmabreak, there came two men and gave me a paper, subscribed by one in Carrick, in name of all therein between Cree and Dee, and also in the name of the whole: which paper overturns many noble pieces of our Reformation, calling hearing of curates, paying of cess, and swearing the abjuration oath, debateable principles, and above their capacity to determine. It bears also a viperous protestation against my preaching, besides many other absurdities in it, which when I read, I gave my animadversions upon it before the two men. On the Thursday following, we kept a public day meeting in the fields, between Cree and Dee. I thought fit, after lecture, which was one upon the xv. Psalm, and sermon, which was upon Song 'of Solomon' ii. 2. to read over the paper before the multitude, that I might let them know what was done in their names, giving my own animadversions upon the same, and exhorting them, if any such were there, who had given their countenance and concurrence to it, that they would speedily with sorrow draw back their hand from such an iniquity. Those who were free to take their protestation before the Lord that they were innocent, and did resent the doing of such a deed in their name, ought to do so. Withal I warned them of the dangerousness of that course, and of the spirit of that party. Likewise, when I came to Irongray, Cornlee came unto me, and before some few, who were meeting for examination, and some others who accompanied me in my

travels, he took instruments against me, and against
my entering into Irongray. Whereupon I gave some
weighty reasons, wherefore I could not look upon his
deed as the deed of a faithful elder in that parish, and
I also cleared some controverted points of our testimony. But he was so drunk, either with wine, or with
the fury of the Lord, or with both, that he could hear
nothing, and he answered with nothing but with
clamour and crying (O the depths of Satan!) that I had
destroyed the church, and that the ministers had a libel
drawn up against me. Whereupon I declared that none
of these things did terrify me, and that this was the
work of the Lord, and that I was resolved, in His
strength, to go on in it, while my breath governed my
joints, and I enjoined silence upon him. I think, by
such an attempt that he hath done no skaith either to
the work or to the owners of it.

Now, Right Honourable Sir, you see some of my conflicts. I bless the Lord, none of these things terrify
me. I think, they are very pusillanimous, who do not
find such hot bickerings a mean to ding a spirit into
them. O that we might be such as could say, Isa. viii.
9, 10, "Associate yourselves, O ye people, and ye shall
be broken in pieces. Gird yourselves, and ye shall be
broken in pieces. Take counsel together, and it shall
come to nought; speak the word, and it shall not
stand; for God is with us." But, further, as to the Societies in Galloway, there are some of them simple,
whom we have much ado to keep right, do what we
can. But there are some others, both in Glenkers and
other places, whom I look upon as bows of steel in the
Lord's hand, and who, I hope, through His grace, shall
abide in strength.

Now, Right noble and dear Sir, I hope not to forget
you, but to mind your case in my weak addresses to the
Lord. I may say, you are very often brought before
me, and, next to my own case, and the church's case,
the case of you and your family, those abroad and those
at home, do lie upon my heart. Lie near the Lord and

wait upon Him. Who knoweth what the Lord may do with you, and for you? He may be humbling and polishing you for some great piece of work. As to our way at last meeting with Mr David Houston and Mr Alexander Shields, you will see it in the letter directed to your worthy brother, to whom I desire you may send this, and the other directed for yourself, for his information; at least so much may be extracted out of this, as you think fit, because I cannot have time to write anent the same things unto him. I commend you to your God, and am, your Honour's obliged friend, and servant in the Lord,   JAMES RENWICK.

The next letter is without date, but may be suitably introduced in this place. It is Renwick's reply to the paper already mentioned, signed by a respected minister in Carrick "in name of all therein between Cree and Dee, and also in name of the whole."

LETTER LV.

As it doth not a little grieve me that such a paper should have come from your hands, who profess adherence to Presbyterian government, who have suffered so much at the hands of the common enemy, and with whom, at least with some of you, I have gone some time to the house of God in company, and have been in some perils because of the sword of the adversary;

So, albeit I am conscious to myself of no desire nor delight in keeping up needless strifes, and vain janglings, of no design to render any persons or party odious, also of no inclination to resent private and personal injuries: yet, when I perceive the truths of God and the work of Reformation, which have been transmitted to us through the wrestlings and blood of our worthy martyrs, in a great measure, like to be buried, and many valiant and honourable contendings and sufferings of Christ's witnesses in our age, condemned and forgotten, I say, when I perceive this, I cannot, I dare not keep silence.

Therefore your paper being given unto me, November 2d, 1686, and finding it so prejudicial to the interest of Christ, I have thought fit, with sorrow, sobriety, and candour, to make some animadversions upon it.

1. The scope and design of it is, to stop the preaching of the gospel.

2. When you speak of division, you do not deduce the same from its own original. For you say that the cause thereof partly proceeds from some paying cess, hearing curates, and taking the late abjuration oath ; and partly from others condemning these things, adhering to the late Declaration on church doors, and receiving of, and adhering to Mr James Renwick, without the consent and approbation of the remnant of godly and faithful ministers, &c. Whereas it is well known to all who are not strangers to the case of our church, that divisions abounded as much before there were any thoughts of that Declaration, and before I, though most unworthy of such an honour, did put my hand to the public work. I judge our divisions have their more native rise and real progress from a party who still cleave to the malignant interest, and who fell upon public resolutions to bring known malignants into places of power and trust :—from the many Presbyterian ministers, who changed their commission, and exercised their ministry under this abjured Anti-christian Prelacy :—from others, who took a new holding of their ministry from an arrogated headship over the church, by accepting indulgences, warrants, and restrictions from the usurper of their Master's crown :—from others, who did meet in Presbyteries to censure the more faithful, for discovering the sin of the Indulgence :—from others who at Bothwell opposed the keeping of a day of humiliation for the sins of the time, and foisted in the late tyrant's interest into the declaration of the army :—from others, who after Bothwell induced the prisoners, taken at that fatal defeat, to subscribe the

o

conscience-defiling bond of peace :—from others, who tolerated, or advised people to compliance with other abominations of the time :—from others, who have been unfaithful in not applying their doctrine against the prevailing sins of our day :—from others, who have satisfied themselves to lie by from the exercise of their ministry, and desisted from the work of the Lord, and that when His vineyard stood most in need :—and from others who have gone into, carried on, or countenanced a hotch-potch confederacy with malignants and sectaries, and temporizing compliers ; and finally, from all, whether ministers or people, who have carried on, plaistered, or strengthened any course of defection, through the course of this church's sinful and lamentable revolt.

3. You very inconsiderately say, "that the cause of "this division proceeds partly from some paying cess, "hearing curates, and taking the late abjuration oath ; "and partly from others condemning these things, ad- "hering to the late Declaration, and receiving of, and "adhering to Mr James Renwick, without the consent "of the remnant of godly and faithful ministers of the "church of Scotland." Herein no small contradiction and absurdity are implied. For, in your accounts, the paying of cess, the hearing of curates, and taking the abjuration oath, have caused division, and the con-demning the foresaids hath done the like. Now a practical condemning of these things is a not doing of them, and the same charge laid against the doing of a thing, and the not doing of the same thing, is flatly contradictory. You judge that the condemning of sin as well as the practising of it must, either in part or in whole, bear the blame of division.

Is not this most absurd ? Is not this sad misreckon-ing ? Though you should say that the practising of the foresaid evils hath caused a sad division, and the con-demning of the same a just and warrantable division, yet that cannot be here meant, because you speak only of the division which hath scandalous and woeful effects. As to the forementioned Declaration, I know some of

the ministers and many of yourselves opened not a
mouth against it, when they thought it subservient to
their designs. And as for the receiving of, and adhering
to Mr James Renwick, as you say, without the consent
of the godly and faithful ministers of the church of Scotland, it is not pertinent for me to answer much unto it,
as you give it forth. Only seeing there are so many
ministers, and fractions of parties, I desire to know
to whom, or if to all, you give that signature FAITHFUL ;
and whether or not, you judge that I ought to have
sought the consent, and approbation of any that are
UNFAITHFUL. Whereas you speak of this receiving and
adhering, as you term it, as being contrary to the laudable practice of this church, and Acts of the General
Assemblies, you would be pleased to consider the
broken and declining state of this church, and then
instance either practice, or Act, whereof you speak.

4. You overturn some material pieces of our attained
Reformation. For, the paying of cess, hearing the
curates, and taking the abjuration oath are brought in
debate, and exhibited as above your capacity to decide
and determine. You do tacitly insinuate a forbearance
to meddle in these things, as if they were not worthy to
be contended against; but you say you will submit yourselves, in all the foresaids, to an Assembly, as you say, of
faithful ministers and elders.

Where can you get a more faithful Assembly to decide these matters, than our venerable Assemblies, that
have decided the same already ? Where can you have a
more faithful decision than they have given, by their
Acts, according to the word of God ? As for the paying
of cess, does not the Act of the General Assembly,
June 17th, 1646, Sess. 14, for censuring compliers with
the enemies of this kirk and kingdom, sufficiently determine the same ? As for hearing the curates—do not our
Covenants, National and Solemn League, convincingly
condemn the same ? As for the Abjuration Oath—does
not the Act of the Assembly, June 28th, 1648, Sess. 14,
against all oaths and bonds in the common cause with-

out the consent of the church, clearly decide the same? If these things be now debateable principles, all the actings and sufferings that have been these twenty-six years and more may be brought in debate and the justness thereof questioned.

Had our Assemblies no authority? or did they not give right decisions in these matters, that are now resiled from, and their sentences referred to the decision of others? Yea, where shall so many ministers now be had, as to make up an Assembly, except those who are practising or tolerating the foresaid evils? Moreover, if an Assembly, less or greater, should give out an Act or sentence, for the lawfulness of paying the cess, hearing the curates, and taking the abjuration oath, would you stand to it? If you would stand to it, would not that be an implicit submission, and an obeying of man, rather than God? If you would not stand to it, where is your submission in these points? For my part, what is clearly decided already, both divinely and ecclesiastically, I will never refer to the decision of any man. Shall I submit it to man to determine whether or not the soul of man is immortal? Or whether there be more sacraments than two? Let Assemblies confirm, ratify, and approve undoubted, uncontroverted truths, and those things that have been already justly and clearly decided; but let none give unto them the determination and decision of these things.

5. "You give forth the paying of cess, the hearing "of curates, and the taking the Abjuration Oath, upon "the one hand, and, upon the other hand, the condemn-"ing of these things, the adhering to the foresaid "Declaration, and receiving of, and adhering to Mr "James Renwick," &c., as debateable principles, and practices, and matters above our capacity to decide. Then you assume to yourselves the determining that none shall call or join with the said Mr James Renwick. Doth not this imply, first, a contradiction? You cannot determine, and yet you do determine; you will not decide, and yet you do decide. Does it not import,

secondly, that it is a matter in debate with you, whether or not people may hear the curates? It is out of our debate with you, whether or not people may hear the curates. But it is out of all debate with you, that you ought not to join with me in my ministry; and yet, in what precedes in your paper, you give forth the receiving of me, only as a debateable thing. How sufficient a ground is a matter debateable with the Protesters, to enter such a resolved Protestation upon, let any man of reason judge.

6. The ground you walk upon, in your paper, in forbearing to call or join with Mr James Renwick, and for marching in such violent opposition against him, is because his ordination is not seen, and approved, as you say, by the faithful ministers of the Church of Scotland. This, in your account, albeit in the broken and declined state of the church, is more sinful, scandalous, and offensive than all that can be tabled against the curates. For this gives you ground to determine not only a forbearance to join with, but also a direct opposition unto my ministry. Whereas, all that you have against the curates is in debate, as is said, whether or not they may be heard.

Howbeit, as to my ordination, it is valid and lawful, and I refuse not to give all possible satisfaction to any who may be conscientiously desirous to hear. Neither refuse I to satisfy any faithful minister thereanent, who may seek the same. Yea, hearing that a certain minister of the Church of Scotland was desirous of information anent my ordination, I did write unto him a true transcript of the certificate of the same, with my judgment as to the chief things controverted in our day; but I never received an answer. Likewise, some other ministers, whom you know, Messrs Barclay and Langlands, shewed their willingness to have a concurrence between them and me, and to lay all debates aside; which I could not do, except these offensive courses were resented and relinquished. They made no exception against me on account of my ordination not having been seen and approved by the ministers, &c.

I refuse not to satisfy any faithful ministers upon that head,—and I am willing to yield all due subjection unto them in the Lord. Nevertheless, I humbly conceive, that those bear not the signatures of faithful ministers, and of such as I am subject unto, who have directly and actually complied with the enemies of this covenanted church and kingdom ; or who defend, excuse, plaister, or cover and tolerate compliances with the foresaid enemies, and their palpable defection from the reformation of this church ; or who pervert their ministry by contradicting our present Testimony, founded upon and agreeable to the Scriptures, our Confession and Covenants ; or who have deserted ministerial duties, and desisted from the public work of preaching the gospel, for fear of hazard ; or who have divided the church, and calumniated and condemned the more faithful.

Now, passing by others whom I might mention, I say I humbly conceive that ministers, guilty of all or any, more or less of the foresaids, are not such as in conscience I can be subject to, considering these charges with application to ministers of this organical church, under the same bond of Covenant with us, and obliged to maintain the same word of testimony, and with respect to the broken and declined state of this church. These things will be found sufficient to warrant my non-subjection to those, while such, to whom they are duly applicable.

7. You call the foresaid Mr James Renwick's preaching upon a call, without previous submission to ministers, against whom he has just exceptions, "a horrid and abominable usurpation and intrusion." Whereas, it cannot be called usurpation, because I have a protestative mission to exercise all the parts of my ministry. Neither can it be called intrusion upon the labours of any faithful minister of Christ. For I declare, with grief and lamentation, that I travelled for a consider-

able space of time through the country of Scotland,
where professors and sufferers did most abound, and in
all my journeys I never heard of any labouring, save the
indulged for a season, and the curates. I think I may
say before God, that it was pity toward the scattered
sheep of Christ in this land, who were fainting and
swooning through the famine of public ordinances, that
moved me to subject myself, in such a weak condition,
to so great a work, and to undergo so many perils and
wanderings. It is most likely, if labourers had been
faithful and laborious, I had laboured none to this very
day.

8. You signify your resolution to protest against the
foresaid Mr Renwick's preaching, as "horrid and
abominable usurpation and intrusion upon you and
your labours, till such time (mark it) as you have the
mind of your faithful ministers anent the foresaid
things."

What are these things? They are nothing, if they
be not the cess-paying, hearing curates, and taking the
Abjuration Oath upon the one hand, and, upon the other
hand, the condemning these things, and adhering to the
foresaid Declaration, and receiving of, and adhering to
the above-named person, without the consent and
approbation, as you say, of the remnant of godly and
faithful ministers, &c.

I am content indeed, that you cast upon the receivers
of my ministry the brand of condemning these iniquities;
but does not this that you say confirm what I have instructed in animadversion fourth, namely, that you
have overturned some great and material pieces of
our Reformation, and brought in debate what was out
of debate, and that you will have a new decision of what
has been by the authority of the Church of Scotland,
long ago, very well decided? What if these faithful
ministers shall counsel you to pay the cess, hear the
curates, and allow taking the Abjuration Oath? If you
follow their counsel, where will you be? and if you
follow it not, how can you hang your resolved Protesta-

tion upon it? But herein you have inveigled yourselves in a great intricacy: for some of the ministers, whom you account faithful, will tolerate, if not defend, the paying of cess, and others will condemn it. Some of them will allow of taking the Abjuration Oath, and others will, at least did, disapprove of it. Some of them will wink at hearing of curates, and others will testify against it. Now, whom will you follow? and whose determination will you follow in your appeal? Have you not brought yourselves by this into a great difficulty?

9. You express yourselves with such confusion, as I know not whether to look upon you as men in office or out of office, or both. You speak with one breath as if you were ministers, and yet also, only as people: for you say, "If the foresaid Mr James Renwick, at the desire of strangers, or any of your brethren dividing from you, shall intrude himself on your labours, without your call or consent, till such time as you have the mind of your faithful ministers anent the foresaid things, you will protest against it as a horrid intrusion on your labours." If you be people, your labours cannot be intruded upon by the exercise of the ministerial function. If you be ministers, how come you to say, "That you must have the mind of your faithful ministers?" I never knew ministers speak so. Though you should say that you are both ministers and people, yet none can free such a speech of worse than an error in language. I do verily wonder, how you can build such absurdities upon some expressions in some of our former papers, which many of you once owned, and which can bear a far other and better sense than you put upon them: and, in the meantime, you yourselves fall into a greater fault. If I thought that any clergyman had penned your paper, I would take a little liberty to discover its contradictions and confusions, to say no worse, and that he hath not adverted to his work when he wrote it. To what I have observed in it, giving me occasion to take it as the draft of illiterate

men, who sometimes cannot aptly express their meaning, I shall be the more favourable, and shall forbear.

10. You say, "that you will look upon Mr James Renwick's preaching the gospel, without subjection to such ministers as he hath sufficient exceptions against, to be divisive and destructive to the poor suffering remnant of this church." Whereunto I shall reply nothing, but that the faithful remnant of this church, who suffer most, both by the hands and tongues of men, do not look with your eyes.

11. You give in your paper subscribed by a faithful and creditable man indeed, William M'Hutchison, in the name of that place of the Stewartry of Galloway, betwixt Cree and Dee :—whereby you have done an injury to some conscientious sufferers and owners of truth in that place, who do abominate your deed. You also do injury to yourselves by using a designation so comprehensive as to exclude none, either Papists or malignants, who reside there. And again you say,— "in the name of the whole." Is that of the whole of your party? Does not this give just ground of exception against the whole of your party?

Now, having in weakness, though with studied candour and sobriety, briefly animadverted upon some things in your paper, wherein I conceived to lie the greatest prejudices to the work of the Lord, I shall not touch some other things in it, which may be looked upon as importing only weakness, choosing rather to cover these, and pass them in silence.

Notwithstanding of all that you have done against me, I have love to you, and desire to behave myself as a friend. Yea, I may say, I am filled with a great measure of sorrow and amazement when I consider your present course and carriage, and compare it with your former. Many of you and I have wandered in the silent watches of the night together, been in perils together, fled from the sword of the common adversary together: and I appeal to yourselves, if you have not found sometimes something of the power of God in our solemnities together. You have suffered much at the hand of the enemy, even to the shedding of the blood of many of you, which I hope was acceptable to God, and is a part of the seed of the church. You professed with us the same thing that we own and profess this day; you were the most forward for action, and we gloried in you, and boasted of you, and I think this hath been our sin, and a part of the cause of your judgment.

Howbeit, there are some things wherein you have greatly wronged the cause of Christ, which, out of respect to that cause, and love to your souls, I shall bring to your remembrance, and set before you, for your serious consideration.

Therefore, I say, consider, when you were professing a concurrence with us in the stated testimony of our day, what underhand dealing you had with other parties, without once acquainting us therewith, from which both you and we were obliged to stand at a due distance.

Consider how you divided from us, and joined with ministers chargeable with sundry offences, still defended, and who have now gone that length that I know not any ministers, however sadly turned aside, from whom you stand at a distance. Yea, do not some of them, whom you call and embrace, calumniate and condemn the more faithful remnant, uttering as untender and uncharitable expressions concerning them, as they can do of the persecuting enemy?

By what warrant should they be heard preach, who speak lies in the name of the Lord? Consider, whether are the ministers who lurk and reside at Edinburgh, and who are chargeable with other things than at present I shall name,—I say, are they now become such unto you, that you will receive no ministers but such as have an approbation and warrant from them? Consider, also, how many temporizing compliers you have received into your select societies.

Consider how you came to our General Meeting, Jan. 28th, 1686, with what purpose of uniting with us the Lord knows; and, when we were using all means to

conciliate a union in the Lord, you dealt very disingen-
uously with us. When we, because of your sundry
offences no way resented by you, did conscientiously, in
our own names, refuse your concurrence with us in
selected Christian fellowship, you went away and did
spread sad lies and calumnies of us.

Consider how you have dispersed your papers and
pamphlets,—with what truth and tenderness, as to the
charges therein contained, we leave to every conscientious Christian who knows us to judge.

Consider how you have by letters, informations,
counsels, and protestations, with more zeal, opposed and
contended against an afflicted witnessing remnant, than
ever you did against the anti-christian hierarchy. And
though the Lord knows, as far as I can see into my
heart, I mention it not to resent any injury done unto
myself, yet I must desire you to consider how when I
came to your border, offering to converse with you, and
willing to preach the gospel, as formerly I had done in
that place, you would let none speak with me but such
as you pleased. You separated from me when I was
going about family exercise, and you also protested
against both my preaching and converse.

Consider what errors, absurdities, contradictions, &c.,
are stuffed into your paper prefixed. O, I say, consider
and take a look of these things ; how thereby you have
sadly wronged the interest of Christ,—have made the
enemy to blaspheme,—made conscientious sufferers to
stumble and fall,—to grope in the dark, not knowing
what to choose or refuse,—have hardened the hearts, and
strengthened the hands of those who are engaged in a
course of defection, so that they do not turn from the
evil of their ways,—have done so much to deprive
posterity of the truths which ought to be transmitted to
them ; and, finally, how you have thereby sinned against
your own souls.

Now, I beseech you, consider your ways. And that
the Lord may pour out on you the spirit of mourning
and turning, is the prayer of him, who is your soul's
well-wisher, JAMES RENWICK.

The next letter is addressed to a Dutch minister, the
Rev. Jacob Koelman, who had been a warm friend of
Renwick, but whose mind had recently been pre-
judiced against him.

Letter LVI.

April 4, 1687.

Right Reverend and beloved brother,—I received
your letter in Latin, but, knowing that you are well
versed in English, I need not write back to you in
that same language. I beg your excuse for so long
delaying an answer; for, as it was a considerable space
of time after the date of your letter, before it came to
my hand, so, since I received it, I have been in such
a measure busied with weighty work and excessive
travel, that scarcely could I borrow one hour from the
one or from the other.

I thankfully accept of your ministerial, friendly, and
brotherly advice unto union. So far as I can see into
my heart (but a man cannot see far into a millstone), I
am as much for a right qualified union as any, and look
upon that as good and pleasant, as Psal. cxxxiii. i.
But, the union which is had without truth and holiness
I can call no other thing but a conspiracy, such as was
found among the men of Judah, Jer. xi. 9. and the
prophets of Jerusalem, Ezek. xxii. 25. I cannot unite,
where I must thereby harden the hearts and strengthen
the hands of such as are engaged in, and carrying on a
course of defection and backsliding from the Lord,
and so partake of their sins, and render myself obnoxious to their plagues. I cannot unite, where I
cannot expect the propagating of the words of Christ's
patience, deposited to us at this time to contend and
suffer for. In reference to both cases, in regulating
my carriage toward ministers of this organical church,
in this her broken and declining state, I desire to mind
what is given in command to Jeremiah, chap. xv. 19,

"Let them return unto thee, but return not thou unto them." I must not divide from the Head to unite with any professed members. But ministers, even of this church, who are clothed with Christ's commission, who are free of censurable personal scandal, who do own and maintain this church's testimony, and who either have kept free of the palpable and gross defections of the time, or else do relinquish and resent the same, I say, with all such I account it my joy, honour and duty to unite, and my practice proveth as much as I say. As for my principles, I am able to manifest them to have their warrant both from the supreme divine authority in the word of God in the Scriptures, and the subordinate ecclesiastical authority of our church constitutions. So this is no new way that I am following, but the good old way, wherein I see the footsteps of our Lord, *cujus vita nos omnia docere potest,** and the print of the feet of our worthy and resolute Reformers, and those who in our day have valiantly and faithfully maintained and sealed with their blood the received and sworn principles of our Reformation.

I acknowledge, as you write, Reverend and beloved, that I may learn many things from my brethren into which I have not enough penetrated, for I am but of yesterday, and what know I? Though they were in a worse course than they are, I would learn what is good from them, for *Fas est ab hoste doceri.†* I acknowledge many of them to be pious and learned, and I will imitate them in what I find to be right. But ah, I cannot see, as they now stand, how I can learn faithfulness and zeal from them; and as for their worldly prudentials, I hope not to learn these. They have lost a good special for the general; they have quit the Presbyterian plea for the Protestant, as is clear in their declaration, wherein malignants and sectaries may compear for their interest. But for my part, I much rather agree with our venerable Assembly,

* Whose life can teach us all things.
† It is lawful to be taught by an enemy.

who, in a paper bearing the date of July 25th, 1648, in answer to the offer of the Committee of Estates, do show, that they had represented to the high court of Parliament, that for securing of religion it was necessary that the Popish, Prelatical and malignant party be declared enemies to the cause, upon the one hand, as well as sectaries, upon the other, and that all associations, either in forces or counsels, with the former, as well as the latter, be avoided. I cannot see, that those means that have destroyed the work of the Lord shall ever be made use of by Him, for raising up the same again. You say well, that *vis irruita longe fortior est quam dispersa ;* * yet that must be taken with a grain of salt, for I must take heed *in quo et cum quibus vis irruita.*† I must unite my poor force both in a good cause, and with such persons as I may lawfully do it. —Now, I hope you will not take it in ill part that I desire you to beware of precipitancy, in receiving and spreading informations against us. I know you are informed in many falsities, and you do credulously believe and sedulously spread the same. This from the hand of famous, learned and godly Koelman is most wounding to me. But you will find in the end that they have not been your friends who have prompted you to such a work.

I cannot but wonder at the difference of your discourse with Mr Hamilton at Leewarden, from the strain of your discreet letter unto me. We little need any to cast oil into our flames. For my part, it is my study not to be bitter against the bitterness of others, not to be reviled into a reviler, nor scoffed into a scoffer, so as to return the same to others as they are to me, neither to throw back my brother's fire-balls into his own face, lest in censuring him I also be my own judge. Though the sourness of others offend me, yet it should not. But I will quiet my spirit in waiting upon the Lord, until

* A force acting together is much more powerful than one divided and scattered.

† In what and with whom the power is acting together.

He bring forth the righteousness of His cause, and the innocence of His servants. I know some can accuse or excuse as they see it makes for their purpose. I can prove it by many witnesses, that Mr George Barclay, and Mr Robert Langlands, before a multitude, accused the church of Holland of Popery, in using three sprinklings in baptism; and of the grossest Erastianism, saying that the magistrate would send the minister a pair of shoes, and dismiss him when he pleased. This was exhibited as a charge against your whole church; but now I am informed, that Mr Barclay flatly denieth such a thing. I desire to know whether or not you judge the church of Holland wronged by this means. And certain I am that a cause maintained after such a manner shall not succeed. Likewise I must say, that I think it strange that any of our ministers should seek to have a union procured betwixt them and us, while they do represent us to be as bad as heretics, and look upon us as unworthy of a charitable construction. I like not to beg charity, but I would not desire (if I may say, demand) what is not right. However, until we be melted, we can never be moulded up into one. If we had nothing a-do but to please one another, and if we were once set right in our ends, an accommodation about all the differences as to the means would be the more facile and feasible (Prov. xi. 3, 5).

Now, Right Reverend, I shall not detain you further. I do thankfully accept your necessary and Christian advices, toward the close of your letter. It is my prayer to the Lord, that I may be helped to follow them. I heartily wish you may soon come to a better understanding of this poor afflicted, reproached Remnant. I am, Right Reverend and beloved brother, your affectionate friend, and servant in the Lord,

JAMES RENWICK.

Letter LVII.

Those to whom this letter is addressed had recently been condemned to banishment. During the twenty-eight years of persecution in Scotland, a very large number suffered in this way. According to the Author of the "Scots Worthies," no fewer than "1700 were shipped to the plantations, besides 750 who were banished to the northern islands."

April, 1687.

Beloved friends,—As my time will not allow me to write largely unto you, so you must accept this short and insignificant line, as a token of my consideration of your lot, and concernedness with it. Your case is somewhat singular, for banishment will readily be looked upon as a great trial for you, through the prospect of many snares, fears and distresses, whereunto you may be subjected. Howbeit, you may have no small peace and consolation from the consideration that you could not evade it, unless you had denied truth. Whatever sufferings you may meet with from your countrymen, from the seas, and from foreigners, you may reckon it all upon the honourable account of your duty. But, my friends, O do not fear the difficulties and perplexities that sense and reason may apprehend to be abiding you. For the Lord's children have often found it by experience, that their present fears have been greater than their future troubles, and that they have oftentimes been more frightened than hurt. He that made a passage for His chosen through the Red Sea and the swellings of Jordan can give you a dry foot passage through all the waters and floods of your afflictions. Take your eyes off the vain things of this world. Look not back on old lovers, but delight yourselves in Christ alone, who is your exceeding rich reward, your satisfying and everlasting portion. Take Him with you. O He is sweet company! and He "will never leave you, nor forsake you." Yea, in the time of your greatest trouble He will be most near you, and in your greatest distresses He will be most kind. Be careful of nothing but how to please Him, and to honour Him in all places whither you may be scattered.

Now, commending you to His grace, which I pray may be sufficient for you, I am, your sympathising friend and servant in the Lord,   JAMES RENWICK.

LETTER LVIII.

July 15, 1687.

Honourable and dear Sir,—You may readily be offended with my long delay in writing to you, but your knowing the cause thereof, I am hopeful, will remove it. My business was never so weighty, so multiplied, and so ill to be guided, to my apprehension, as it hath been this year ; and my body was never so frail. Excessive travel, night wanderings, unseasonable sleep and diet, and frequent preaching in all seasons of weather, especially in the night, have so debilitated me, that I am often incapable for any work. I find myself greatly weakened inwardly, so that I sometimes fall into fits of swooning and fainting. I take seldom any meat or drink, but it fights with my stomach ; and for strong drink, I can take almost none of it. When I use means for my recovery, I find it someways effectual ; but my desire to the work, and the necessity and importunity of people, prompts me to do more than my natural strength will well allow, and to undertake such toilsome business as casts my body presently down again. I mention not this through any anxiety, quarrelling, or discontent, but to show you my condition in this respect. I may say, that, under all my frailties and distempers, I find great peace and sweetness in reflecting upon the occasion thereof. It is a part of my glory and joy to bear such infirmities, contracted through my poor and small labour, in my Master's

P

vineyard. But to leave this, I tell you truly, that I have no more jealousy of you than ever, for I know no ground for it, and I hope you will not take up any suspicion of me. Therefore though multitude of business, or bodily sickness, may divert me from so frequent writing unto you, as need were, you would have me excused, and construct rightly and favourably of me. I say not this, that I purpose to neglect it, or that I will allow myself in that neglect, but to prevent my need of using any further apology of this kind.

Right Honourable and dear Sir, if I had the tongue of the eloquent, and the pen of a ready writer, my desire would be to employ both in praise of the Great King. O! "Who is like the Lord amongst the gods? Who is like Him, glorious in holiness, fearful in praises, doing wonders!" We are rebels and outlaws, we are lost and undone for ever; but He hath made a covenant with us, and given Himself a ransom. This covenant is everlasting, "well ordered in all things and sure." It hath all fulness in it, for the matter; all wisdom, for the manner; all condescendence, in the terms. It is most engaging in its end, being made to bring about the peace and salvation of sinners; and it is most necessary, for there is no journeying to heaven without it. This then is the chariot that will carry us into the joy and rest of our Lord; this is the chariot wherein His glory and our good ride triumphantly together, for it is made for Himself and the daughters of Jerusalem. This is the chariot that hath "the pillars of silver, the bottom of gold, the covering of purple, and the midst of it paved with love." O what a pavement is there! what lining and stuffing is there! O happy are they who are taken up into this chariot! They stand upon love, they sit upon love, they lie upon love, and, if they fall, they fall soft, for they fall upon love. Those who are without may see somewhat of its glittering and beauty, yet none can know the heart and the bowels of it and the love that is there, but those that are within. O! Sir, can you not say, you are taken in with the King into this glorious piece of His workmanship? Then why should you fear? Though Satan and his instruments compass you about, and shoot at you upon all hands, yet you are well guarded. You are not only riding with the King in His chariot, but lying with Him in His bed, which has round about it threescore valiant men, of the valiant of Israel, standing well appointed, and in a ready posture, for your defence. The angels and the attributes of God are a good and sure defence. However you may be surrounded with the world's malice and hatred, His love is still about you, and always next unto you. O advance with that princely disposition and carriage that becometh one of so royal a descent, being a son of the great King, the Almighty Lord God, by your adoption and regeneration. Fear not what the worms of the earth can do unto you; they are His poor, chained, weak creatures. Let them be counted as ashes under the soles of your feet. Your cause is glorious, your leader gracious, your victory certain, your reward sure, and your triumph everlasting. O let all your care be to choose and do, every thing, what may please Him; and encourage yourself in Him, for He will not leave you nor forsake you. You know not what great things He may do for you, and by you, ere you pass your sojourning and pilgrimage in this earth. The more dark and stormy that our night may be, the nearer is our morning. The hour of our great tribulation and temptation is coming: it is fast approaching, and it will haste to its end; and blessed shall every one be who keepeth the word of Christ's patience.

I can inform you of little, as to the case of this land, but what you know. The enemies are restrained from the execution of their rage in the former measure, but they are consulting and plotting the utter ruin and razing of the interests and followers of Christ: for they neither follow their nature nor designs, whatever method they follow. If this were believed, people would not so readily be hood-winked with their pretences of favour;

but, after so much sad experience, none who will not wilfully blindfold themselves need to be beguiled. There is a liberty now issued forth from the arrogant, absolute, and uncontrollable power of the intruder and usurper, upon the prerogative of the great God, bounded with the restriction that his government may not be spoken against, and nothing said that may alienate the hearts of the people from him ; prescribing the place of preaching to be only in houses, inhibiting the worship of God in the fields, commanding the severe execution of all the iniquitous laws against all such meetings, and requiring ministers to give up their names to some one or other of the civil powers ; which restricted and strangely qualified liberty to Presbyterians is conveyed through the ceasing and disenabling of all our penal laws and statutes enacted against Papists, and the toleration of all heresies and sects.

The generality of this generation esteem peace as their great good, and they covet and desiderate it upon any terms. But the Lord saith, "They shall not have peace :" they have left the way of peace, and He will trouble them. The cloud is fast fast gathering, which will fall down as the irruption and inundation of a flood, and overflow the land. Happy are they who have fled into their city of refuge.

Before the publication of this Indulgence, sundry Presbyterian ministers, who had been more lurking formerly, began to travel through the country, and officiate in houses, and that in somewhat of a public manner. Mr Samuel Arnot preaching upon a Sabbath, in the daylight, about a mile from Glasgow, a considerable company of people being within and without doors, a party of soldiers went out of the town, and scattered the meeting, apprehending near to a hundred men and women, stripping them of their clothes, and taking their money from them, and laying them in prison. These were afterwards sent to Edinburgh, and, as I am informed, are all liberated, save one man, who would not call Bothwell-bridge rebellion. But now the ministers are all generally preaching, and some who had been hearing the curates are falling to again; but I hear of little freedom amongst them anent the sins of the time. Some of them who had professed clearness against paying the cess begin now to tolerate it, saying, that the narrative of the Act falls, seeing the term is expired, though the cess be continued, and so it is not sinful. Others say, there is no scandal in paying it, because they allege it to be an epidemical fault, if they make it a fault (O such horrid juggling with God !). I know none of them who do not preach in houses ; and I see not but that they must be interpreted to officiate under the cover and colour of this churlish liberty. Beside what compliance is with it, I hear not of a conscionable and practical testimony given against it. They do generally show themselves more than formerly to be of the contrary part, and set against this poor witnessing and suffering handful. They fail not to cry out against us ; they charge us with false and gross transgressions. They press people every way to discourage and discountenance us ; they carry as if their great design were to crush and ruin us ; they spare no pains in preaching, converse, and writing to effectuate this. Hereby they make many violent upon their way ; but some are questioning, and likely to come freely off from them. The course they take is ready to let none halt between them and us. None are more brisk and headstrong than Mr Gabriel Semple, Mr W. Erskine, Mr Robert Langlands, particularly Mr Samuel Arnot, who by sundry means discovers no small biasedness, credulity, and impertinence, to say no worse. I fear, ere all be done, that it will come to the putting forth of the hand with some of the parties ; but, if it were once at this, I hope our trial would not be much prolonged, whatever might be our extremity and perplexity for a time. Since I knew any thing of the corruptness of their way, I thought they were men of a strange spirit ; but now I think them more strange than ever. O to live near God, that we may endure the storm !

Mr Flint and Mr Russel are parted; the number of their followers is not increasing. I have been often informed of Mr Ross's preaching one time with a curate. But my great discouragement is from ourselves. Though there be one part of the people that is straight and stedfast in the matters of God, yet there is another part that is inclined to laxness and instability. They will not leave us, and we have not as yet sufficient enough ground to refuse their concurrence; but they are as weights upon our hands, and are always to be drawn, because they will not follow. I think some will yet scour off, for, alas! we are not all right in heart with God.

As for Mr David Houston, he carries very straight. I think him both learned and zealous. He seems to have much of the spirit of our worthy professors; for he much opposes the passing from any part of our testimony, yea, and sticks close to every form and order whereunto we have attained, asserting pertinently that if we follow not even the method wherein God hath countenanced us, and keep not by every orderly form, we cannot but be jostled out of the matter. He hath authority with him, which some way dashes those who oppose themselves. He discovers the mystery of the working of the spirit of Antichrist more fully and clearly than ever I have heard it.

As for Mr Kersland, I know nothing of his carriage here, but that it is most humble and straight. I am informed by some very zealous, that, in conference both with ministers and professors of the contrary part, he hath spoken pertinently; yea, I have been witness to somewhat of it. I have heard him condemn the business of the association wherein we condemn it; but he much denies his being embodied with them. He takes upon him very much toil and travel to serve the Societies in the corner where he wanders, and to further and attend the work of the gospel amongst them. And to speak freely, according to my conceptions, I am afraid of him in nothing so much as in the business of Mr Boyd.

There are sundry Societies in Ireland that have come out from the defections of the time, who are keeping correspondence with us. I am desired to visit them, and I purpose, God willing, to do it. When Mr David Houston was there in the end of the spring, he was very free, and considerable numbers attended his preaching. I suppose ere this time he hath admitted some elders in Galloway or Nithsdale, and I am to set about it the week following. But a part of my business this while hath been, to travel through some places of the country where I had not been heretofore, and I hope not without some fruit. When I was last at Edinburgh, a considerable number of choice friends were banished to Barbadoes. Mrs Binning is gone to Ireland.

I am glad of your travels through other churches. Your difficulties have been many, yet the Lord hath been with you. I am affrighted and astonished with the abounding of iniquity amongst them. The Lord hath a controversy with all flesh, and He will plead it. Let us look through the whole world,—they are but very few whom we can see or say that they are for Him.

As to the letters of information that are to be sent abroad, I shall endeavour that it be done, and I shall send you some sermons ; but I have so much upon my hand, that I cannot get it all done. For some weeks together, I scarcely get one night's rest, or am two days in one place ; and, where I am, there I am so taken up, either with preaching, examination, or conference, that I almost can get no other thing done. I would gladly hear if you have seen the Vindication,* and what are your thoughts of it ; and if you and Mr Alexander Shields have met, and how you have accorded. I am hopeful, if you did not mistake one another, there would be little or no dissension between you. As to your

---

* The Informatory Vindication, generally regarded as Renwick's masterpiece. It was printed abroad, and having been brought to Scotland was sold "at eight-pence per book and at seven-pence unstitched." We learn this from a Society minute of date Dec. 7th, 1687.

coming to Scotland, I can say no other thing now, than I said in my former letter.

Now, the Lord be with you. I forget you not. I seldom go to God but you go with me : and I have some confidence that I need not desire you to remember him, who is, Honourable and dear Sir, yours as formerly,

JAMES RENWICK.

LETTER LIX.

Right Honourable Sir,—Since my last, I have travelled through many damps and deeps, and seen many discoveries of many things. The Lord by all dispensations is saying, that He will have malice and mistakes, right and wrong, righteousness and unrighteousness, brought to light. O noble contrivance! O noble way! What shall the upshot of all the losses, sufferings, contendings, and difficulties of the remnant be, but the clearing of the cause to all beholders, so that he that runs may read the righteousness of it? Shall not truth thereby be made more precious and known? The Lord will have a people to reap the sweet fruit of that we are put to this day. Let us then be content to lay name, credit, enjoyments, life, and all, under His feet, that He may stand thereupon, to advance the glory of His own name, and to bring about the advancement of His kingdom.

As to what friends have written to you, I hope you will not be troubled thereat, but take it in good part, for it hath flowed from real respect to the cause, and love and tenderness toward you in the most part. Whatever you were prevailed with to cede unto, through your own confusion, simplicity, and inadvertency, by the overpowering of a furious biased party, at Bothwell, I would advise your Honour to this anent it—to write to the remnant the way, and any reality thereof, expressing your own sense thereof, together with your willingness to make acknowledgment thereof, according to the degree of the offence, in the true church of Scotland. This, I think, would be most for the glory of

God, the vindication of His cause, your own honour, and the endearing of the remnant unto you. Also you must write your innocency of what other things are laid to your charge, with what probation thereof can be had, with this bearer; and if we had these we could then stop the mouths of slanderers. Likewise, you must not be offended that Robert is not sent unto you, for the meeting did it not out of any dissatisfaction with him, or with your desiring of him, but as a mean to wipe away that malice-like aspersion, that we are all led by you, and that by the mouth of more witnesses words may be more confirmed. Also I hope you will find the young man both distinct and honest anent matters; and I doubt nothing but you will be well pleased with him. Moreover, friends are most desirous to know how it is with Thomas, and if he be found, in some measure, qualified, as to zeal, piety and parts, they would gladly have all means used for his ordination. And I must join my desire with theirs; for there is as much work to be had in Scotland, notwithstanding of all the persecution, as would hold ten ministers busy (O blessed be the name of the Lord) and if I had some with me to help to plenish the country, and to act more judicially and authoritatively, through the Lord's assistance, the cruelty of the enemy and the malice and underminings of other parties would not be able to mar the work in our hands.

And as to foreign churches, I would offer your Honour my humble advice, that, considering the bad information that they have got from those that have passed as sufferers, you would with patience wait on them, for a little time will give them a clearer insight of our matters. I think no wonder, that the various confusions of Scotland jumble them anent the uptaking of Scotland's cause. And give not over to deal with such as are not possessed with prejudice and malice. And as for ordination for Thomas, if no other thing stood in the way of it, I could be clear that you sought it from the purest amongst the Reformed. Though they cannot win the length of approving all the circumstances of our cause, provided they be faithful against the sins of their own place, and have not, with prejudice at us, sided with the backsliders in the church of Scotland. For there is a great difference between joining with ministers of a foreign church, and ministers of our own church. For the former (as I have often told those who objected against my ordination) come under a general consideration as Protestants, but the latter under a far more special consideration, as may be clear from the supposed example. The Reformed ministers abroad, who keep up a testimony against the sins of their own place, and side not themselves against us, I could lawfully join with them, though they cry not out against the steps of our defection, because that is not the matter of their present testimony. Yet if any of them were coming to Scotland, and offering themselves ministers to us of one organical church, we could not accept them, unless they would keep up our present testimony against all the sins of our place.

As for what passed betwixt these ministers and us, I can inform your Honour no more fully than our friend's letter doth. And as to the present state of the country, Clydesdale continueth firm as it was; Nithsdale is as one man upon their former ground, together with Annandale; some in Kyle are gone off, but many continue; many in Carrick are jumbled, some (for the time) are quite off, and some few continue; the few that are in Livingston and Calder are put all in a reel; —the Lord knoweth how they will settle. Since our last meeting with these ministers, I made a progress through Galloway, and found never such an open door for preaching the gospel, the people coming far better out than they did before. And we got eight field-meetings kept there without any disturbance, and six in Nithsdale, many coming out who were not wont to come, and none in any of these places staying away that came out formerly. Mr W. Boyd hath made his escape out of Dunnottar, and is clear in our controversies against these ministers. Robert Goodwin hath made his escape likewise, and continues also clear in our matters. George Hill's family hath all been sick, and Mrs B. hath been long sick in prison; but this is but the ordinary calamity of the country, for I never heard of such a general sickness in Scotland.

As for choosing of elders, according to your desire, we have some honest old men, members of our Societies, who were elders in our settled state; and we are resolving to set about the choosing of more, with some deacons. But our various confusions and debates have much retarded this and other things hitherto.

In what I have here written, I entreat your Honour that I may not be mistaken; for, the Lord knoweth, I am the same both anent the cause and toward you that ever I was. All that biased folk can say doth neither lessen my confidence in, nor estimation of you. And what I have said of Thomas, understand me so, that I would most gladly have him for a help, but I would rather want him ere he should be a hindrance. But because I judge him not to be of a dangerous spirit, I suspect him less than many others. Also I think it is more simplicity of nature than want of honesty that is with him. Also you should speak with this bearer anent setting forward to the work, for he hath past his course at the college, and, I think, hath the cause honestly stated in his heart, though he hath but small means for enduing him with gifts; yet he wants not a spirit for contending for the honest side. As for ordination abroad, I would have all means essayed before we took another course; for we cannot defend our doing any thing of that nature, before all other lawful ways essayed do fail us, while we are in such a case. I thought fit also to inform you, that there is a general desire among friends that you should come home on a visit, and return again, through the apprehension that they have of your doing a great good at this time; but, since our debates were brought to some close, I cannot be so anxious for it as I was.

Now, dear Sir, take heed to yourself. There are many

looking out for your halting, many nets are spread against you, both at home and abroad. But exercise yourself in this, to keep a conscience void of offence toward God and man, and the Lord shall bring forth your righteousness as the noon-tide of the day. Remember me kindly to your worthy dear sister, to Thomas, and all the family. Pray for him who is ever as formerly,   J. R.

'P.S.'—I have here written to the Presbytery of Groningen, informing them of what the ministers have said that they might render my ordination odious, and I hope that you will press them to give me answer, they being so much concerned. Also the relation that friends have sent unto you may be shown unto them, if they enquire any further knowledge of what passed in our conference.

Letter LX.

Aug. 13, 1687.

Much Honoured Ladies,—The zeal which I desire to have for the advancement of Christ's kingdom, the love which I bear to your souls, and my sense of the obligations which I stand under unto you in particular, have moved me to salute you with this line. There is not a rational creature, that doth not propone unto itself some chief good, the obtaining and enjoying whereof is the great intent and end of all its actions. "Who will shew us any good?" But the woful evil among men is, their setting up to themselves some naughty, vain, and petty nothing, and despising that wherein their real and chief happiness doth only lie,—"rejecting the counsel of God against themselves." This mistake is deplorable, for man is an infinite loser by it; it is desperate, for he refuseth to be instructed. Hence so many different prevailing natural inclinations and predominating lusts as there are among the children of Adam, so many different chief goods; "There be gods many, and lords many." I am sad to think upon the

folly and madness of the poor creature, that thus doth
forsake its own mercy; but let the world choose and
follow what they please,—"to us there is but one Lord."

I am hopeful, much honoured Ladies, that you are
turning your backs upon created and carnal delights,
and setting your faces toward Christ, seeking after
union and communion with Him. It is my soul's
earnest desire, that it should be so. If the comfortless
and distracting vanities of a present perishing world
shall wheedle and bewitch you, that you study not the
wisdom of God, it shall bring great grief and sorrow of
heart unto me. I say, I am carried betwixt hope and
fear. I hope the Lord will work a good work in you.
I hope it will be, for I would have it to be, and there
are some appearances of it. I fear that the pleasant
and easy yoke of Christ be looked upon as irksome and
wearisome by you, when I consider your temptations,
and the seemingly promising beginnings, and fair
blossoms that I have seen in many, which have fallen
away, without bringing forth mature fruit. Do not
take my freedom in ill part, neither be offended with it,
for it cometh from affection; my ardent desire is that
you do not neglect the great salvation. Religion is
a great mystery, and a far other thing than even the
professing world taketh it to be. There are many hindrances in the way of fleeing to Christ, and closing with
him. The natural blindness that is in man, whereby he
neither sees his sin and danger, nor his Saviour, is a
great hindrance, Rev. iii. 17, 18; his natural unwillingness and flat aversion to the way of salvation laid
down in the covenant, and held forth in the gospel,
John v. 40; his hard-hearted unbelief, whereby he
giveth no assent to the righteousness of Scripture
precept and doctrine, and the justice of Scripture
threatening, nor consent to Scripture promises, making
fiducial application of them, John v. 38; Heb. xi. 6; his
whorish addictedness to his lusts, idols, and carnal
entanglements, whereby he doth not quit his profanity,
nor leave the honour, applause, profit, and pleasure of

this world, Psal. xiv. 10, 11; Song iii. 11; iv. 8; his mistaking the government of Christ, counting it hard, melancholy and unpleasant, Matt. xi. 28, 29, 30; his judging religion but a fancy, and a politic invention to amaze and amuse the minds of men, Matt. xxii. 5; his conceiving a facility in religion, thinking there needeth not be so much ado about it, and that he can do all that is needful, when he pleaseth, Matt. viii. 19, John vi. 44; his postponing the business of life eternal from time to time, leaving that last in doing, which ought to be first done, resolving to amend ere he end, whereby his vain heart deceives him, and Satan jostles him out of all time, Luke ix. 61; his peevish and foolish impatience, whereby he doth not forsake present imaginary good, for a future real happiness. A man may think it a good thing to enjoy everlasting life; but, because that is a happiness hereafter, and lieth now only in promise, he cannot wait for it and take it as his portion, but grasps at what is present, though it be neither contending nor constant, Psal. iv. 6; 2 Tim. iv. 10. I say, all these are great hindrances: see that you get over these, and all other obstructions, and lay hold upon Christ. O that I could bewail the lamentable condition of man, who is held in so many chains, from this work of great concern and eternal moment!

O, much honoured Ladies, consider the indispensable and absolute need you have of a Saviour. Consider the awful commands, full promises, free offers, hearty invitations, and serious requests given forth in the Word, all crying aloud with one voice unto you, to match with the Lord of glory. Consider the assurance that His own testimony hath given you, of dwelling with Him throughout eternity, in his heavenly mansions, where you shall see Him as He is, have a full sense of His love, and a perfect love to Him again, and ever drink of the rivers of pleasure that flow at His right hand, if you shall embrace Him upon His own terms. Consider the peremptory certification of everlasting destruction, of

dwelling with continual burnings, and lying under the
burden of His wrath ; a curse running always out upon
you in the overflowing flood, if you shall neglect to make
your peace with Him, and reject His salvation. I say,
consider these things, "and give all diligence to make
your calling and election sure ;" and see well that you be
not deceived, for there are many mistakes, and a great
mystery in that business. Many think themselves to be
something when they are nothing, and so deceive themselves, and come short of the grace of God. Instead of
founding upon the immovable Rock of Ages, they build
upon the sand of their own attainments. For folk may
go a great length, and yet be void of true saving grace.
They may have a great speculative knowledge of the
matters of God and mystery of salvation, and strong
gifts, 1 Cor. xiii. 2. They may abstain from many
pollutions, and the gross evils that others are given
unto, Luke xviii. 11-14. They may externally per-
form many duties, as reading, prayer, and be very
much in these, Luke xviii. 11-14. They may have
a very great sorrow for sin, not because of the dishonour done to God, but of the hurt to themselves,
not because they are polluted, but because they are
destroyed by it, Matt. xxvii. 3 ; Heb. xii. 17. They
may have a desire after grace, though not for grace's
sake, but for heaven's sake, Matt. xxv. 8. They may
have a historical faith, and give an assent of the mind
to all that is revealed in the Word, yea, to the spiritual
meaning of the law, Mark xii. 32-34. They may
have big hopes, and that in the mercy of God, which
nevertheless is but presumption ; for they forget that
He is just, and they neglect to lay hold upon Christ for
satisfaction of His justice, whereas, He is merciful to
none out of Christ, Job viii. 13, 14. They may have
the common operations of the Spirit, and a taste of
"the heavenly gift, and of the powers of the world to
come," Heb. vi. 4-6. They may be convinced that it is
good to close with Christ, and comfort themselves as if
they had done it, whereas they are still in their

natural state, Hos. viii. 2, 3. They may suffer many
things materially for the cause of God, and toil much
in following ordinances, undergoing the same out of
respect to their own credit, 1 Cor. xiii. 3. I say, people
may, and many do arrive at all these and such like
attainments, and notwithstanding remain in the gall
of bitterness and bond of iniquity. It may make us
all tremble to think what a length folk may go, and
yet never have gone out of themselves, and passed
through the steps of effectual calling. Many will say
to Him in that day, "We have eaten and drunk in
Thy presence, and Thou hast taught in our streets.
Have we not prophesied in Thy name? and in Thy
name cast out devils? and in Thy name done many
wonderful works?" whom He will chase away from
His presence, with that awful sentence, DEPART
YE, professing unto them that He never knew
them.

Let this alarm you to make sure work in this great
concern, and not deceive yourselves with a counterfeit,
instead of a reality, with a flash instead of conversion,
and a delusion instead of Christ. But get you a sight
of your sinful and miserable state,—a sense and feeling
thereof, putting you in a perplexity, and discouraging
you from resting in it; a conviction of your inability
to help yourselves, and of your unworthiness that God
should help you out of it. Look unto Christ, as your
alone Saviour, receiving Him wholly in His threefold offices of King, Priest, and Prophet, welcoming
Him, and taking up His cross against the world, the
devil, and the flesh, and resting upon Him alone for
salvation; and then the business will be done, and all
will be sure, and you may defy devils and men to pluck
you out of His hand.

If you have thus closed the bargain with Him,
then you will find in you a war declared and maintained
against all sin, Rom. vii. 15; Ezek. xviii. 21; 1 John
iii. 9;—a respect to all the commandments of the
Lord, Ezek. xviii. 21;—a liking of the way of happi-

ness, as well as happiness itself, John iii. 14, 15 ;—a high esteem of justification and sanctification, Psal. xxxii. 2 ;—a prizing of Christ, and a longing to be with Him, Phil. i. 23 ;—and an admirable change wrought in you, a new judgment, new will, new conscience, new memory, new affections. In a word, all the faculties of the soul will be new, in regard of their qualifications ; and all the members of the body, in regard of their use, 2 Cor. v. 17. Now, if you have attained to a saving interest in Christ, you may find these, and the like marks and evidences of it.

O halt not in this great matter, rest not in uncertainty, and satisfy not yourselves with a maybe. But "examine yourselves, whether ye be in the faith ; prove your own selves ; know ye not your own selves, how that Jesus Christ is in you, except ye be reprobates ?" In setting your faces toward Zion, you may expect that Satan will raise all his storms against you ; but fear him not, for the grace of God is sufficient for you. Give yourselves wholly to the Lord, to serve Him, and to love His name, to choose and follow the things that please Him. Your greatest honour lieth in this, your greatest duty, your greatest profit, and your greatest pleasure. Count the cost of religion. God is a liberal dealer. Deal not niggardly with Him, prig not with Him about your estates. Who is in heaven like unto Him ? and who in earth is to be desired like Him ? Lay down to Him your names, your enjoyments, your lives, and your all at His feet, for He is only worthy to have the disposal of them. The sufferings of this present time are not worthy to be compared with the glory that shall be revealed in us. Think not much to quit the vain and carnal delights of the world ; they cannot satisfy your senses, and much less your souls. The earth is round, and the heart of man three-cornered ; therefore, this cannot be filled by that. Though you could find content in them, yet how vain were it, because inconstant ! and how unsolid, because uncertain !

Q

Regard not men's reproach, for so reproached they our Lord and the prophets. Yea, there can be no contempt or calumny cast upon you, for the gospel's sake, but what hath been cast upon the faithful in all ages. Remember "Moses, who esteemed the reproach of Christ greater riches than the treasures of Egypt:" and "go ye forth without the camp bearing His reproach." Christ's new name will more than enough recompense the world's nick-name. Advance resolutely in the way of godliness. Your Guide is faithful, your victory is certain, your reward sure, and your triumph everlasting. Stumble not, because religion is mocked at; for it is not the worse that man thinketh so little of it. Count it not a fancy, because men desert it; but "taste and see that God is good." Follow no man farther than he follows Christ. Divide not from the Head, to unite with any professed members. Walk not with them who renounce their dependence upon Christ, or who are carrying on a course of defection, pressing a relinquishing of the present Testimony, and casting reproaches upon the way of God. Keep yourselves from the pollutions of this time, and partake not with other men in their sins. But study to have a good conscience. A good conscience will be a peaceable conscience, and a peaceable conscience will be a fat feast. Shun as much as you can the company of carnal and vain persons. You will not get this wholly evaded; but you may avoid unnecessary converse, frequency and familiarity with them. We are obliged to carry ourselves with courtesy, humanity, and pity towards all, but not with friendliness and familiarity. You know, evil company and communications corrupt good manners. O! what shall I say? Watch always, be much in secret prayer, self-examination, spiritual meditation. Read the Word of God; seek to have your minds understanding it, your hearts affected by it, and your consciences and actions guided by it. Get His Spirit to dwell in you, directing you into all truth, reproving you for sin, bringing every thought into obedience to Christ, and leading you into supplication. Lay aside every weight, and run the race that is set before you with cheerfulness and alacrity. Despise every opposition and obstruction in the way, and keep your eyes still upon the prize, having respect to the recompence of reward.

Now, "The very God of peace sanctify you wholly, and I pray God your whole spirit and soul and body be preserved blameless, unto the coming of our Lord Jesus Christ." I am, much honoured Ladies, your assured and obliged friend and servant in the Lord,

JAMES RENWICK.

LETTER LXI.

Nov. 5, 1687.

Right Honourable and dear Sir,—Our troubles are growing, enemies are stretching forth their hands violently to persecute and they want not instigations from our false brethren ; so we are made the contempt of the proud, and the scorn of them that are at ease. Our sufferings were always rightly stated, but never so clearly as now ; and why should we not endure these trials, for they shall work for truth's victory, and Christ's glory. O let all the suffering remnant keep clean hands, for therein shall be their strength, and wait with patience, for He will not tarry, who cometh to plead His own cause, to lay claim to His own interest, that is basely and deceitfully abandoned and betrayed into the hands of man, and to give a fair decision. They whose souls are vexed with the now abounding abomination shall have a Zoar to flee unto, when the fire of God shall fall down upon our Sodom. I am certain the Lord will have a sanctuary for His people. We must once be brought to that extremity, wherein there can be no longer subsistence without present help ; but God will not leave His people there. O this liberty hath let Satan loose, and brought the truths of God, and the faithful, into great bondage. But God will loose His judgments, and pour them out upon this woeful generation, that will not see, till they be made to feel. There is now strange thirsting after my blood, but that moves me not ; though they had it, they would not be satisfied, for nothing will quench them till they get their own blood to drink.

As to Mr B.,* he came to our last General Correspondence, and desired, that, seeing he knew there was something, wherefore we were dissatisfied with him, as he also was with us, we might commune with him freely upon the same. So, first, we showed our dissatisfaction with his taking licence without our knowledge, which was contrary to his own engagement, at least declared purpose and resolution. Next, we took his paper, which he left in our hands when he went abroad, wherein (amongst other things) he asserted, that his withdrawing out of the land was no way to separate or disjoin from us, and signified his dislike of countenancing those ministers against whom we had valid exceptions. When we asked, How could his declaring, that he neither was oined, nor would join with us, nor any other party, consist with the former ; and 'when' from the latter we desired to know, if he judged the accepting of this liberty (as they call it) a sufficient ground of discountenancing ministers ? his answer to the first of these did no way help him or satisfy us, his answer to the last was, If the question was concerning such ministers, as might sit in Assemblies with the addressers, and go out to places of the country at their direction and preach, he would not forbid people to hear them, whatever he would do himself. So after some debating against his mind in this, I showed the meeting that I neither could nor would determine matters of such extent and importance without my brethren, who by providence were not present ; yet, in the meantime, I would keep at a distance and not concur with him in the public work. And they concluded and signified unto him that they would not

* Mr Boyd, referred to also in next letter.

call him nor hear him elicitly, yet they would not discourage and discountenance him so far as not to hear him in case of necessity, as if they should be providentially cast with him into one family, and he going about exercise, or the like. Moreover, he himself was not desirous to incorporate with us ; what he may do after, I know not. There were also other particulars wherewith we were dissatisfied ; but the foresaid were the most material, and also included sundry of the others, and much time was spent in reasoning about them.

My fears concerning Kersland in this affair were altogether disappointed. The bearer can write to you what was concluded concerning himself and what news are heard. I have seen your letter concerning the money that was borrowed for Mr A. his use, and I have used my endeavour to get it advanced. I have got the third and expect more, if not all, to-night ; and what I get I shall commit to the bearer, Th. L.*

I have also seen the account which you gave to your sister, Mrs Jean, of Euph. B. V., her affair : you would not be over much pressed with it. The Lord is taking all pains to wean you more and more from the world, and win you more and more to Himself. Remember Joseph in the dungeon. God hath vindicated, and will yet vindicate you. Friends are very desirous to have you at home, and I shall endeavour to manage that business seasonably, and as may be most for the advantage of the cause.

Now, the Lord be your guide, and your guard, and heap the blessings of the everlasting covenant upon your head. Pray that the Lord may spare His people ; pray that He may purge His house ; and pray for him, who is, Right honourable and dear sir, yours as formerly,

JAMES BRUCE.

* Thomas Linning, who was being sent abroad for another season to the University.

LETTER LXII.

Dec. 29, 1687.

Hon. and dear Sir,—Though I know not how this shall be transmitted to your hands, yet I judge it my duty to write a brief account of some things occurring at present amongst us. Mr Boyd came to our last General Correspondence, professing his agreement with our Testimony, and his willingness to join with us. When we came to speak about the duty of teaching the people the necessity of abstracting themselves from the acceptors of the present Toleration, he granted that it is lawful to teach it, but the expediency of it he did not see. However, he had endeavoured to discover the sin of the Toleration being accepted : thus he stood at this time. When we were reasoning with him, he said that, ere he were the instrument of a breach amongst us, he would leave Scotland. But it was no small perplexity for us to know how to carry anent him. It was thought that the refusing either to call or hear him would cause a very great animosity and breach, and the ground of it was not valid enough. They came at length to conclude (with some averseness in the most part) that, until the time of our next meeting, those who had not clearness to call and hear him should not be offended with those that might do it, and those again that might do it should not be offended with those who had not clearness for it. Howbeit, they were not for entirely incorporating with him, and giving him a joint solemn call. As I declined to preach with him, so I denied my consent to the foresaid conclusion, and was put in a perplexity, not knowing what to do, seeing many sad inconveniences to follow, if I had opposed their determination. So, with a full heart, I forbore : but afterwards I opened my heart to Mr Boyd himself. I heard that K. was of my judgment in this matter.

As for Mr David Houston, he went long ago into Ireland, and is not yet returned, whereby we have suffered no small loss. I am certain some strange thing hath happened him. The report is, that he hath been sore sick. I hear that many in Ireland are turning Dissenters. Kersland hath taken from his factors about sixteen hundred merks of his own rents. For what was communed anent yourself and Mr Thomas Douglas, your letter from the meeting will inform you. We have written a Testimony of about five or six sheets of paper, witnessing against this Toleration, the accepting of it, addressing for it, and hearing the acceptors :— testifying also for the obligation of our covenants, and showing the necessary duty of field-preaching, in the present circumstances of this church.

I have been at Peebles this week, and through the Lord's providence wonderfully escaped. Our intended meeting near to the town, about nine of the clock at night, in the time of our gathering, was by a strange providence discovered. It is a place I had not been in before, and we had no armed men ; there are four taken and imprisoned. Sir, I hear Stansfield * is murdered by his own family : his eldest son had a chief hand in it.

Now, Honourable and dear Sir, I have no more at the time to inform you of, but I have much to write if time would allow me. My fears were never greater anent the interest of Christ in these lands ; there is such an inclinableness in people to defection. But I believe the Lord will not want some to own His controverted truths. The next time I write to you, I purpose to write also to Leewarden friends. The Lord be with you. I am, Right Honourable and dear Sir, your sympathising friend and servant in the Lord,

JAMES RENWICK.

* Sir James Stansfield of Newmills, whose son was condemned for his murder on 6th Feb. next.

1687.

Beloved Friends,—It is both my duty and desire to sympathise with all who are suffering for the precious name of Christ, especially with you who are called to partake so deeply of the afflictions of the children of Zion. You are now to be banished out of your native land; but your enemies could not have appointed that for you, unless the Lord had from all eternity ordained it. His infinite love and wisdom have consulted and measured out your lot; and as this should make you despise the instruments of your afflictions, so it may help you to stoop, and cheerfully submit unto the providence of God, who "is of one mind, and who can turn him?" Yea, considering the preciousness of the cause for which you are persecuted, you may rejoice that you are counted worthy to suffer such things. It is no less than the gospel of Christ, and His great prerogatives, as He is King of His own church, which He hath purchased with His own blood, and as He is supreme Governor and Sovereign of the whole world. Oh is not this a precious cause? Are not these great heads of suffering? If every one of you had a thousand worlds of enjoyments, and a thousand lives, they would be all too little to signify your love to Christ, and your respect to so honourable a cause. You cannot glorify your Lord so much on earth, as by being faithful to the word of your testimony, and suffering for Him now, when men are declaredly topping with Him about His supremacy both in His kingdom of grace and power. O, my friends, regard not what you meet with in this present world, but be careful to have matters standing right between God and you. See that you attain to a saving interest in Christ, for, if that be not secured, your duties will not be acceptable, your sufferings will not be acceptable: and, whatever you have here for a possession, you may lay your account with lying under His curse and wrath, and the immediate strokes of His severe vengeance, to all eternity. O make Christ your own, and then you may defy devils and men to come between you and your happy state. Give yourselves wholly to His disposal, for He is gracious and faithful, and will order every thing for His own glory and your good. Study to maintain His cause whole, and, wherever your lot may be, keep up the testimony of the church of Scotland. Quit none of your sworn and received principles, whatever way those may insinuate upon you, who are engaged and persisting in a course of defection. Make no tampering or bargaining with any, when it will infer a condemning of the cause of your sufferings, and a justifying of the iniquitous sentence that men have passed upon you. Keep all stedfast and united together in the truths of God, and beware of defection, which breedeth division. Fall not away from any of the words of Christ's patience, but shun all unnecessary questions, needless strifes, and vain janglings. Live at peace amongst yourselves, so far as holiness may sustain no prejudice by it, and this will be both pleasant and profitable for you.

Now, O beloved, what shall I say unto you? I have no time to enlarge. Do not say because of your banishment, is there any sorrow like unto your sorrow? For I am persuaded, that those whom you leave behind you have a greater sorrow. I do not say, that any should flee out of Scotland, or leave it without a necessary or sufficient call. Yet that is coming upon the inhabitants, which will make the ears of them that hear thereof to tingle. The consumption determined shall pass through, and the Lord will quiet His Spirit in our destruction; for His "soul shall be avenged on such a nation as this." And who knoweth, but your banishment may be for the preservation and hiding of at least some of you, until the indignation overpass? But when the time of gathering cometh, the Lord will bring again His banished. He will bring them from all places whither they have been driven ; He will say to the east, give up, and to the west, keep not back. Fear not a long sea-voyage ; for "they that go down to the sea in ships, that do business in the great waters, these see the works of the Lord, and his wonders in the deep." Yea, though the deep should be your grave, or though you should die in a strange land, yet your death of that kind shall be a testimony, and shall cry for vengeance upon persecutors ; it will be also an outlet of all your misery, and an inlet of your everlasting glory. But if the Lord shall meet you with providential mercies, whither you are carried, and give you any tolerable ease, safety, or sustenance, then, I say, as you would not have your blessings cursed, and would not lose the badge of Christians and sufferers, sit not down upon these things, content not yourselves with these things, and forget not the case of the remnant whom you leave behind you.

Now, I commend you all to the grace of God, hoping not to forget you in my weak addresses to the throne of Him who is the hearer of prayer, and hoping to be remembered by you in like sort. I am, beloved friends, your sympathizing friend and servant in the Lord,

JAMES RENWICK.

CHAPTER X.

THE END.

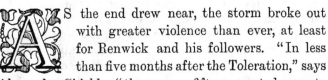S the end drew near, the storm broke out with greater violence than ever, at least for Renwick and his followers. "In less than five months after the Toleration," says Alexander Shields, "there were fifteen most desperate searches, particularly for him, both of foot and horse, in which they were very outrageous, breaking into cellars and breaking down the ceilings of houses in their search for him." Indeed, as we have already had occasion to observe, the larger amount of liberty enjoyed by the moderate Presbyterians was obtained only at the price of greater severity to the persecuted. This, however, did not prevent Renwick from responding to the numerous calls which reached him from different parts of the country. In the next letter, which is addressed to Mr Alexander Shields, he refers to his escape at Peebles two weeks before.

Letter LXIV.

Jan. 12, 1688.

Dear Brother,—I long to hear much how you are. The third night after I parted with you, I had a sore fit of sickness, but it lasted not, and through the goodness of God, I have been in ordinary health since. However, it occasioned a disappointment of a meeting for examination. I came forward to Peebles, where our meeting in the time of gathering was discovered by a wonderful providence, namely, as I am informed, the pursuing of some for theft, when people were observed to crowd out of the town; which made the Clerk to enquire what they were, and whither they were going. The report whereof coming unto me, being lodged in a most suspected house, I went forth, and passed on towards the place of meeting, until I came within speaking and hearing of the Clerk and of some with him, who were without the town challenging people: and, being in no capacity to resist, I turned again into the town, where there was some little uproar, and went forth of it another way, where I waited a considerable space for my horse, which was at length got unto me, with some difficulty. Finding that the meeting could not be kept, I came away; but there were four persons taken. Since I came to this place, I have lodged with Thomas and John, and, lest I should trouble mine own spirit, I have not desired any to keep silent anent my being here, nor reproved any for coming into my quarters, whatever the hazard might be. I left that to the providence of God, and people to their own discretion, and I find it not the worst way.

As for the books, they have come safely in boxes to Wooler. I have inserted, in the papers which you left, what you desired to be transcribed out of Durham upon the Revelation; but I thought I could not fitly add what concerneth Kersland, because I know not distinctly the manner of it, and how to express it suitably to the matter of fact. But I have written to the Lady, desiring that she may give to Mr Had. and Mr Lin. a plain and full account of it, and I have written also to them that they may insert it, and shown distinctly the place where it is added. I thought this the fittest way, because people might possibly carp, if they were not acquainted with what concerneth them so nearly. Again, it will prevent any cavil about misrepresentation of a matter of fact. As for the Testimony, the publishing of it is longer retarded than I expected because Michael Shields * was not in health for writing; but I shall be careful about it. I have added what

* Brother of Alexander Shields, and clerk to the United Societie .

was to be transcribed out of Durham upon Scandal, and did oversee the writing of the most difficult places, and taken out some of the "bigots," because the recurring of such epithets makes them unsavoury. I have not got any of the letters sent abroad, but I am using diligence. There are little news here. They are to proceed against Sir James Stanfield's family for the murder. Mr Hardie * is still in prison, but it is thought he will be liberated. He refused to tell the Council what he had preached, but put them to prove what they could against him. Whereupon they called some of his hearers, but they said they were either sleeping, or at a greater distance, and could not hear ; so they were not the nearer their purpose. There are orders given forth for a day of thanksgiving, for the conception of the queen, and, as is reported, to pray that she may have a man-child. I am detained in this place some few days beyond my purpose, through the want of a guide, but I am now about to remove.

Now, being in great haste, I must desist. Your direction, encouragement, strengthening, comfort, health, and protection are prayed for by him, who is, your brother and servant,   JAMES RENWICK.

Proceeding now to Edinburgh, he lodged in the hands of their Moderator a protest against the Toleration, which he wished to be laid before an early meeting of the Indulged Ministers. He then crossed into Fife, where he held numerous conventicles, preaching on the 24th from Ps. xlv. 10, and on the 27th from Luke xii. 32. His last sermon was preached at Bo'ness on the 29th of the same month from Isa. liii. 1 : "Who hath believed our report, and to whom is the arm of the Lord revealed ?" Returning to Edinburgh two days afterwards, he repaired to the house of a friend on the Castle Hill,

* Minister of Gordon in Berwickshire, who was tried for treason but acquitted. See *The Covenanters of the Merse*, p. 238.

where, next morning, he was discovered, and, after a severe struggle and flight, was apprehended and taken to the guard-house. The Captain of the Guard, on learning who he was, exclaimed with surprise, "What! is this boy the James Renwick that the whole nation has been so troubled with?"

When in prison he was more concerned about others than himself, fearing lest, through the severity of his examination and the threatened application of torture, he might have betrayed any of his friends. To this he refers in the following letter to an unknown correspondent, of date Feb. 6th.

LETTER LXV.

February 6, 1688.

Dear Friend in the Lord,—I have no cause to complain of my lot : there is a great necessity for it, and the Lord hath seen it for His glory, and He maketh me joyful in it. But there is one thing that doth a little trouble me, and yet when I look upon it again I think there is not much cause of trouble. The matter is this. When I was apprehended and searched, there was found upon me a little memorandum, containing the names of some persons, to whom I had lent, and from whom I had borrowed some books, as also a direction of letters to some doctors of divinity, or ministers abroad. Upon this I was interrogated in the tolbooth, by a committee, who said, they had orders to torture me if I was not ingenuous. So as to the direction to the doctors, or ministers abroad, which were full in the memorandum, I told them that there was a purpose of writing letters to them, but that none were written. Being asked about the scope and design of the letters, I told them that it was to represent our sufferings, and to procure their sympathy. It was asked me, with whom I kept correspondence abroad? I told them with Mr

Robert Hamilton, which, I thought, could do no injury.
As to the names of other persons, which were written
short, I judged there was no hazard in explaining their
names, who were in the same hazard already. So I told
them that A. S. was Alexander Shields; and being
asked if he was in Scotland? I, thinking that his public preaching would not let him be hid, said, I supposed
he was, but told no definite place; that M. S. was
Michael Shields, but told no place of his abode; that
Ja. Wil. and Ar. Wil. was James and Archibald Wilson,
and, being asked about the place of their abode, I
answered, only in Clydesdale; that C. A. was Colin
Alison, but I spoke of no place of abode; that Peter
R. was Peter Raining, for I thought he was without
their reach; and being asked about his occupation and
abode, I told them, he trafficked within the border of
England. Peter Aird's name was written full, and, being
asked particularly about him, I told them he was a man
of the country of New-mills, Galston, or Evandale, I
knew not whether. James Colstoun's name was thus
full, and, being asked of his abode, I told them he lived
in the Newtown of Galloway, or thereabout. You know
the man, and this was true of him, wherever he is now.
That M. was my mother, but spoke of no place of her
abode. I was most pressed to tell who M. M. at Gl. was,
with whom a hat was left; and I answered, that I was
not free to bring any other person into trouble, whatever
they might do with me. They said that the business
could not bring any into trouble, for they did not now
proceed against folk for such matters; and that their
design was only to save me from torture, which they
could not do, unless I would be ingenuous about that
name. I answered, that I would in no ways explain
the name, unless they would not trouble the person.
They said, they would endeavour to prevent all trouble
of that kind. Therefore, I thinking that the person's
name was already among enemies in the place, and
supposing there were some others of that name, and
also conceiving, that trouble upon that account could

hardly be expected, they guessing that Gl. was Glasgow, I told the advocate alone, that M. M. was Mrs Millar. Her name was not set down in writing by their clerk as the rest were, and he hath no witnesses upon it; so I think it not probable that they can incur any injury, for I was not more particular.

Now, I shall say no more as to this, but only advise persons in my circumstances, either not to write such memorandums, or not to keep them upon them, which I did inadvertently and inconsiderately. You may communicate this to whom you think fit, especially to the persons concerned, but see that you take along with you all the circumstances. I studied to save myself from lying, to preserve them from trouble, and to evite the threatened torture. I was pressed much to tell my haunts and abodes these several years by past; and I told them I sometimes resorted to John Lookup's house, where the officers came upon me, but further I would give them no notice; so I passed.

Now, if there be anything in this that may be offensive to friends, I seek their forgiveness for it; for if I had apprehended any sin in all this, or that any person would thereby incur injury, I would then, and now also, rather undergo all the threatened torture.

The keepers of the tolbooth have frequently told me of my having married the herd in the Leeps, and some persons in Pentland. Alexander Weir, who is with the Provost, told me of baptising a child to one —— Scott's husband, but I endeavoured to boast them out of it. As for my pocket-book, which contained only the sum of my two last sermons at Braid's Craigs, with the time and place, I owned such doctrine.

I have no further matters to write at the time, for I resolve to write some after this, which I would have more public than this. I desire that none may be troubled upon my behalf, but that they rather rejoice with him, who, with hope and joy, is waiting for his marriage, and coronation hour. I am, your friend and servant in the Lord,   JAMES RENWICK.

Shortly before his trial his mother was admitted to see him, and in an agony of grief she one day said to him, "How shall I look upon that head and those hands set up among the rest on the port of the city?" Smiling sweetly, he replied—"I have offered my life unto the Lord, and have sought that He may bind them up, and I am persuaded that they shall not be permitted to torture my body nor touch one hair of my head further." Afterwards, surmounting even the fear of torture, of which he had always had a great dread, he said—"The terror of it is so removed that I would rather be cast into a caldron of boiling oil than do anything to wrong truth."

On the 8th February he appeared before the Council for the last time, when he openly adhered to all that he had previously said, practically admitting the various heads of his indictment, and justifying his conduct as opportunity offered. When asked if he owned the King's authority, he replied—"I own all authority that hath its prescriptions and limitations from the Word of God, but I cannot own this usurper as lawful king, seeing both by the Word of God such an one is incapable to bear rule, and likewise by the ancient laws of the kingdom, which admit none to the Crown of Scotland until he swear to defend the Protestant religion, which a man of his profession cannot do." When asked regarding the lawfulness of paying the Cess or War-tax, he replied, "For the present Cess, enacted for the present usurper, I hold it unlawful to pay it, both because it is oppressive to the subjects for the maintenance of tyranny, and because it is imposed for suppressing the Gospel. Would it have been thought lawful for the Jews, in the days of Nebuchadnezzar, to have brought every one a coal to augment the flame of the furnace,

R

to devour the three children, if so they had been required by that tyrant? And how can it be lawful
either to oppress poor people for not bowing to the
idols the king sets up, or for their brethren to contribute what may help forward their oppression on that
account?" Asked next if he had taught his hearers
to come armed to their meetings, and in case of opposition to resist, he immediately answered—"It were
inconsistent with reason and religion to do otherwise.
Yourselves would do it in the like circumstances. I own
that I taught them to carry arms to defend themselves
and to resist your unjust violence." Sentence having
been given that he should be executed in the Grass-
market within three days, the Judge enquired if he
wished a longer time, whereupon he replied, with
great composure—"It is all one to me. If protracted it
is welcome : if shortened it is welcome. My Master's
time is the best."

Strenuous efforts were now made even by many
influential persons to save his life. During a reprieve
which was obtained while these were in progress, the
following letters were written to some Christian
friends :—

Letter LXVI.

In the "Cloud of Witnesses," where this was first printed,
it is said to have been "emitted from his own hand the
day before his suffering," but it was written some days
earlier, and indeed is dated February 13th, 1688. His
friend Alexander Shields mentions that "his begun
Testimony, which he was writing, was taken from him,
and pen, ink, and paper removed : yet by secret convey-
ance he got a short word sent out the night before his

suffering.' The original MS., as well as that of the letter which he wrote on the 15th of February, is preserved in the Library of the New College, Edinburgh.

My dear friends in Christ,—It hath pleased the Lord to deliver me up to the hands of men, and I think it fit to send you this salutation which I expect will be the last. When I posed my heart upon it before God I dare not desire to have excepted this lot, for no less could be for His glory and the vindication of His cause on my behalf. And as I am free before Him of the profanity which some either naughty, wicked, or strangers to me have reported that I have been sometimes guilty of, so He hath kept me from the womb free of the ordinary pollutions of children, as these that have been acquainted with me through the tract of my time do know. And now my blood shall either more silence reproaches or more ripen them for judgment. But I hope it shall make some more sparing to speak of those who shall come after me. And so I am the more willing to pay this cost both for their instruction and my succeeders' ease. Since I came to prison the Lord hath been wonderfully kind. He hath made His word to give me light, life, joy, courage, strength, yea, it hath dropped with sweet smelling myrrh into me : particularly these psalms and promises, Gen. xxii. 12 (latter part of the verse); Neh. viii. 10 (latter part of the verse); Job iii. 17; Job xxiii. 10, 11, 12, 13, 14 ; Ps. cv. 19 (latter part of the verse) ; James iv. 28, 29, 30, 31; Jer. i. 17, 18, 19 ; Jer. xvii. 12, 13, 14 ; Zech. ii. 8 (latter part of the verse) ; Luke xxi. 12, 13, 19 ; St John's Gospel ; Heb. xii. 2, 3 ; James i. 12 ; 1 Pet. i. 6, 7, 8 ; Rev. iii. 8-12 ; Rev. xix., xx., xxi., xxii., and several other Scriptures. O what can I say to the Lord's praise? It was but little that I knew of Him before I came to prison. I have found sensibly much of His divine strength, much of the joy of His spirit, and much assurance from His word and spirit concerning my salvation. My sufferings are stated upon the matters of my doctrine, for there was found with me the sum of my two last sermons at Braids Craigs which I wrote after I did preach them : the former whereof was upon Ps. xlvi. 10, and the latter upon Heb. x. 38. And I was examined upon the application made therein unto the sins of the time, all which I owned once and again, as is to be seen in my indictment; and, being tried, and an assize set, I adhered to my former confessions explicitly. So my sentence of death was drawn forth upon these three heads (1) because I could not own James the seventh to be my lawful Sovereign, (2) because I taught the unlawfulness of paying the Cess expressly exacted for suppressing the faithful and free preaching of the Gospel, (3) because I taught it was people's duty to carry arms at the preaching of the Gospel now when it is persecuted, for defending of themselves and re-sisting unjust violence. I think such a Testimony is worthy of many lives, and I praise the Lord for His enabling me to be plain and positive in all my Confessions, for therein I found peace, joy, strength, boldness. I have met with many assaults in prison, some from some of the Indulged party and some from some of the Prelatic. But by the strength of God I was enabled to stand that they could neither bow me nor break me. I was also assaulted by some of the Popish party : I suppose they were of their ecclesiastic creatures : but they found none of their own stuff in me. I told them after sundry debatings that I had lived and should die an enemy to their way. However, some that knew me not reproached me with Jesuitism : but I was most dealt with by sundry to seek a reprieve : and my answer was always that I adhered to my former confession, and that if they pleased to let their appointed time of my death stand, let it stand, and if they pleased to protract it, let them protract it, for I was ready and willing both to live and to die. Howbeit there came a reprieve for eight days, but I had no hand in it.

They still urged, would I but say that I desired time for conference with some persons anent my principles. I answered that my time was in the Lord's hand and I

was in no hesitation or doubt about my principles
myself. I would not be so rude as to decline converse
with any, so far as it might not be inconvenient for me
in my present circumstances, but I would speak it with
none. I have no more to say upon this head, but my
heart doth not smite me for anything in the matters of
my God since I came to prison. And I can further say
to His praise with some consciousness of integrity that
I have walked in His way and kept His charge throughout much weakness and many infirmities whereof you
have been witnesses.

Now my dear friends in precious Christ, I think I
need not tell you that as I have lived, so I die, in the
same persuasion with the true Reformed and Covenanted Presbyterian Church of Scotland. I adhere to
the testimony of this day as it is held forth in our
Informatory Vindication and in the testimony against
the present Toleration, and I own and seal with my
blood all the precious truths, even the controverted
truths that I have taught. So I would entreat every
one of you to make sure your personal reconciliation
with God in Christ: for I fear many of you have that
yet to do, and, when you come where I am to look
pale death in the face, you will be not a little shaken
and terrified if you have not laid hold on eternal life.
I would entreat you to much diligence in the use of
the means, to be careful in keeping your Societies, to
be frequent and fervent in secret prayer, to read much
the written Word of God, and to examine yourselves
by it. Do not weary to maintain in your places and
stations the present testimony: for when Christ goeth
forth to defeat Antichrist, with that name written on
His thigh and on His vesture, King of kings and Lord
of lords, He will make it glorious in the earth, and if
you can but transmit it to posterity you may count
it a great generative work. But beware of the
ministers that have accepted this Toleration and all
others that bend that way, and follow them not, for
the sun hath gone down on them. Do not fear that

the Lord will cast off Scotland, for He will certainly return and show Himself glorious in our land: but watch and pray, for He is bringing on a sad over-throwing stroke which shall make men say that they have got easily through that have got a scaffold for Christ, and do not regard the sufferings of this present world, for they are not worthy to be compared with the glory that shall be revealed. I may say to His praise, that I have found His cross sweet and lovely unto me, for I have had many joyful hours and not a fearful thought since I came to prison. He hath strengthened me to outbrave men and outface death, and I am now longing for the joyful ban of my dissolution, and there is nothing in the world that I am sorry to leave but you. But I go unto better company, and so I must take my leave of you all. Farewell, beloved sufferers and followers of the Lamb; farewell, Christian inti-mates; farewell, Christian and comfortable mother and sisters; farewell, sweet Societies; farewell, desirable General Meetings; farewell, night wanderings, cold and weariness for Christ; farewell, sweet Bible and preaching of the Gospel; farewell, sun, moon, and stars, and all sublunary things, and farewell, conflicts with a body of death. Welcome scaffold for precious Christ, welcome heavenly Jerusalem, welcome innumer-able companies of angels, welcome General Assembly and Church of the First-born, welcome crown of glory, white robes, and song of Moses and the Lamb, and above all, welcome, O Thou blessed Trinity and one God; O Eternal One, I commit my soul into Thy eternal rest,

Sic subscribitur,

Feb. 13th, 1688.   JAMES RENWICK.

LETTER LXVII

My dear friends in Christ,—I see then what hath been the language of my reprieve. It hath been that I might be further tempted and tried, and I praise the

Lord He hath assisted me to give further proof of
stedfastness. I have been often assaulted by some
Popish priests, but the last time that they came I told
them that I would debate no more with such as they
were, and that I have lived and would die a Presbyterian Protestant, and testified against the idolatrous
heresies, superstitions, and errors of their Anti-christian
way. But yesterday I was cast into a deep exercise
and made to dwell under the impression of the dread-
fulness of everything that might grieve the Spirit of
God. I found sin to be more bitter than death, and
an hour's hiding of God's face more insupportable.
And then at night I was called before a party of the
Council, and the Chancellor produced the Informatory
Vindication and asked if I knew it. I answered I did
know it : and, being interrogated, I confessed that I
had a great hand in writing of it. They pressed me
to tell my assistants. I told them they were those
they were persecuting, but would satisfy them no
further. They also urged me, upon pain of torture,
to tell what were our Societies, who kept our General
Correspondences, and where they were kept. I answered,
though they should torture me, which was contrary to
all law after the sentence of death, I would give them
no further notice than the book gave. I was, moreover, threatened to tell of my haunts and quarters,
but I refused to make known any such thing to them ;
so I was returned to prison again. Such an exercise
as I had was very needful for such a trial, and I would
rather have endured what they could do unto me than
have dishonoured Christ, offended you, and brought
you into trouble. But I hope that in less than three
days to be without the reach of all temptation. Now
I have no more to say. Farewell, again, in our blessed
Lord Jesus,   JAMES RENWICK.

Feb. 15, 1688.

Two days later, on the morning of his execution, he

wrote a very touching letter to his friend and benefactor, Sir Robert Hamilton. It is as follows :

LETTER LXVIII.

Feb. 17, 1688.

Right hon. and dear Sir,—This being my last day
upon earth, I thought it my duty to send you this my
last salutation. The Lord hath been wonderfully
gracious to me since I came to prison, He hath assured
me of His salvation, helped me to give a testimony for
Him, and own before His enemies all that I have
taught, and strengthened me to resist and repel many
temptations and assaults, O ! praise to His name.

Now, as to my Testimony, which I left in your hands,
when I entered into the work of the ministry, I do still
adhere unto *the matter* of it ; but I think *the manner of
expression* is in some things too tart, and it containeth
sundry men's names, some whereof are now in eternity.
It is not so pertinent to our present affairs, for the state
of our controversies is altered. Therefore I judge it
may be destroyed, for I have testimony sufficient left
behind me in my written Sermons, and in my Letters.
But if this trouble you, and if you desire to keep it for
yourself, and your own use, you should keep this letter
with it, and not publish it further abroad. Yet you
may make use of any part of the matter of it, that may
conduce to the clearing of any controversy. As for
the direction of it unto you, if I had lived, and been
qualified for writing a book, and if it had been dedicated to any man, you would have been the man. For
I have loved you, and I have peace before God in that ;
and I bless His name that I have been acquainted with
you.

Remember me to all that are friends to you, particularly to the Ladies at Leewarden, to whom I would
have written, if I had not been kept close in prison,
and pen, ink, and paper kept from me. But I must

break off. *I go to your God and my God.* DEATH TO
ME IS AS A BED TO THE WEARY. Now, be not anxious;
—the Lord will maintain His cause, and own His
people. He will show His glory yet in Scotland.
Farewell, beloved and comfortable Sir,

JAMES RENWICK.

When the drum beat the first warning for his execution, he was at table with his mother, sisters, and
some Christian friends. As soon as he heard it, he
burst out into rapturous exclamations, saying, "Let
us be glad and rejoice, for the marriage of the Lamb
is come, and in some measure I think I can say,
the Bride, the Lamb's wife, hath made herself ready."
On the scaffold he sang a part of the 103rd Psalm
and read the 19th chapter of Revelation. He also
prayed and attempted to address the people, but, the
drums being beat all the time, only a few who were
close to him could hear what was said. To a friend
beside him, he said—"Farewell. Be diligent in duty;
make your peace with God through Christ. There is
a great trial coming. As to the remnant I leave, I
have committed them to God. Tell them from me
not to weary, nor be discouraged in maintaining the
Testimony. Let them not quit nor forego one of these
despised truths. Keep your ground, and the Lord will
provide you teachers and ministers, and when He comes
He will make these despised truths glorious upon the
earth." The last words which passed his lips were
these—"Lord into Thy hands I commit my spirit, for
Thou hast redeemed me, Lord God of truth."

As we bid farewell to this servant of Christ, besides
lovingly cherishing his memory let us humbly yet
firmly resolve through grace to follow in his steps, and
like him in our several positions to remain faithful

unto death. Every age has its peculiar dangers and difficulties, but fidelity to Christ and to His cause is always our duty and is never without a great reward. But for Renwick and his friends, the Revolution of 1688 might never have been effected, and we might still have been groaning under civil and ecclesiastical tyranny.

Making allowance for the age in which they lived, and the infirmities and imperfections which are incident to human nature, we need not hesitate to think and speak of them as the true friends of liberty. As has well been said, the banners which they kept waving on the mountains and moors of Scotland, and which, when dropped by one, were taken up and displayed by another, were descried by William in Holland, and encouraged him to make the attempt which finally issued in the deliverance of Britain. Moreover, the conduct of our martyrs was publicly vindicated at the Revolution, when the Parliament of Scotland rescinded all the measures passed against them, and pronounced these "void and null from the beginning." Even Renwick's strongest utterances against the Stuart dynasty were fully borne out by the Scottish Convention when it declared "that King James, by his abuse of power, had forfeited all title to the Crown," while the declaration of the English Parliament was equally explicit—"that King James the Second, having endeavoured to subvert the Constitution, by breaking the original contract between the king and the people, did abdicate the throne."

That Renwick and his friends made some mistakes we are not eager to deny, as this is only a proof that they were human, and that the times were out of joint. Taking everything into account, indeed, the wonder is that they were able to conduct themselves as they did.

But those who characterise them as ignorant, foolish, and violent fanatics might profitably read the *Informatory Vindication*, generally regarded as Renwick's masterpiece, and might take special note of the spirit of candour and moderation which breathes in such a sentence as the following : "If in anything we have, in the manner of managing affairs in reference to the public cause, through ignorance or imprudence, jointly miscarried, having good designs, and the thing not attended with obstinacy, our weakness and insufficiency in the abounding confusions of these preceding times (our faithful guides and men of understanding by death and otherwise being removed) should be compassionately looked upon and tenderly handled."

We do not presume at present to say wherein they "jointly miscarried," if indeed they did in anything, but surely we cannot refuse this touching appeal to our better nature, in the judgment we form and express regarding both their character and conduct.

Let us also shew our appreciation of their faithful contendings and sufferings by the use we make of our dearly-bought rights and liberties, and let us seek to be able always and truly to say—

> " We 're the sons of sires that baffled
> Crowned and mitred tyranny ;
> They defied the field and scaffold
> For their birthrights—so will we ! "

NOTE to Letter of date August 13th, 1686, in connection with the expression at beginning of second paragraph, "I have been for a season in England," page 182.

From the Privy Council papers we learn that during the previous month he had presided at a conventicle in a retired glen called the Greencleugh, near Braidshaw Rig in Lammermoor. It appears that, in consequence of the discovery of this meeting, a very strict search was made for him, and probably he found it necessary to go for a time to England. See *The Covenanters of the Merse*, pp. 228-234.

OTHER SOLID GROUND TITLES

We recently celebrated our eighth anniversary of uncovering buried treasure to the glory of God. During these eight years we have produced over 225 volumes. A sample is listed below:

Biblical & Theological Studies: *Addresses to Commemorate the 100th Anniversary of Princeton Theological Seminary in 1912* by Allis, Machen, Wilson, Vos, Warfield and many more.

Notes on Galatians by J. Gresham Machen

The Origin of Paul's Religion by J. Gresham Machen

A Scientific Investigation of the Old Testament by R.D. Wilson

Theology on Fire: *Sermons from Joseph A. Alexander*

Evangelical Truth: *Sermons for the Family* by Archibald Alexander

A Shepherd's Heart: *Pastoral Sermons of James W. Alexander*

Grace & Glory: *Sermons from Princeton Chapel* by Geerhardus Vos

The Lord of Glory by Benjamin B. Warfield

The Person & Work of the Holy Spirit by Benjamin B. Warfield

The Power of God unto Salvation by Benjamin B. Warfield

Calvin Memorial Addresses by Warfield, Johnson, Orr, Webb...

The Five Points of Calvinism by Robert Lewis Dabney

Annals of the American Presbyterian Pulpit by W.B. Sprague

The Word & Prayer: *Classic Devotions from the Pen of John Calvin*

A Body of Divinity: *Sum and Substance of Christian Doctrine* by Ussher

The Complete Works of Thomas Manton (in 22 volumes)

A Puritan New Testament Commentary by John Trapp

Exposition of the Epistle to the Hebrews by William Gouge

Exposition of the Epistle of Jude by William Jenkyn

Lectures on the Book of Esther by Thomas M'Crie

Lectures on the Book of Acts by John Dick

To order any of our titles please contact us in one of three ways:

Call us at **1-866-789-7423**

Email us at **sgcb@charter.net**

Visit our website at **www.solid-ground-books.com**

9 781599 252049